United Nations.
ECONOMIC COMMISSION FOR EUROPE,
Geneva

THE ECONOMIC ROLE OF WOMEN
IN THE ECE REGION

Developments 1975/85

UNITED NATIONS
New York, 1985

The designations employed and the presentation of the material in this publication do not imply the expression of any opinion whatsoever on the part of the Secretariat of the United Nations concerning the legal status of any country or territory or of its authorities, or concerning the delimitation of its frontiers.

E/ECE/1100

UNITED NATIONS PUBLICATION

Sales No. E.85.II.E.20

ISBN 91-1-116333-1

01250P

CONTENTS

LIST OF TABLES

Chapter II

LIST OF FIGURES

Chapter III

Chapter IV

Chapter V

EXPLANATORY NOTES

The following symbols have been used in the tables:

    .. = not available or not pertinent;

    – = nil or negligible.

Minor discrepancies in totals and percentages are due to rounding.

Unless otherwise indicated, the designation "Great Britain" used in this study signifies the United Kingdom, excluding Northern Ireland.

ABBREVIATIONS

CFR	Coefficients of female representation
CMR	Coefficients of male representation
DI index	Dissimilarity index
ECE	Economic Commission for Europe
EEC	European Economic Community
EUROSTAT	Statistical Office of the European Communities
GDP	gross domestic product
GNP	gross national product
ICLS	International Conference of Labour Statisticians
ILO	International Labour Organisation
INTER	Interaction term
ISCO	International Standard Classification of Occupations
ISIC	International Standard Industrial Classification of all economic activities
NMP	net material product
OECD	Organisation for Economic Co-operation and Development
WE index	Women employment index

CHAPTER I

BACKGROUND AND INTRODUCTION

This study has been prepared in accordance with decisions D(XXXVIII) and J(XXXIX) taken by the Economic Commission for Europe at its 38th and 39th sessions, which requested the Executive Secretary to revise the 1980 study on "The Economic Role of Women in the ECE Region" for submission to the 1985 World Conference to Review and Appraise the Achievements of the United Nations Decade for Women. In the same decisions the Commission also requested the Executive Secretary to convene a seminar in 1984 on the economic role of women in the ECE region. The present study and the conclusions and recommendations of the Seminar constitute the Commission's contribution to the 1985 World Conference, due to be held in Nairobi from 15 to 26 July 1985.

In view of the fact that the study and Seminar dealt with the same subject, it was decided that the basic documentation submitted to the Seminar would constitute the draft chapters for the study. Accordingly, the present study is largely based on the documentation submitted to the Seminar, which was held in Vienna from 15 to 19 October 1984, at the invitation of the Government of Austria. The report of the Seminar is contained in document ECE/SEM.6/2 and the conclusions and recommendations adopted by the Seminar appear in the annex to that report.

The former study, bearing the same title,[1] was prepared for the mid-decade World Conference of the United Nations Decade for Women: Equality, Development and Peace (Copenhagen, 14 to 30 July 1980). In this revised version, special attention has been given to changes in the economic role of women which have taken place since the beginning of the Women's Decade. Accordingly, the chapters in this study focus on recent economic, social and demographic developments which have influenced the economic situation of women (chapter II); trends in labour force participation, employment and unemployment (chapter III); sectoral and occupational distribution in the labour market (chapter IV); and pay differentials between women and men (chapter V). A final section (chapter VI) summarizes the main findings and conclusions of the preceding chapters. Several topics, not covered in the present study, but for which the results of the previous study remain generally valid, include: education and training, reasons for male and female occupational differentials, and the use of time. As a background to the discussion in the following chapters, the remainder of this chapter comprises a brief review of the summary and conclusions of the 1980 study.

That study was concerned with various aspects of the role of women in the production of goods and services. It noted that women, far more than men, combine economic activity, in the sense of paid employment, with "non-economic activities" in the household. These activities, even though they do not figure in conventional forms of economic accounting, are at least as essential as traditional "economic activity" to the welfare of society and also have a positive impact on the economy.

As regards women's participation in the labour force, the 1980 study noted a general tendency of increasing women's participation, despite the existence of large differences in levels of activity rates between countries. The increasing participation of women mainly resulted from a significant rise in the activity rates of married women, including those with young children. Because the male labour force had either expanded slowly or not at all, in the majority of countries women accounted for most of the growth in, and comprised an increasing share of, the total labour force.

However, in the market-economy countries the rising number of women in the labour force was accompanied by higher unemployment. In several countries, women's unemployment rates were higher than those for men, especially in the younger age groups. Part of this increase in unemployment was found to be attributable to the business cycle, although it was difficult to determine whether the negative impact of the recession was more serious for women or for men. On the one hand, employment is more stable in some sectors in which a large proportion of women work. On the other hand, women tend to be more vulnerable to lay-offs than men because of factors such as less training, less seniority and employment conditions providing less job security.

The 1980 study also noted that the increase in the number of women in the labour force did not necessarily imply a proportionate increase in total labour supply or employment. In a number of countries, a substantial proportion of working women are employed on a part-time basis. Part-time work, most of which is found in the service sectors and particularly in public services, had accounted for a large share of the observed increase in women's employment.

The service sector is the primary employer of women in many countries, and the expansion of the female labour force is to some extent linked with the growth of service sector employment. As regards occupational distribution, the data showed a strong tendency for women to be concentrated in certain occupations. In addition, there was evidence that the occupational specialization of women had changed very little in recent years. The structure of the demand for labour was such that much of the increase in female employment occurred in those occupations in which there was already a high concentration of women.

With respect to pay differentials between men and women, the 1980 study confirmed the existence of lower average earnings of women, although differences between countries were considerable. The results,

[1] *The Economic Role of Women in the ECE Region* (United Nations publication, Sales No. E.80.II.E.6).

however, also indicated a narrowing of the gap between men's and women's pay over the previous decades. Some of the measurable factors for the pay differentials included: differences between men and women in the number of hours worked; differences in the age distribution of workers, particularly the concentration of women workers in the younger age groups; the different sectoral distribution of men and women; and most importantly, occupational differentiation between the sexes.

The previous study also discussed some causes of the specific features of women's activity rates, occupational concentration and relative earnings. Among the demographic changes, declining fertility was identified as being directly associated with increasing female labour force participation.

It was also found that educational systems and training provisions for employment tended to prepare women for a narrower range of jobs than men. Differences in educational attainment and qualifications began to appear at the secondary level in most countries. For the population as a whole, the proportion of women who had completed secondary education was generally lower than that of men and this disparity was even more marked at higher levels of education. However, the development of educational systems in recent decades has changed considerably. Enrolment statistics show that in most countries there is presently at least equal participation of boys and girls in secondary education. Moreover, women's enrolment in higher education has grown faster than men's in most countries. There had been little change, however, as regards the choice of subjects for study, a major difference between men and women. Women are concentrated in humanities and education, and are under-represented in most science subjects.

The 1980 study also included a brief review of other factors affecting labour market differences between men and women, including "sex stereotype" concepts and management attitudes and practices. The final chapter of the study analysed available evidence regarding the use of time. International comparisons revealed certain common features, including the time pressures on women who combine paid employment with housework. The findings also indicated an uneven pattern in the division of labour within the family. They also suggested the emergence of attitudinal changes toward a more equitable sharing of household and child-care responsibilities and the implementation of social provisions in favour of working mothers.

Whereas many of the conclusions reached in the 1980 study remain valid, there have nevertheless been some recent developments regarding the economic role of women. The period since the beginning of the Women's Decade has been one of significant changes in levels and patterns of labour force participation, unemployment, sectoral and occupational distribution and pay differentials of women. The economic, social and demographic determinants of women's economic situation and role have also changed considerably. Statistics and other data which have become available since the completion of the 1980 study shed some light on these different aspects. Even so, as was the case with the previous study, gaps in detailed and recent statistics have hampered the scope and content of the analysis. While the original version had to rely to a large part on statistics dating back to 1970, the present revision was limited by the fact that detailed statistics from the 1980 round of censuses are not yet available in many cases. Data from other sources could only partially compensate for these limitations. As a result, the discussion in the following chapters is less extensive, both geographically and substantively, than would have been desirable.

CHAPTER II

RECENT DEVELOPMENTS AFFECTING THE ECONOMIC ROLE
OF WOMEN IN THE ECE REGION

Introduction

Economic, demographic and social factors and, in a broader context, the evolution of society as a whole all affect the role of women in the economy. Since 1975, which marked the beginning of the United Nations Decade for Women, significant changes have taken place in the ECE countries which have affected the economic situation both of women and men. The evolution of the economic role of women in the recent past and its prospects for the future should be viewed in the context of these general developments. Moreover, policies aimed at improving the economic and social situation of women will not be fully effective unless they are integrated within society's comprehensive development objectives. As stated in the Programme of Action for the Second Half of the United Nations Decade for Women, the historical perspective "proves that any measures for women isolated from the major priorities, strategies and sectors of development cannot result in any substantial progress towards attaining the goals of the Decade".[1]

The purpose of the present chapter is to review briefly, as the Decade for Women draws to a close, some of the recent developments which have affected, both positively and negatively, the economic role of women in the ECE region. With a view to formulating strategies for the future, the discussion also refers to some likely future developments concerning some of the crucial variables considered.

A. Economic developments

1. ECONOMIC GROWTH

Economic growth in the ECE region has slowed down considerably since the early 1970s. On the basis of tentative data on output growth for the region as a whole, it is estimated that, while the growth of output averaged 5% per year between 1970 and 1973, it dropped to approximately 2.5% per year between 1974 and 1983. In the industrialized market economies, the average annual increase in output declined from over 4% in the early 1970s to less than 2% during the period from 1974 to 1983. An even sharper drop occurred in output growth, from nearly 6.5% to less than 3%, in the countries of southern Europe. The previous decade was also marked by a slow-down in growth in the centrally planned economies of Europe and the Union of Soviet Socialist Republics. However, growth levelled off later and less markedly in those countries than in the market econ-

omies. Estimates indicate that, whereas from 1970 to 1973 growth in the centrally planned economies was increasing at an annual rate of 7%, the corresponding average between 1974 and 1983 was slightly above 4%.

The loss in growth momentum in the market economies was associated with a number of factors, among which were pronounced increases in inflation and unemployment. Prices, which had been going up gradually in the course of the 1960s, rose sharply in 1973–74. In addition to the oil price shock and rising commodity prices, which occurred during these years and again in 1979, structural factors affecting wages and labour costs as well as public sector spending and deficits, also contributed to the persistent rise in inflation from the early 1970s to the beginning of the 1980s. It has been argued that, among the structural causes, long-term labour market developments played a particularly important role in the case of Europe.[2] During the 1960s, domestic sources of labour and, in particular, the potential for the transfer of agricultural labour to the non-agricultural sectors, declined considerably. The combination of a slowly increasing labour supply and nearly full employment resulted in strong upward pressures on wages and labour costs in the general climate of rigidities in the labour market existing in most European market-economy countries. The labour market in the United States of America proved to be far more responsive to economic conditions: real wages increased little after 1973 and also adjusted more rapidly to the recessions of the 1970s and early 1980s than in Europe.

Apart from labour market developments, public sector deficits and efforts to control them emerged in the 1970s as a major constraint on economic growth in the industrial market economies. The public sector's share in the total gross domestic product (GDP) of the industrialized countries began to increase sharply in the second half of the 1960s. Whereas in the first half of that decade the public sector's share increased by approximately 1.3 percentage points (reaching approximately 30% of total GDP by 1965), during the remainder of the decade the rise was more than twice as high (2.8 percentage points). The proportion rose even more rapidly (by some 4.5 percentage points) during the first half of the 1970s. Although the expansion of the public sector subsequently slowed down, by 1980 it accounted for two fifths of the total GDP in the industrial market economies. In many of these countries, this expansion was accompanied by sharply increasing budget deficits. As the deficits increased from year to year, a growing number of countries tightened fiscal policies, restricted public expenditures and reduced the services rendered by the public sector.

[1] Report of the World Conference of the United Nations Decade for Women: Equality, Development and Peace, Copenhagen, 14–30 July (United Nations publication, Sales No. E.80.IV.3), p. 11.

[2] A. Boltho, "Growth", A. Boltho ed., The European Economy; Growth and Crisis (Oxford University Press, 1982).

The recent economic recovery in most of these countries should be viewed against this background. As had been estimated, the recovery had manifested itself in most countries of western Europe by the end of 1983 and continued through 1984. The generally accepted forecast for 1985 is for a GDP growth of over 2% in western Europe. In the United States, growth in 1984 was significantly higher than in western Europe, but this gap is expected to decrease in 1985. The longevity of the present recovery and the medium-term growth prospects thereafter will depend, as suggested above, on a number of factors. The estimates for the rest of the decade are for a relatively modest annual growth of between 2.5 and 3.0% in the industrialized countries.[3]

The deceleration in economic growth in the centrally planned economies can be associated with declining trends in factor inputs and with developments in the efficiency with which they were used. The factor most often mentioned as limiting the possibilities of expansion at the historically observed rates is the constraint due to labour resources. Although the scarcity of labour did not affect all countries to the same extent, it played an important role in the economic development of most of the centrally planned economies in the latter part of the 1970s. For eastern Europe (excluding the USSR), the increase in the active population, which was over 3 million in 1966–70 and close to 2.5 million in 1971–75, dropped to less than 600,000 in 1976–80. During the latter period, only the German Democratic Republic experienced a higher growth than in the preceding five-year period. The active population in the USSR increased by some 10 and 11 million respectively during the first two periods in question, followed by a reduction of the increase by more than one quarter, to 8 million in 1976–80.[4] Low population growth and dwindling traditional labour reserves in agriculture, as well as the already very high level of women's economic activity in the countries concerned, point to a continuation, and possibly an aggravation, of the constraints of labour resources in the future.

Another major cause of the deceleration of economic growth in the centrally planned economies during the latter part of the 1970s, was the increasing scarcity and rising costs of material inputs. Investment levels acted as an additional constraint on growth. Net capital formation in 1976–80 slowed down considerably in comparison with earlier periods. The fall was especially large in some countries, such as Hungary and Poland, where the growth rates in 1976–80 were negative while, in the other four east European countries, rates of capital formation were from 30% to 80% lower than the respective growth rates of net material product (NMP) distributed.[5]

An upturn in economic growth, which was already under way in the USSR in 1982, characterized overall developments in the centrally planned economies in 1983. The NMP of the USSR is reported to have increased by approximately 4%, whereas the growth rate of the east European planned economies in 1983 was of the order of 3.5%. With the exception of Bulgaria and Hungary, the recent slow-down in growth in this group of countries came to an end. In 1984, the centrally planned economies of the region maintained the recent rates of growth. The 3–4% growth rate in the USSR is expected to continue in 1985 and, in the east European countries, the outlook for a similar aggregate growth rate also seems to be fairly good. Nevertheless, these prospects for the near future would constitute considerably slower growth than that which occurred in the 1960s and early 1970s. The longer-term outlook is more difficult to predict. A broad assessment of medium-term prospects for economic growth in the centrally planned economies, based on the likely developments regarding factor inputs and efficiency in their use, led to the conclusion that, while there is little reason to expect a deceleration of growth, there are also little grounds for anticipating a significant acceleration. On the whole it therefore seems likely that, in the medium term, growth in the USSR and eastern Europe will not differ much from that of recent years.[6]

General economic developments obviously have a significant effect on the economic role and status of women, as well as men. The most obvious are the repercussions on women's status in the labour market. It has been recognized that the pace of economic change is not only an important determinant of women's participation in the labour force, but also their levels of employment and unemployment, the degree of their integration in the labour market and the levels and trends of their earnings. Nevertheless, the precise effect of economic conditions on the situation of women is not yet known. For instance, the discussion on the relative importance of the "discouraged worker" and "added worker" effect during periods of economic slow-down or recession remains inconclusive. Moreover, there is evidence which suggests that the relative importance of each of these phenomena can vary over time. Data indicate a weakening of the "discouraged worker" effect during the recent recessions. The same is true for some of the other aspects referred to above. Although the following discussion is mainly concerned with women's role in the labour market, the pace of economic development also determines the extent to which the economy will be able to satisfy the social and related needs of women. Whereas women are increasingly in the labour force for a significant part of their active lives, there are still many women (such as those who are older, widowed, unmarried or heads of single-parent families) who are economically dependent. Slow economic growth, in combination with efforts to reduce public sector spending, negatively affect the situation of increasing numbers of women living in precarious economic conditions.

2. SECTORAL CHANGES IN EMPLOYMENT

A major characteristic of labour market development in recent decades has been the shift in the sectoral distribution of the labour force. The most notable change was the high rate of expansion of service sector employment, accompanied, in many cases, by a stagnation or even a contraction of employment in industry. The historical phase of the transformation from an agricultural to an industrial economy has been followed by a new phase, marked by the emergence of a service economy, especially in the industrialized market economies. Signs of this latest transformation already began to appear in the

[3] United Nations, *Review and Appraisal of the International Development Strategy for the Third United Nations Development Decade* (A/39/115; E/1984/49), p. 12.

[4] *Economic Survey of Europe in 1981* (United Nations publication, Sales No. E.82.II.E.1), p. 135.

[5] *Ibid.*, pp. 135–136.

[6] *Economic Survey of Europe in 1983* (United Nations publication, Sales No. E.84.II.E.1), p. 123.

TABLE II.1

Employment by sector

(*Percentages*)

| Country | Total employment in | | | | | |
| | Industry | | | Services | | |
	1960	1970	1980	1960	1970	1980
Austria	40.6	41.3	39.8	36.9	44.1	51.2
Belgium	43.5	42.1	33.6	48.0	53.3	63.4
Canada	32.0	30.6	28.3	53.6	61.9	66.3
Finland	31.8	35.3	34.2	32.0	42.1	53.4
France	36.7	38.7	35.0	41.7	47.9	56.5
Germany, Federal Republic of ..	46.4	47.5	43.9	40.1	44.0	50.2
Netherlands	40.4	39.0	31.9	48.2	53.9	62.1
Sweden	40.3	38.4	32.2	44.0	53.5	62.2
Switzerland	46.5	46.0	39.8	38.9	45.4	53.0
United Kingdom	46.8	44.1	37.6	46.5	52.7	59.7
United States	32.3	33.0	29.9	59.7	62.6	66.6

Source: Economic Survey of Europe in 1982 (United Nations publication, Sales Number E.83.II.E.1), p. 67.

TABLE II.2

Service sector employment, in terms of hours worked and numbers employed, 1973–1980

(*Percentages*)

| Country | Shares in total employment | | | | Annual average growth rates 1973–1980 | |
| | Hours worked | | Numbers employed | | Hours worked | Numbers employed |
	1973	1980	1973	1980		
Finland............................	53.1	56.8	54.7	58.2	1.0	1.4
Norway	51.0	58.0	55.3	61.9	2.6	3.9
Sweden............................	57.6	63.2	60.0	65.5	1.4	2.6
United States......................	65.2	68.4	67.9	70.9	2.6	2.6

Source: See table II.1.

1960s and, in some countries, even in the 1950s. However, it gained momentum in the 1970s and despite the slow growth in overall employment in the 1970s, the employment structure continued to change rapidly.

Table II.1 presents data on the structure of employment by sector in selected ECE countries for 1970 and 1980 and, for comparative purposes, for 1960 as well. The table shows that, in 1960, employment in services accounted for less than half of total employment in all countries except Canada and the United States. In 1970, service employment represented more than half of total employment in the majority of countries and, by 1980, this was true for all of them. By contrast, the proportion of employment in industry which, between 1960 and 1970 was still increasing in several countries, decreased between 1970 and 1980 in all cases. However, as indicated by the table, the rate and degree of change in sectoral employment varied considerably. In 1980, the service sector absorbed nearly two thirds of total employment in Canada and the United States. In Belgium, the Netherlands, Sweden and the United Kingdom, the corresponding proportions were close to or over 60%. Lower percentages, between 50% and 56%, were found in the remaining countries.

An important feature of the growth of the service sector has been that much of this growth took the form of part-time employment. Data for a few countries on the

share of service employment in total employment, both in terms of absolute numbers and of hours worked, are presented in table II.2. The share of employment in the service sector is, as the data show, lower on the basis of hours worked than of numbers employed in all countries, the largest difference being found in Norway (4 percentage points). More important are the differences in growth rates between the two measures. The annual growth rate of service employment in Sweden, in terms of hours worked, is almost half of that corresponding to the number of employed; it is one third lower in the cases of Finland and Norway. By contrast, in the United States there was no difference in these growth rates, which implies a similar rate of expansion for both part-time and full-time employment. A second noteworthy feature concerns the growth of employment in public, as distinct from private, services. A considerable proportion of the change in the structure of service employment during the 1970s in a number of countries could be attributed to the public sector. Together with financial and business services, the major gains in service employment took place in the government sector.

The evolution of the sectoral distribution of the labour force, and the generally increasing share of employment in the service sector, is of special importance for the labour force participation and employment of women. Historically, women's employment has been strongly concentrated in certain sectors of the economy. In pre-industrial societies, the large majority of women were active in agriculture, usually as family workers in subsistence agriculture. By contrast, comparatively few women worked in industry and, as a result, female participation in the labour force generally declined during the phase of rapid industrialization. Unlike the industrial sector, the service sector is an important source of female employment. The emergence of the service sector, therefore, led to a rapid expansion of the female labour force and employment, a phenomenon which has dominated labour market developments in recent years in a large number of countries.

B. Demographic trends

1. POPULATION GROWTH AND AGE STRUCTURE

Since 1975, the trend of declining population growth characteristic for the industrialized countries continued to dominate the demographic evolution in the ECE region, where the rate of population growth fell from approximately 1.3% annually in the early 1950s to roughly 0.7% at present, a reduction of nearly 50%. On a global scale, current growth in the region compares with a rate of approximately 2% for the rest of the world, approaching a one to three ratio. However, changes in population growth since the beginning of the Decade for Women have been relatively small. Generally speaking, two phases in the slow-down of the population growth in the ECE region since the 1950s can be distinguished. In the first phase, between 1950 and 1965, the annual growth rate of the population was of the order of 1.3%. The second phase began in the latter half of the 1960s with a sharp drop in growth, to less than 0.9%. Since then the decline has continued, but at a much slower pace. It is estimated that, between 1975 and 1985, the annual rate of population increase for the region as a whole slowed down only slightly, from approximately 0.8% to 0.7%.

The regional averages referred to above conceal significant differences between countries and groups of countries within the region. When the countries are arranged in broad categories according to current growth rates, the range observed is considerable (see table II.3). At the lower end of the scale are countries with near-zero

TABLE II.3

Countries grouped according to levels of population growth, 1975–1980

(*Percentages*)

Average annual rates of population growth	Country
Under 0.5	Austria; Belgium; Cyprus; Denmark; Finland; France; German Democratic Republic; Germany, Federal Republic of; Hungary; Italy; Luxembourg; Norway; Sweden; Switzerland; United Kingdom.
0.5–0.99	Bulgaria; Czechoslovakia; Greece; Malta; Netherlands; Portugal; Spain; Romania; United States; USSR; Yugoslavia.
1.0–1.5	Canada; Iceland; Ireland; Poland.
Over 1.5	Albania; Turkey.

Source: Demographic Indicators of Countries: Estimates and Projections as Assessed in 1980 (ST/ESA/SER.A/82).

growth, while in the upper range, growth rates of up to 2.5% are still found. At the same time, certain regional patterns in growth come to light. In the majority of the west European countries, the annual population increase is less than 0.5% and, in a number of cases, it is even negative. Half of the east European countries and the USSR fall within the group with intermediate growth rates, from 0.5% to 0.99%. Most of the south European countries are also characterized by moderate growth, although both Albania and Turkey have more in common with the developing countries as regards their demographic characteristics, than with the rest of the region. As for North America, population growth in the United States is in the upper range of the intermediate group, whereas in Canada it is even higher.

It is likely, however, that the decline in population growth will continue. According to United Nations projections, the population of the ECE region is expected to increase by approximately 0.6% annually by the end of the century and, by the year 2025, the increase should amount to no more than 0.3% per year. Moreover, by the year 2000, 21 out of 32 ECE countries are projected to have growth rates of less than 0.5% (compared with 14 countries in 1975–1980). Population growth is projected to be negative or practically zero (less than 0.1% annual increase) in at least one third of the countries.

Considerable controversy exists with regard to the economic consequences of a slow or negative population growth. Even less is known about the direct impact of such trends on the economic role of women. Although the adverse effects of a low or negative population growth have occasionally been stressed, there exists a consensus that the decline of population growth as such would not have major economic consequences. The fact that few developed countries view their low or negative growth of population as a serious economic handicap also emerged from the ECE Regional Meeting on Population.[7] However, the consequences of the actual or virtual cessation of population growth cannot be considered independently from the changes in the age composition which accompany the decline in growth (and ultimately in that of fertility as the main causative factor).

There is more agreement as regards the effect on the economy of changes in the age structure of population resulting from the decline in population growth. The ramifications of such changes for the economic role of women are also much more evident. One of the major implications of the slow-down in population growth, particularly the underlying decline in fertility, is the progressive aging of populations, defined as the increased proportion of people in older age groups. From a global perspective it is evident that the process of the aging of the population is by far the most advanced in the ECE region where, in 1975, the proportion of those aged 60 years and over was about 15%, compared with under 7% in the rest of the world. The degree to which the population of the region has aged can also be seen from the fact that, whereas in 1980 the total population of the region represented less than one quarter of the world's total, more than two fifths of people aged 60 years or over in the world lived in the ECE region.

---

[7] *Report of the Meeting on Population,* held in Sofia, Bulgaria, 6–12 October 1983, in preparation for the International Conference on Population in Mexico, 6–12 August 1984 (ECE/AC.9/2) annex, para. 14.

The rate at which the aging of populations in the region has progressed over the last three decades has been considerable: the share of those aged 60 years and over in the total population, increased from 11.6% in 1950 to about 15% currently. Although a relative slow-down in the aging process occurred in the last ten years or so, demographic projections show that until the year 2000 the proportion of the aged will continue to grow, albeit at a slower absolute and relative pace than in the past. Nevertheless, between the mid-1980s and the end of the century, the share of the aged in the population is projected to increase considerably: from its present level of about 15% to more than 17% by the year 2000. The increase will be particularly pronounced in western Europe (see table II.4).

The effect of the aging process over the past three decades has been both to raise the proportion of the old and to decrease that of the young, a trend which had no significant effect on the relative size of the population of working age and thus the potential labour force. The working age population was growing at a somewhat lower rate than the total population in the 1950s, but this situation was reversed in the 1970s when those born during the post-war "baby boom" were reaching working age. Data for the region as a whole show that, in spite of the strong aging trend, the total dependency ratio (i.e. the ratio of the number of people under 15 years old plus those aged 60 years and over to that of people in the 15–59-year-old age group) remained virtually unchanged between 1950 and 1980 and is projected to remain fairly stable until the year 2000. As the growth of the working-age population has generally been about the same as that of the total population growth without affecting the potential dependency burden, the impact of the aging process *per se* on labour supply was limited. Changing labour force participation rates, rather than demographic changes, determined labour supply in most countries. In eastern Europe, however, where the slowing-down of the natural growth of the labour force was associated with already high participation rates of women, and the virtual disappearance of the traditional labour reserves in agriculture, labour shortages resulted, especially in the industrial and related sectors.

The major impact of the aging process relates to the changes in demand patterns resulting from the shifts from youth to old-age dependency. Most of the available evidence suggests that low (or zero) population growth and aging have only a relatively small effect on household or private consumption. In addition, although the demand for certain goods and services may be affected by these demographic changes, their total effect on consumption

patterns also seems to be relatively weak.[8] One possible explanation for this is that the consequences of changes in these demographic variables are offset by shifts in the number, size and composition of households, which are associated with a slow-down of population growth and with the aging process. Whereas the effect of a low population growth and aging on private household demand may be modest, the same cannot be said of the impact on the public or state sectors. In most countries of the region, a broad range of social services is provided by the Government or the State, so that the aging of the population has a significant effect on public sector expenditures. In general, expenditures in a number of these sectors differ because they are limited to certain segments of the population (e.g. education and old-age pensions) or concentrated in certain age groups (e.g. infants and old people who account for a large proportion of health expenditures). Although detailed studies on the subject are rare, it has been estimated that the cost to society of an old person may be, on the average, between two and three times higher than that of a child.

This factor becomes especially important in view of the fact that women account for a high proportion of the aging population, and thus will be most affected by government policies pertaining to social needs and services. In 1950, women represented nearly 58% of the population of 60 years of age and over in the ECE region. Between 1950 and 1980, the number of women in this age group increased at a considerably higher rate (85%) than that of men in the same age group (65%). The proportion of women of these ages consequently rose to more than 60% by 1980. Although this growth differential is projected to be reversed between 1980 and 2000, the ratio between the sexes will continue to be seriously unbalanced. Moreover, the differential is even more pronounced for the so-called "aged aged", i.e. those of 75 years and over. In 1980, nearly two thirds of the population of 75 and over, which typically includes a significant proportion of the poor and needy, were women. The social, economic and policy implications of these features of the age distribution are obviously far-reaching.

2. FERTILITY

Levels and trends of reproduction are relevant, not only because fertility changes have been the major factor in the changes in population growth and age composition

[8] See, for instance, "Economic Implications of Aging in the ECE Region", *Economic Bulletin for Europe*, vol. 35, No. 3 (Pergamon Press for the United Nations, September 1983), pp. 320–323.

TABLE II.4

Population distribution by broad age groups, ECE subregions, 1950–2025

(Percentage of total)

Region	1950			1980			2000			2025		
	0–14	15–59	60 and over	0–14	15–59	60 and over	0–14	15–59	60 and over	0–14	15–59	60 and over
Western Europe.............	24.0	61.7	14.3	20.9	60.8	18.3	17.9	61.2	20.9	17.5	55.8	26.7
North America	27.1	60.8	12.1	22.9	62.1	15.0	22.0	63.0	15.0	20.5	57.2	22.3
Eastern Europe and USSR	29.0	61.4	9.6	24.1	62.2	13.7	22.9	59.3	17.8	21.6	57.8	20.6
Southern Europe.............	31.3	59.6	9.1	30.2	58.4	11.4	26.6	59.4	14.0	22.6	59.6	17.8

Source: Demographic Indicators of Countries: Estimates and Projections as Assessed in 1980 (ST/ESA/SER.A/82).

in the region over the past decades. More important, reproductive behaviour has a direct and significant impact on the economic role of women. The extent of women's participation in the labour force has traditionally been closely linked to, and conditioned by, childbearing and the number of children in the family or union.

Data on fertility clearly show that the ECE region is characterized by low levels of reproduction. The average total fertility rate for all countries is estimated to have been somewhat below 2.2 children per woman in 1975–80, just above the long-term level needed to ensure replacement. The corresponding figure for the rest of the world was of the order of 4.5 children per woman. The diffusion of low fertility levels in the region is evident from a comparison with the situation at the beginning of the 1970s. Whereas, at that time, the total fertility rate in nine countries was below the long-term level needed to ensure replacement (about 2.1 children per woman), this applied to nineteen countries by the end of the decade. Recent data suggest that fertility may have subsequently fallen to below the critical level in another four countries. Thus, fertility is currently below the long-term level required for replacement in 23 out of 32 ECE countries. It remains comparatively high in only three of the remaining countries: Albania (with an estimated total fertility rate of about 4); Ireland (3.2); and Turkey (estimated at 4.7). Table II.5 illustrates the shift in reproductive behaviour since 1970. The tendency toward the small family can also be seen from the decline in the number of births within larger families. The decline in fertility has been associated with an especially steep drop in the number of third and further births. In western Europe, where fertility declined most, the proportion of third and further births dropped from about 35% of total births in the early 1960s, to less than 20% at the end of the 1970s.

An important aspect of the change in reproductive behaviour, with potentially significant implications for women's economic role, is the general reduction of the childbearing period. While, in the past, childbearing continued through the reproductive period, in the low fertility countries there has been a consistent tendency towards having children during the early part of the childbearing years. In 20 of the 23 ECE countries for which

recent data are available, women under 30 years of age accounted for more than 90% of total births and, in more than two-thirds of these countries, childbearing was virtually completed by the age of 35 years. There are indications, at least in some countries, of an additional change in the timing of childbearing, namely a delay in childbearing after marriage. According to fertility surveys carried out in the second half of the 1970s in the United Kingdom and the United States, the interval between marriage and the first birth for women married after 1970 was significantly longer compared to those married earlier. In the case of women married in 1971 or later in the United Kingdom, nearly 35 months elapsed between marriage and the first birth, compared with 25 months for those married between 1966 and 1970. The corresponding figures for the United States were 31 and 23 months. This trend, combined with the lowering of the age at which women bear their last child, implies an increasing concentration of childbearing within a relatively short time span.

The evolution of fertility levels and patterns in the course of the last decade or so reflects the continuation and extension of the longer-term declining trend typical for the industrialized countries. The future course of fertility will, to a large extent, depend on whether these changes represent a transitory phase or a more permanent phenomenon. Data on past and current general fertility levels can provide only limited information in this regard. A more detailed analysis of the components of fertility changes, however, gives some insight into the role of the different factors involved, over time. Changes in the crude birth rate can be broken down into three underlying factors: changes in sex-age composition, in nuptiality and in marital fertility. The results of this analysis for those countries where fertility levels have been lowest since 1970, suggest that whereas lower levels of marital fertility accounted for most of the decline in the earlier years, the predominant factor affecting the decline in the recent period was changes in nuptiality. With some reservations, the data suggest that, in the low fertility countries, the decline of marital fertility may have come to a halt. A comparison of the results of fertility surveys in these countries lends some support to this hypothesis. The data generally show only a small difference in the ultimate expected number of children of couples who have been married for less than 5 years and those married for between 5 and 9 years. However, there is a significant difference between the number of expected children of these groups, and of those married for 10 or more years.

The past decline in marital fertility corresponded both to a decline in unwanted children and to a reduction in the number of wanted births. According to the results of an ECE comparative analysis of fertility surveys in fifteen countries of the region, the average expected size of family in the mid-1970s to the end of the decade, varied between 2.1 and 2.5 children. Only in Spain was the number notably higher (2.8). In all countries, 40% or more of women expected to have only two children, while the proportion of those anticipating having three children in no case exceeded 30% The extent to which the birth rate has come under control can be deduced from the fact that, for the eight countries for which data were available, the average of unwanted pregnancies represented a maximum of just over 15% of all pregnancies and, in half of the countries concerned, the proportion was 10% or less.

Another development with potentially significant implications for the economic role of women is the

TABLE II.5

Countries grouped according to total fertility rates, 1970 and 1980

Below 2.11 in 1970 and 1980	2.11 and over in 1970, below 2.11 in 1980	2.11 and over in 1970 and 1980
Denmark	Australia	Albania
Finland	Belgium	Cyprus
Germany, Federal	Bulgaria	Czechoslovakia
Republic of	Canada	Greece
Hungary	France	Iceland
Luxembourg	German Democratic	Ireland
Malta	Republic	Poland
Sweden	Italy	Portugal
Switzerland	Netherlands	Romania
United Kingdom	Norway	Spain
	United States	Turkey
		Yugoslavia
		USSR

Sources: National data and secretariat estimates.

increased incidence of births outside marriage. Whereas in the low fertility countries marital fertility appears to have shown a trend towards stabilization, childbirth outside (formal) marriage has been increasing rapidly in many countries. The tendency towards an abrupt increase in these births is found both in countries where the incidence of extra-marital births was already high and in those where it was negligible. Data on extra-marital births as a proportion of total births, the "illegitimacy ratio", in countries for which data were available around 1975 and a subsequent year, are shown in table II.6. The range in these illegitimacy ratios is wide (in 1975 the percentages in the countries included varied from as little as 2% to as much as 32%) but, in all cases, they increased significantly in recent years. In Denmark and Sweden, extra-marital births represent approximately two fifths of total births. However, the current situation with respect to these countries seems to represent a departure from past trends, when illegitimate births were mainly to young unmarried women. At present, a large proportion of extra-marital births occurs amongst older women, who cohabit without formal marriage. Contrary to the past, when illegitimate children were also usually first children, these women often bear a second or a third child outside marriage.

3. NUPTIALITY AND THE FAMILY

In the course of the last decade, changes in fertility in the developed countries have been associated with, and

TABLE II.6

Illegitimacy ratios, in selected ECE countries, around 1975 and in recent years

Country	Year	Illegitimacy ratios
Austria	1975	13.0
	1982	21.6
Belgium	1977	3.1
	1981	4.5
Canada	1975	7.2
	1982	15.1
Denmark	1975	21.7
	1982	38.3
Finland	1975	10.1
	1981	13.3
France	1975	8.5
	1981	12.7
German Democratic Republic	1975	16.1
	1981	25.6
Germany, Federal Republic of	1975	6.1
	1982	8.5
Hungary	1975	5.6
	1982	7.7
Netherlands	1975	2.1
	1982	5.9
Norway	1975	10.3
	1982	17.6
Sweden	1975	32.4
	1982	42.0
United Kingdom [a]	1975	9.1
	1982	14.4

Sources: National data and secretariat estimates.

[a] Relates to England and Wales only.

are to some extent manifestations of, profound alterations in the role and institution of marriage and the family. Marriage and divorce rates, as well as the structure of the family, have undergone a considerable transformation in recent years. Several of these changes are likely to have repercussions on the economic situation and role of women.

One such change has been the downward trend in marriages which, by the mid-1970s, had manifested itself in most countries of the region. Throughout most of the post-war period, crude marriage rates varied considerably from one country to another and over time. Most countries experienced a rise in marriage rates in the years immediately after the Second World War. The subsequent decline stabilized in the late 1950s or early 1960s and marriage rates started to rise again in the majority of countries. The upturn, however, did not occur everywhere: rates continued to fall in some countries and the upturn lasted for only a short time in others. This pattern of declining crude marriage rates, which had started in some countries in the 1960s, gradually spread to other countries and, by 1980, had become nearly universal. In 23 out of the 26 ECE countries for which data are available, crude marriage rates in 1980 had fallen substantially from the previous peak. The significance of the decline can be inferred from the fact that, in countries where the decline in nuptiality started comparatively early (around 1965), crude marriage rates fell by at least 20% and, in most cases, by approximately 40%. It has been argued that the drop in marriage rates is only temporary and is caused *inter alia* by unfavourable economic conditions leading to the postponement of, rather than abstention from, marriage. However, if the past trends reflect a secular change and not an ephemeral phenomenon, current marriage rates would imply a significant rise in the number of those who never marry.

The changes during the last ten years or so have already had a significant impact on the distribution of women by marital status, especially in the younger marriage ages. Table II.7 presents data for 1970 and 1980 on the percentages of women in fourteen countries, aged 20 to 24 and 25 to 29 years, who were married. The decline in the proportion of those married is particularly marked in those countries where marriage rates have been declining for a longer period of time. In Denmark, for instance, the proportion of young married women aged from 20 to 24 years dropped, from more than half (54%) to just over one fifth (22%). The corresponding decrease relating to women 25 to 29 years old was from more than four fifths (83%) to less than three fifths (58%). In Sweden, less than 15% of women 20 to 24 years old were married in 1981, compared with nearly 40% in 1970 and, in the 25 to 29-year age group, the proportion of married women declined from nearly 75% in 1970 to well below 50% in 1981. Smaller, although significant, changes were observed in other countries, mostly in western Europe and North America, where the downward trend in marriages started in the 1960s or early 1970s. The effect of the changes in marital composition is not yet evident in the remaining countries, which experienced a declining marriage trend only after about 1975.

Another development which became more important during the 1970s was the increase in divorce levels. Whereas, until the mid-1960s, divorce rates remained relatively stable, they subsequently began to rise considerably in most countries. This trend has continued: data for

TABLE II. 7

**Percentages of women aged 20–24 and 25–29 years
who are married**

Country	Year	Ages	
		20–24 years	25–29 years
Austria	1971	52.8	76.5
	1981	39.6	67.5
Belgium	1970	59.4	86.6
	1981	52.0	81.6
Canada	1971	55.7	82.7
	1981	48.0	76.8
Czechoslovakia	1970	63.2	85.5
	1980	64.5	84.2
Denmark	1970	54.0	82.5
	1981	22.0	58.0
Finland	1970	47.0	75.5
	1981	29.3	63.1
France	1970	53.8	81.2
	1981	43.5	72.6
German Democratic Republic	1970	63.4	85.6
	1981	54.6	79.1
Germany, Federal Republic of	1970	56.9	82.7
	1981	36.2	70.0
Hungary	1970	65.4	85.2
	1981	66.0	82.5
Netherlands	1970	51.8	84.5
	1981	39.2	74.3
Norway	1970	53.1	81.8
	1981	36.0	71.6
Poland	1970	52.5	83.1
	1978	52.2	82.2
Sweden	1970	39.7	73.9
	1981	14.9	45.4
Switzerland	1970	44.5	75.9
	1980	26.5	63.6
United Kingdom [a]	1970	58.6	84.8
	1980	48.0	78.7
United States	1970	60.5	82.5
	1981	44.2	68.9

Sources: National data and secretariat estimates.

[a] England and Wales only.

1970 and 1981, which are available for 22 countries, indicate an increase in divorce rates in all but two countries. Moreover, the extent of the change was considerable in most of these countries, in nearly half of which current crude divorce rates reveal that each year 2% of existing marriages are being terminated by divorce. In addition, although the incidence of remarriage among the divorced persons is generally very high, this trend has also weakened. According to recent data, the remarriage rates of divorced women varied between 5% to more than 18% per year. Comparisons with data for earlier periods show that these rates are currently considerably lower in nearly all countries concerned, implying that increasing proportions of divorced women do not remarry.

Another feature of marital patterns, although difficult to document, has been the increasing incidence of non-marital cohabitation. The impact of this phenomenon on long-term marriage patterns is not clear. While cohabiting couples may eventually marry, thus taking the first step in the process of forming a family, cohabitation may also be a more permanent arrangement, thus making it a substitute for marriage. Statistical data on the characteristics of cohabitation are very limited but nevertheless provide some indication of the extent of this phenomenon. In the mid-1970s, 13% of women aged 18 to 44 years in Sweden and 11% of those between 18 and 49 years in Denmark lived in a condition of "paperless marriage". The proportion of women between 20 and 24 years of age in non-legal unions in both countries, however, was close to one third. According to data for Norway, about 5% of women in the 18 to 44 years age group lived in such unions in 1977. Similar estimates were obtained for France and the United States in the years around 1980. More detailed data for Finland provide further insight into the evolution of this phenomenon. The number of couples living in consensual unions as a percentage of all couples, whether legally married or cohabiting, is estimated to have increased from slightly less than 2% in 1970 to nearly 8% in 1979, and to close to 11% in 1982. In the course of the 1970–1979 period, the proportion of all recently established couples who lived in consensual unions increased from approximately 30% in the first year to 65% in the latter. Moreover, the increase over time in the number of consensual unions was not limited to younger new couples (under 25 years) but was also found among those who were already older when establishing such a union. Finally, the data suggested a tendency towards a longer duration of consensual unions; whereas those living in such unions for 4 years or more represented only 1% of the total in the beginning of the 1970s, towards the end of the decade the proportion had risen to 8%.

CHAPTER III

LABOUR FORCE PARTICIPATION, EMPLOYMENT AND UNEMPLOYMENT

Introduction

Since the beginning of the United Nations Decade for Women, there have been significant changes in the economic role of women in the ECE region. Some of these changes may be viewed as a continuation of historical trends, while others reflect new developments. Demographic changes, a rising level of education, and sectoral shifts in the economy are among the longer-term trends which have continued to influence women's labour force participation over the past ten years. Economic developments in the last decade or so are among the more recent factors contributing to new patterns of labour market behaviour in many countries of the region.

A persistent problem in analysing and interpreting the changes which affect women's role in the labour market is that of the measurement of women's economic activity. In outlining problems of this nature, the 1980 study [1] noted that not only do concepts and definitions vary between countries, thus affecting inter-country comparisons, but that such comparisons are often limited within countries over time. Although the standardization of labour force concepts has been an objective of the International Conference of Labour Statisticians (ICLS) since the 1920s and despite international recommendations on definitions and classifications, practices still vary from one country to another. In addition, there may be differences within countries, over time and among different agencies and programmes of data collection.

One of the important areas where there are major differences between countries concerns the definition of those who are counted as being in the labour force, and the classification of unpaid family workers. While housewives are not considered as being part of the labour force, those who work as unpaid helpers in family businesses or farms are normally included in the economically active population. The 1980 study drew attention to the fact that, because women are often engaged in various unpaid productive activities, or are occupied simultaneously in income- and non-income-producing activities, there may be a tendency to underestimate the number of women who are economically active. However, as was also observed, since almost all countries in the ECE region have reached a level of development and industrialization where relatively few people work in small family enterprises, different practices in remunerating women in these enterprises no longer have such significant adverse effects on data comparability.

Various problems associated with data comparability continue to hamper the analysis of female participation in the labour force and its characteristics. Nevertheless, the data base has improved: current statistics are more

readily available and they are more comparable. Data from the 1980 round of population censuses, undertaken by most countries of the region, provide new information on labour market trends during the 1970s. However, some of the conclusions drawn from these data must still be considered as tentative, because the detailed results of all recent censuses are not yet available. However, the census and other data which do exist provide evidence of various important new developments in women's labour force participation and its patterns.

A. Women in the labour force

During recent decades, one of the outstanding features of labour market developments in the ECE region has been the dynamics of the participation of women. Whereas, for some time the activity rates of men have been showing a tendency to decline, those of women have generally been rising, very rapidly in a number of countries. As a result, the growth of the female labour force has become a major determinant of the evolution of the work force. General, and admittedly rough, estimates of labour force trends for the whole of the ECE region provide evidence to this effect.

According to these estimates, women accounted for more than three fifths (63%) of the expansion of the labour force in the region from 1960 to the present. The number of women in the labour force increased by more than 60% over this period, compared with a rise of just over 20% for men. These different growth trends for males and females have resulted in the share of women in the labour force rising from less than 37% in about 1960 to nearly 44% currently. Moreover, the trends show an acceleration over time: while, between 1960 and 1975, the rate of growth of the female labour force had already been more than twice as high as that of males, since 1975 the rate of labour force growth slowed down somewhat for men and rose further for women, causing a widening of the growth differential. It is thus estimated that, between 1975 and 1985, the rate of increase in the number of women in the labour force was three times that of men, and that women accounted for two thirds of the expansion of the work force during this period.

Labour force estimates for individual countries confirm the above trends in the large majority of cases. Data on labour force growth by sex and on the share of women in the total labour force are set out in table III.1. The estimates refer to the period from 1975 to 1984 for the market-economy countries and from 1975 to 1982 for the countries with centrally planned economies. In addition, it should be noted that the data for the latter countries relate to the socialized sectors or certain segments of the socialized economy (such as employees and office

---

[1] *The Economic Role of Women in the ECE Region* (United Nations publication, Sales No. E.80.II.E.6).

TABLE III.1

**Percentage change of labour force by sex, and share of women
in total labour force change, 1975–1984**

Region and country	Labour force change			Share of women in total labour force change
	Both sexes	Males	Females	
Western Europe				
Austria..................................	2.6	1.0	5.0	77.4
Belgium.................................	5.4	−0.8	17.4	110.1
Denmark................................	10.1	2.5	20.9	85.6
Finland	13.4	10.7	16.6	57.4
France	5.5	1.2	12.7	85.8
Germany, Federal Republic of..............	1.8	−0.1	5.0	104.8
Ireland..................................	15.2	11.1	26.2	46.2
Italy	10.7	3.5	27.3	76.9
Netherlands..............................	18.7	7.4	47.3	71.6
Norway	16.3	6.5	32.3	75.0
Sweden	6.3	−1.8	17.4	116.4
Switzerland	−0.3	−2.2	3.3	a
United Kingdom	5.0	0.4	12.5	94.7
North America				
Canada	24.0	13.6	41.9	64.0
United States	20.7	12.8	33.0	62.4
Eastern Europe and USSR				
Bulgaria.................................	9.8	4.7	15.7	74.3
Czechoslovakia...........................	5.2	5.1	5.4	46.6
German Democratic Republic	5.3	0.0	10.5	99.0
Hungary	−1.8	−3.7	0.1	a
Poland	−1.3	−2.9	0.7	a
Romania	18.9	11.8	31.6	60.0
USSR	9.1	10.2	8.1	45.3
Southern Europe				
Greece	14.8	12.3	20.8	41.4
Portugal	20.6	10.9	36.1	67.2
Spain	4.9	−7.0	48.8	213.5
Turkey..................................	14.7	17.8	19.3	22.9
Yugoslavia	9.3	6.8	13.3	54.1

Sources: National statistics and secretariat estimates.

a Not applicable because change of total labour force was negative.

workers) [2] and are therefore not strictly comparable with the results from the market economy countries. Notwithstanding these differences, the data show that the growth of the female labour force was more rapid than that for males in all but two countries: Turkey and the Union of Soviet Socialist Republics, where the relative increase was higher for men than for women. In the former case, this may reflect the effect of the structural transformation of the economy from agriculture to non-agriculture, which often leads to a decline in the number of women working or reported as unpaid family workers in subsistence agriculture. Such changes would tend to slow down the growth of the female work force. The USSR is also a unique case in that female labour force participation has been very high for quite some time. In fact, the Soviet Union is the only country in the region where, as early as 1975, women workers outnumbered male workers (about 50.5% of those employed in the socialized sectors were women). Under such conditions, the main reason for a further growth of the female labour force—rising participation rates—disappears and demographic changes as

[2] For Poland and Romania in particular and, to a lesser extent, for Bulgaria, the data used differ significantly from those of the labour force according to census concepts.

well as minor shifts in participation levels determine the male-female growth differential.

Table III.1 also shows that, over the period, the number of men in the labour force was stagnant or even declined in absolute terms in: Belgium; German Democratic Republic; Germany, Federal Republic of; Hungary; Poland; Spain; Sweden and Switzerland. However, the female labour force increased in all countries, although there were large differences in this regard. The percentage increase was very high in Canada, the Netherlands, Norway, Portugal, Spain, Romania and the United States, averaging more than 3% annually between 1975 and 1984 (between 1975 and 1982 in the case of Romania). In other countries, such as Austria, Czechoslovakia, the Federal Republic of Germany and Switzerland, the rate of increase was much slower. In Hungary and Poland, the female labour force grew negligibly. In most of these countries the male labour force either increased slowly or declined, suggesting that stagnation of labour force growth can be partly attributed to demographic factors and, in particular, to a slow growth of the working age population. The opposite factor, a rapid increase of the working age population, may have been responsible to some extent for the rapid expansion of the female labour force in the first group of countries.

The share of women in the total growth of the labour force in individual countries, also shown in table III.1, clearly reflects the impact of the high growth rate of the female labour force. Although the percentage share depends not only on the difference in the rate of increase of the number of men and women in the labour force, but also on their initial relative shares, women represented more than half of the increase in the labour force in all but five countries: Czechoslovakia, Greece, Ireland, Turkey and the USSR. In four countries where the male labour force declined (Belgium, the Federal Republic of Germany, Spain and Sweden), women accounted for more than 100% of the growth in the total labour force. In addition, the total labour force declined in Hungary, Poland and Switzerland, despite a growth in the female labour force. In thirteen of the remaining fifteen countries, more than 60% of the total growth was due to the increasing number of women in the labour force.

As a result of these developments, the female share of the total work force increased in all countries, with the exception of Turkey and the USSR. In general, women constitute the highest percentage of the labour force in the centrally planned economies and in the Nordic countries. In the former, women generally represent well over 40% of the labour force (table III.2). The proportion, as noted above, was already more than half in the USSR in 1975.

TABLE III.2

Female labour force as a percentage of total labour force, 1975 and 1984

	Women in the total labour force	
Region and country	1975	1984
Western Europe		
Austria	40	41
Belgium	34	38
Denmark	41	45
Finland	46	47
France	37	39
Germany, Federal Republic of	37	39
Ireland	27	29
Italy	30	35
Netherlands	28	35
Norway	38	43
Sweden	43	47
Switzerland	34	35
United Kingdom	37	40
North America		
Canada	37	41
United States	39	43
Eastern Europe and USSR		
Bulgaria	47	49
Czechoslovakia	45	46
German Democratic Republic	50	52
Hungary	44	45
Poland	42	43
Romania	36	40
USSR	51	51
Southern Europe		
Greece	30	31
Portugal	38	43
Spain	21	30
Turkey	36	35
Yugoslavia	38	39

Sources: National statistics and secretariat estimates.

By the early 1980s, more than half of all workers in the German Democratic Republic also were women. In the Nordic countries, the share of women varies between 43% and 47% but, it should be noted that, in these countries, approximately half of employed women are part-time workers. The percentage of women in the labour force in the remaining countries of western Europe varies between approximately 35% and 40%, although it is much lower (under 30%) in Ireland. In Canada and the United States, the percentages were 41% and 43% respectively, which places them between those for the Nordic countries and the rest of western Europe. The south European countries consist of two groups: Greece, Spain and Turkey, where women account for between 30% and 35% of the labour force; and Portugal and Yugoslavia where the proportions are considerably higher, 43% and 39% respectively. In addition, changes in these shares over time were considerable. The proportion of women in the labour force increased by only one percentage point over the period considered in Austria, Czechoslovakia, Finland, Greece, Hungary, Poland and Switzerland. Relatively high increases (4 to 5 percentage points) are found in Belgium, Canada, Denmark, Italy, Norway, Portugal, Romania, Sweden and the United States. The share of women rose very sharply in the Netherlands (by 7 percentage points) and even more so in Spain (by 9 percentage points).

The growth difference between the female and male labour force was also associated with a shift in the demographic composition of the labour force. Women currently outnumber prime-age males [3] in the labour force in several countries (table III.3). In North America, as well as in several countries of western Europe, women are the larger demographic group in the labour force, when compared with prime-age males.

TABLE III.3

Demographic composition of the labour force in selected countries

(*Percentages*)

	Prime-age males (25–54 years)[a]		Women (all)	
Country	1975	1982	1975	1982
Canada	40	38	37	41
Finland	38	40[b]	47	47[b]
France	43	44	39	42
Germany, Federal Republic of	44	44[b]	37	38[b]
Italy	58	52[b]	28	34[b]
Netherlands	51	50[b]	27	32[b]
Norway	45	42[b]	38	42[b]
Portugal	35	31[b]	38	42[b]
Spain	46	45[b]	27	28[b]
Sweden	37	36	43	46
United Kingdom	39	38	38	40
United States	37	37	39	43

Sources: OECD, *Labour Force Statistics 1970–1981*; OECD, *Employment Outlook* (Paris, September 1983); and national statistics.

[a] Except for Italy, where prime-age males are those between 25 and 59 years and where older people are those 60 years of age and over.

[b] 1981.

[3] Prime-age is generally taken to be the age group 25–54, except in Italy, where it refers to the age group 25–59.

TABLE III.4

Labour force participation by sex, 1975–1984

(Percentages)

	Labour force as a percentage of population 15–64 years					
	Both sexes		Males		Females	
Region and country	1975	1984	1975	1984	1975	1984
Western Europe						
Austria........................	70.2	66.5	88.2	80.5	53.6	53.1
Belgium	63.8	62.9	83.7	75.8	43.9	49.3
Denmark	76.8	79.5	89.8	85.1	63.5	73.6
Finland	71.6	74.7	77.8	75.6	65.5	73.8
France	67.3	65.5	84.4	79.1	49.9	51.7
Germany, Federal Republic of....	67.9	61.2	87.0	78.8	49.6	45.1
Ireland	61.7	61.1	89.2	85.0	33.4	36.5
Italy	58.9	61.6	84.2	81.2	34.6	42.3
Netherlands...................	57.8	60.1	82.1	76.8	33.1	42.9
Norway	69.7	78.8	85.9	88.8	53.3	68.5
Sweden.......................	78.5	81.1	89.2	85.5	67.6	77.3
Switzerland	73.3	68.5	97.5	88.8	49.6	48.3
United Kingdom...............	73.9	74.2	92.5	88.4	55.4	59.9
North America						
Canada	68.1	72.7	86.2	84.4	50.0	60.9
United States..................	69.1	74.0	85.4	83.0	53.2	64.8
Eastern Europe and USSR						
Czechoslovakia.................	74.2	75.4	81.9	83.0	66.6	68.0
German Democratic Republic	76.0	76.1	81.0	74.8	71.5	77.5
Hungary	72.0	71.0	82.5	79.3	61.9	63.0
USSR	71.5	71.7	74.8	73.7	68.6	70.0
Southern Europe						
Greece	58.8	60.9	84.8	84.9	33.9	37.8
Portugal......................	69.0	75.3	91.1	85.3	49.6	56.3
Spain	56.7	53.1	91.3	74.6	23.7	31.9
Turkey	74.1	65.8	92.0	82.9	55.1	47.3
Yugoslavia....................	62.1	60.7	78.8	74.4	46.0	47.0

Sources: National statistics and secretariat estimates.

These shifts in the demographic composition of the labour force, as well as the differences in overall trends in the male and female work force, reflect to a large extent diverging tendencies in the participation patterns of men and women. For some time now, participation rates for men have been declining, while those for women have been increasing. There are several reasons for men's lower participation. In many countries extended periods of education have reduced activity rates among both young men and young women. Improved retirement options have had the same impact on the participation rates of older workers of both sexes. In a number of countries, however, early retirement appears to have become more widespread among men below the age of traditional retirement, thus also reducing the activity rates of those in the upper and even lower fifties.[4] As far as the participation rates in the prime age groups are concerned, those of women have continued to increase, whereas those for men generally remained stable or even declined somewhat.

The impact of the different pace of male and female labour force growth on total participation rates varies

considerably (see table III.4). In two countries, the German Democratic Republic and the USSR, the overall participation for both sexes combined did not change between the mid-1970s and the early 1980s. The participation rates increased in half of the remaining countries and declined in the other half. Nevertheless, the decreases were generally larger than the increases and, in several countries (Austria, the Federal Republic of Germany, Spain, Switzerland and Turkey), the extent of the decline was considerable (at least 3.5 percentage points). The downward pressure on overall participation was due, as the data of table III.4 also show, to the continuing negative trend in male participation rates. The rates for men were lower at the end of the period in all countries shown in the table, except for Czechoslovakia and Norway where they increased, and Greece where they did not change. Large decreases in male activity rates occurred in: Austria; the German Democratic Republic; Germany, Federal Republic of; Spain; Switzerland and Turkey, mostly countries which also experienced a considerable drop in the overall participation rate.

Whereas the general decline in male participation during the recent period represents a continuation of past trends, the almost universal rise in female participation is a much more recent phenomenon. The 1980 study showed that female participation rates increased between 1960 and 1970 in just over half of the countries. Between 1975

---

[4] Participation rates of men in the 60–64 year age groups have decreased especially sharply in many countries, but rates also declined, though more gradually, for men between 55 and 59 years old and, in some cases, even after the age of 45.

and the early 1980s, however, participation rates of women rose in all but four of the countries included in the table (Austria, the Federal Republic of Germany, Switzerland and Turkey). Despite the general tendency for female participation to rise throughout the region, the levels reached by the end of the period still varied considerably from one country to another. The countries of the centrally planned economies and the Nordic countries have the highest female participation rates: approximately 70% of women of 15 years of age and over are in the work force. These countries are followed by North America, with participation rates of 60% to 65%. Considerable differences exist between the other west European countries, in which the highest female participation rate is that of the United Kingdom, at 60%. The corresponding rates in Austria, Belgium, France and Switzerland are between 45% and 55%. The rates in the Federal Republic of Germany, Italy and the Netherlands are between 40% and 45%, and the lowest participation of women in western Europe is found in Ireland (36%). The degree to which women in southern Europe participate in the labour force also varies considerably. Over 55%, a high rate, is reported for Portugal; Turkey and Yugoslavia each have female participation rates of about 47% and, at the lower end of the scale, are Greece (38%) and Spain (32%).

B. Patterns of women's labour force participation

While aggregate data show that women's participation continued to increase in virtually all ECE countries, only a more detailed analysis, taking account of such factors as age, marital status, fertility, the presence of children and levels of education, can shed further light on these trends.

1. AGE

In many countries, the participation of younger women in the labour force (in the 15 to 19-year age group) declined during the 1970s, doubtless as a result of the extension of the education period. It is believed that this downward trend among young people due to increases in enrolment in education and training, to some extent reflects a pattern of postponement of entry into the labour market in response to high unemployment and declining job opportunities. If so it is possible that participation rates among the young may begin to increase again once economic growth is more strongly established. Among older women, participation rates have also declined in many countries of the region; improved pension provisions in some countries may partly account for this trend. A significant development in women's participation in recent years has been the increase in the activity rates of women in the main childbearing years (age groups 25–29 and 30–34 years). The participation rates of these age cohorts increased in 18 of the 19 countries for which data are available, in some cases quite dramatically (table III.5 and figure III.1).

Differences in the age pattern of women's labour force participation were already pointed out in the 1980 study. In eastern Europe and the USSR, such patterns closely resemble those of men. Activity rates plotted on a chart have the appearance of an inverted "U", with little variation between the ages of 25 and 45 years, when high levels of participation prevail. In western Europe and North America, activity curves have typically revealed an "M"-

TABLE III.5

Increase in labour force participation of women in main childbearing years, in selected countries

(Percentages)

Country and year	Age group 25–29	Age group 25–34	Age group 30–34
Belgium (1970–1977)	30	..	38
Canada (1971–1981)	..	47	..
Denmark (1970–1981)	47	..	56
France (1970–1980)	..	31	..
Italy (1971–1981)	64	..	68
Netherlands (1971–1981)....	81	..	95
Norway (1970–1980)	43	..	68 [a]
Sweden (1970–1980)	37	..	47
United Kingdom (1971–1981)	28	..	18
United States (1970–1980) ..	..	47	..

Source: Calculated from participation rates shown in the figure.
[a] 30–39 year-olds.

shaped pattern, in which labour force activity reaches a peak in the 20–24 year age group, then drops for the age groups 25–29 and 30–34 years, coinciding with childbearing periods, when many women withdraw from the labour force. Participation then reaches a second peak around the ages of 40–50 years, as married women often return to the work force once their children are older. In the countries of southern Europe, the general level of women's labour force participation was much lower, and tended to drop sharply after the age of 25, with little evidence of a second peak.

More recent data show significant changes in the pattern of activity curves in several countries. In the Nordic countries and France, the inverted "U"-shaped curve has replaced the "M"-shaped one. In other countries, such as Austria, Canada, Italy and the United States, the general level of participation has risen and, while there is still some decline after the age of 25 years, the subsequent years are characterized by what appears to be a tapering off from the much higher level, rather than a sharp drop followed by a secondary peak. This pattern can be regarded as a transition from an "M" to a "U"-shaped curve.

It is important to note that labour force activity curves reflect cross-sectional data and do not give any indication of changing longitudinal patterns. In other words, a particular activity curve in a given year does not necessarily reflect the likely future participation pattern at a later age of women in the younger age groups. It cannot be assumed that these younger age cohorts will follow participation patterns similar to those of the previous generation, even at higher levels of participation. The fact that the present participation rates of the age cohorts in the early reproductive ages are so much higher than they were some ten years ago, could be an indication of a new trend, for which several factors may be responsible. Declining fertility means that many women have only one child, or two at most, instead of the larger families which were common in previous generations. The increasing dependence of families on two wage-earners, and the increasing incidence of divorce and female-headed single-parent families, are other factors affecting participation patterns among this younger generation of women. Increasing levels of education and changing attitudes have also had an influence. It has been noted that, if participation rates of the younger age cohorts are observed through succes-

Figure III. 1

Changing patterns of women's labour force participation

(per cent active)

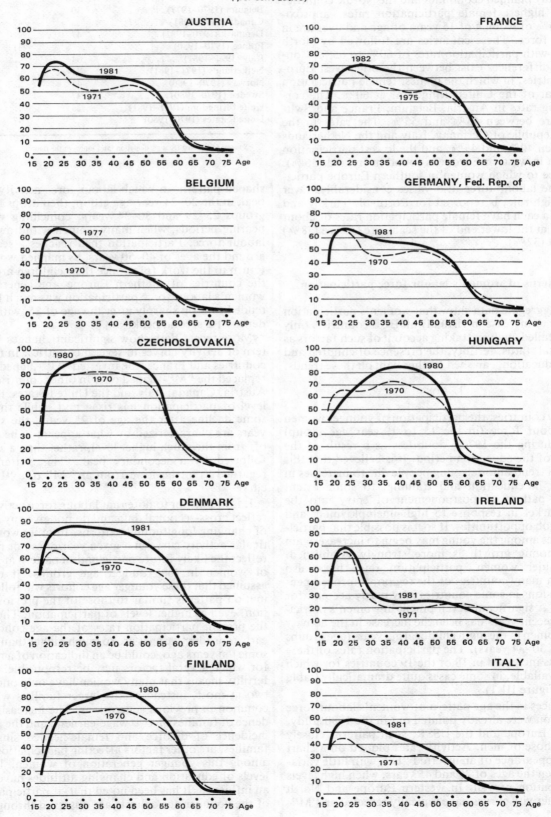

Figure III. 1 (*continued*)

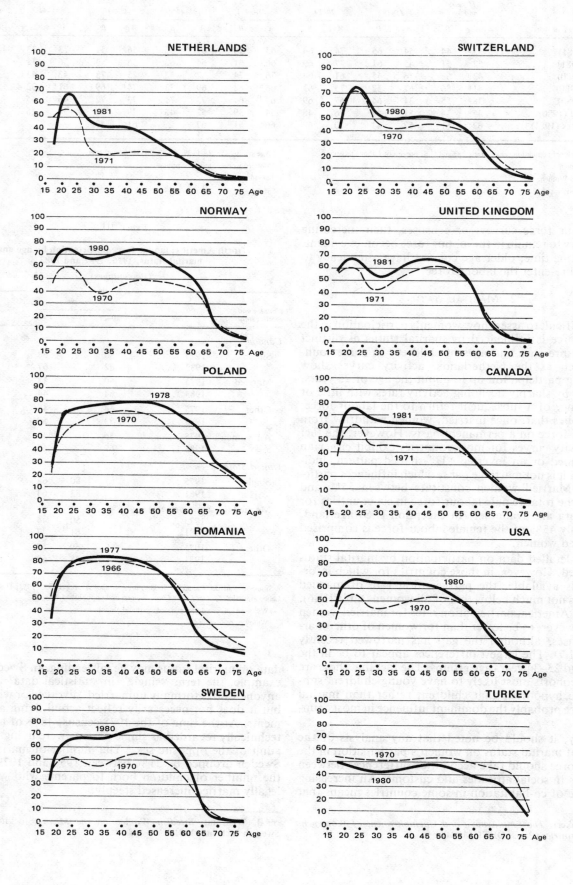

TABLE III.6

Activity rates of women by age and marital status, 1980-1981

(Percentages)

Country and year	Total 15 years and over		15–19		20–24		25–34		35–44		45–54		55–64		65 and over	
	A	B	A	B	A	B	A	B	A	B	A	B	A	B	A	B
Austria (1981).........	35[a]	44	54	65	74	64	63	56	61	56	56	51	23	23	2	3
Canada (1981)	52	51	45	61	77	69	66	61	64	62	56	53	36	31	6	5
Finland (1980)	42[a]	63	16	45	61	64	76	74	82	82	75	75	43	43	2	4
Norway (1980)	41[a]	56	62	52	75	61	66[b]	62	69[b]	73	74[b]	69	61[b]	32	17[b]	..
Sweden (1980).........	38[a]	55	31	64	67	69	67	64	72	71	73	72	46	45	2	2
Switzerland (1980)	35[a]	34	51	49	76	48	54	39	52	43	49	41	34	25	5	4
United States (1981)[c]...	62	51	52	47	70	62	66	61[d]	67	..	61	47[e]	..	..	8	7

Sources: National population census statistics; and U.S. Bureau of Labor Statistics.

A = All women
B = Married Women
[a] Crude activity rate.

[b] Age groups 25–29, 30–39, 40–49, 50–59, 60 and over.
[c] Married women, husband present.
[d] 24–44.
[e] 45–64.

sive labour force surveys or censuses, their increasing propensity to remain in the labour force becomes evident. At the same time, older age cohorts have a tendency to enter and re-enter the labour force.[5]

2. MARITAL STATUS

It is difficult to assess how women's participation in the labour force is influenced by marital status as distinct from the presence and ages of children. In some countries, such as the Netherlands, activity curves show increasing participation up to about the age of 25 years, followed by sharply declining activity rates with little or no evidence of a subsequent return to the labour force. This implies that, once married, women withdraw from the work force on a permanent basis. However, the fact that activity curves for most countries exhibit either an "M"-shaped or an inverted "U"-shaped pattern, indicates that it is not marriage *per se* which influences participation. Married women constitute between 55% and 69% of the total female labour force in six countries for which data are available. An exception is Switzerland, where only 45% of the female labour force is comprised of married women.

More detailed data on participation by marital status are limited. However, in those countries for which information is available, the participation rate of married women is not much below that of all women (table III.6). In North America, participation rates for married women tend, however, to be lower than for women of other marital statuses, although the gap has narrowed recently (table III.7). The largest differences appear to be in the 20–24 and 25–34 years age groups. The fact that these are the age cohorts most likely to have young children, supports the hypothesis that children, rather than marital status, are probably the dominant influence in most countries.

Finally, it should be noted that any analysis of the impact of marital status on women's participation in the labour force should take account of differences between countries in social attitudes and customs. An increasing incidence of co-habitation in some countries means that

TABLE III.7

North America: labour force participation by age and marital status, 1975, 1981 and 1983

(Percentages)

Country and marital status	Year	Age group			All women
		20–24	25–44	45–64	
Canada					
Single	1975	80		68	59
	1983	82		67	64
Married	1975	50		35	42
	1983	64		44	52
Other	1975	64		48	32
	1983	73		50	36
All women	1975	56		39	44
	1983	69		46	53
United States					
Single	1975		80	68	57
	1981		83	64	62
Married (husband present)					
	1975		50	44	44
	1981		61	47	51
Other[a]	1975		69	59	38[b]
	1981		78	60	42[b]

Sources: Statistics Canada, *Labour Force Annual Averages 1975–1983*; U.S. Bureau of Labor Statistics, *Special Labor Force Reports* and unpublished data.

[a] Widowed, divorced and married, husband absent.
[b] Widowed or divorced.

data on marital status may be misleading. In Sweden, for example, the term "single" in statistical data refers to anyone who is formally unmarried, divorced or widowed, but it does not necessarily reflect actual living arrangements. At the time of the 1975 census, 48% of all those technically regarded as single parents were living with an adult of the opposite sex.[6] The number of marriages in Sweden dropped by 31% between 1950 and 1979, while the number of children born to parents who were not legally married increased steeply.

---

[5] L. Paukert, *The Employment and Unemployment of Women in OECD Countries* (Paris, OECD, 1984).

[6] B. Wistrand, *Swedish Women on the Move* (Stockholm, The Swedish Institute, 1981).

3. FERTILITY AND THE PRESENCE OF CHILDREN

It is generally assumed that declining fertility rates in almost all countries of the region have had a major influence on female participation rates. However, the evidence is not conclusive. For instance, despite the fact that women in the east European countries have higher fertility rates than those in the west European countries, female participation is much higher in the former countries. The 1980 study observed that, even though significant changes in reproduction patterns had made it possible for many more women to engage in paid labour, they had not done so to the same extent in all countries. Large differences in women's activity rates remain between countries where the small family norm has existed for decades.[7] The study also pointed out that many other factors, such as education, family income, prevailing wage levels and, perhaps most important of all, societal attitudes and values, considerably influence the extent of women's labour force participation. There are also major differences between the countries of eastern and western Europe in the participation rates of mothers with very young children. Whether or not such women participate in the work force is certainly dependent on a complex combination of factors, but societal factors undoubtedly play a large role.

It has been observed that a major shift in the age pattern of participation rates is taking place as women move through the prime childbearing ages.[8] The traditional relationship between childbearing and the participation rates of women in the prime childbearing age groups was reversed in the United States, beginning in 1976. In that year, women in the age group 25–29 years had a higher participation rate than five years earlier (see also table III.8). It was also noted that, in Canada, there was a significant departure from the traditional female participation pattern beginning with the age cohort born between 1941 and 1950. For the cohort born between 1951 and 1960, sufficient data do not yet exist to establish a trend line. In the west European and North American countries, this age group includes the so-called "baby-boom" children.

As regards the relation between the presence of young children and women's labour force participation, the 1980 study noted an inverse relationship between the activity rates of married women in each age group and the number of children, with a clear positive correlation between the activity rates of these women and the age of the youngest child.[9] Perhaps one of the most significant developments since the mid-1970s has been the marked increase, in several countries, of labour force activity among the mothers of very young children (table III.9). In North America, 50% or more of mothers with children under the age of six are currently in the labour force. In Canada, the labour force participation of married women with husbands present and with children under the age of three rose from 35% in 1975 to 52% in 1983, representing a 58% increase in the participation rate of this group within only eight years. In the United States, 50% of married women with husbands present and with children under six years old now participate in the work force, compared with only 37% in 1975. In some of the Nordic countries, the participation of mothers with young children is even higher. In 1981, 79% of women in Sweden with children under seven and 59% in Norway with children in the 3–6 year age group, were in the labour force, although, as noted above, a high percentage of women workers in these countries have part-time jobs. Data are not available for most of the other countries of the region, although it appears that the trend described above may not be common to all countries. In the United Kingdom, for instance, 67% of children aged between three and four years had mothers who did not engage in any paid work in 1979 whereas, six years earlier, in 1973, the corresponding figure was 72%.

An earlier comparison of the participation rates of mothers in six east and west European countries sheds some light on the apparently different relationship between fertility and labour force participation in the two groups of countries (table III.10). The data show major differences between east European countries and between countries of western Europe and North America. As the results indicate, the negative effect of the presence of young children in respect of labour force participation is much less pronounced in the east European countries.

4. EDUCATION

There is considerable evidence that the higher the level of a person's education, the more likely it is that he or she is in the labour force. This appears to be even more true of women than of men. The existence of such a relation, however, does not necessarily emerge from aggregate data on labour force participation. Table III.11, for instance, does not reveal any obvious correlation between the average educational levels of women and their participation. A more detailed breakdown is needed, if the impact of education on labour force activity is to be assessed more accurately. Table III.12 sets out labour force participation rates by sex and educational level for seven countries. The data generally seem to provide support for the hypothesized positive relation between educational level and labour force participation. It should be noted, however, that there is likely to be a certain bias in the data in so far as older women are concerned. Women in the older age groups generally have had more limited educational opportunities, and also tend to be characterized by lower participation rates.

TABLE III.8

United States: participation rates of women aged 20–24 and 25–29, selected years

(Percentages)

Year	20–24	Year	25–29
1968	54.6	1973	51.8
1969	56.8	1974	54.8
1970	57.8	1975	57.1
1971	57.8	1976	59.3
1972	59.1	1977	61.8
1973	61.2	1978	64.3

Source: U.S. Bureau of Labor Statistics, *Employment and Earnings.*

---

[7] *The Economic Role of Women ...*, p. 77.

[8] D. Curiak and H. Sims, *Participation Rate and Labour Force Growth in Canada,* Department of Finance (Ottawa, April 1980).

---

[9] *The Economic Role of Women ...*, p. 14 and table II.5.

TABLE III.9

Labour force participation of mothers with young children, in selected countries

(Percentages)

Country and family status	1975	1976	1977	1978	1979	1980	1981	1982	1983
Canada									
Female participation rate by age of own children									
Husband present									
With pre-school-age children ..	34	35	37	41	42	44	47	48	52
With children under 3 years ...	31	32	34	38	39	42	45	46	49
Without children under 3 years but at least one 3–5 years ...	39	40	41	46	47	49	51	53	56
No husband present									
With pre-school-age children ..	45	44	47	45	50	53	51	52	51
With children under 3 years ...	38	34	38	40	43	45	42	44	44
Without children under 3 years but at least one 3–5 years ...	51	52	54	50	56	60	60	58	56
All families									
With pre-school-age children ..	35	36	38	41	43	45	48	49	52
With children under 3 years ...	32	32	34	38	40	42	45	46	49
Without children under 3 years but at least one 3–5 years ...	40	41	43	47	48	50	53	54	56
United States									
Labour force participation rates of married women, husband present, by age of own children									
Under 6 years	37	38	39	42	43	45	48	49	50

	1960	1970	1980	1981
By marital status, and age of own children				
Married, husband present, children under 6 years	19	30	45	48
Separated, children under 6 years	..	45	52	51
Divorced, children under 6 years .	..	63	68	65

	Women with children under 16		Age of youngest child			
			0–2 years		3–6 years	
	1979	1981	1979	1981	1979	1981
Norway						
Labour force participation rates of married women by number of children and age of youngest child						
of which:						
With one child	66	69	56	56	58	66
2 children..................	57	62	39	44	56	58
3 children..................	58	60	38	47	58	55
4 and more	46	49	34	33	44	55
Total..................	60	64	45	48	56	59

	1973	1974	1975	1976	1977	1978	1979	1980	1981
Sweden									
Labour force participation rates of women aged 16–64 years by marital status and age of children									
Single women	66	68	71	72	72	73	74	74	74
Married women	61	64	66	68	70	72	74	76	78
Women with children under 7 ...	54	57	61	63	66	69	72	75	79

TABLE III.9 (*continued*)

Country and family status	1973 children aged			1979 children aged		
	0–2 years	3–4 years	All ages under 15	0–2 years	3–4 years	All ages under 15
United Kingdom						
Children by family characteristics						
Paid work done by mother						
None	81	72	55	79	67	50
Part-time	14	20	30	17	27	36
Full-time	5	8	15	4	6	14
Total	100	100	100	100	100	100

Sources: Statistics Canada, *Labour Force Survey*; U.S. Bureau of Labor Statistics, *Monthly Labor Review* (December 1983) and *Special Labour Force Report No. 13*; Norway, Central Bureau of Statistics, *Labour Market Statistics, 1979, 1981*; Swedish National Labour Market Board, *Labour Force Sample Surveys*; and United Kingdom, *General Household Survey, 1973* and *1979*.

C. Some aspects of the changing participation of women

The trend towards greater female participation has been associated with a number of factors which have a bearing on the degree of women's integration into the labour force. Whereas questions related to sectoral concentration, occupational segregation and pay differentials are discussed in later chapters, some of the more general aspects are examined below. These aspects include the increasing participation of women in the labour force, problems of combining household duties with paid employment, the changing occupational status of women, the growing importance of employment in services, and part-time work for women.

1. THE INCREASING ATTACHMENT OF WOMEN TO THE LABOUR FORCE

The tendency towards increasing participation rates of women at the main childbearing ages and of those with young children, clearly suggests a growing desire of women to be employed throughout their working life. In particular, the younger generations may opt for a work pattern of a more permanent nature, different from that of previous generations. Another factor which points to such an increasing attachment to the labour force is the

continuing increase in women's participation even during the recent economic recessions.

In previous recessions, considerable differences were observed in the behaviour of male and female workers in terms of the phenomena described as the "discouraged" and the "added" worker. "Discouraged" workers are those who withdraw from the labour force or refrain from entering it during a recession because they are discouraged about the possibility of finding work. "Added" workers are those who would not normally be in the labour force, and who enter it during a recession because other family members are without employment. There is some disagreement about the net effect of these phenomena. Clearly, if the discouraged-worker effect outweighs the added-worker effect during a recession, total participation rates would decline. Some observers believe that married women are particularly likely to be "added" workers. Paradoxically, women are also believed to be more likely to become "discouraged" workers because they are perceived to have a weaker attachment to the labour force than men. Two studies which examined this question with regard to Canada and the United States [10] concluded that female participation rates are more sensitive to cyclical variation than male participation rates. The OECD has constructed econometric models for seven countries, [11] on the basis of which it concluded that "prime-age males appeared to remain in the labour force irrespective of the economic situation as their participation rate varied very little over the cycle. Other demographic groups such as women, youth and older people tended to withdraw from the labour group, to a greater or lesser extent as the demand for labour declined". [12]

TABLE III.10

Labour force participation of mothers, by age of child, 1976

(*Percentages*)

Country	Age		
	0–3 years	3–6 years	School age
France	43	44	48
German Democratic Republic	80	85	85
Germany, Federal Republic of	32	34	41
Hungary	82 [a]	75	75
Sweden	58	64	78
United States	35	48	56

Source: S. B. Kamerman and A. J. Kahn, *Child Care, Family Benefits and Working Parents: A Study in Comparative Policy* (New York, Columbia University Press, 1981).

[a] Thirty-three per cent excluding women at home on child-care leave, 82% if women on child-care leave are included.

[10] K. B. Clark and L. H. Summers, "Demographic Differences in Cyclical Employment Variation," *Journal of Human Resources* (Winter, 1981), pp. 61–79; and A. S. Roy, "Cyclical Sensitivity of Unemployment and Participation Rates among Demographic Groups in Canada", published as Technical Annex No. 10, in M. Robertson, *A Longitudinal Analysis of the Canadian Labour Market, Employment and Immigration* (Ottawa, June 1982).

[11] Canada; France; Germany, Federal Republic of; Italy; Japan; the United Kingdom and the United States, based on annual data for the period 1961–1981, except for France and the Federal Republic of Germany, where the period related to 1962–1981.

[12] OECD, *Employment Outlook* (Paris, September 1983).

TABLE III.11

Influences on female labour force participation, around 1980

| Region and country | Total female labour force as per cent of female population 15–64, 1980 | Gross enrol- ment ratio of female students at third level, 1977/78 [a] | Proportion of female students registered in | | Total fertility rate, [d] 1970/80 | GNP per capita (US $), 1980 |
			Humanities and arts, [b] 1977/78	Science, engineering, medicine, etc., [c] 1977/78		
Western Europe						
Austria	49	18	34	24	1.73	10 230
Belgium	48	22	13	37	1.68	12 180
Denmark	71 [e]	28	22	29	1.60	12 950
Finland	67	21	21	34	1.64	9 720
France	53	24	–	–	1.88	11 730
Germany, Federal Republic of	49	21	24	37	1.38	13 590
Ireland	35 [e]	15	36	26	3.24	4 880
Italy	40	23	26	36	1.81	6 840
Netherlands..............	35	21	30	21	1.57	11 470
Norway	63	23	19	30	1.72	12 650
Sweden	74	34	5	41	1.68	13 520
Switzerland	50	10	32	25	1.50	16 440
United Kingdom	58	14	22	22	1.70 [f]	7 920
North America						
Canada	57	38	26	22	1.77	10 130
United States	60	39	..	..	1.85	11 360
Eastern Europe and USSR						
Bulgaria.................	72 [g]	21	17	48	2.15	..
Czechoslovakia...........	75	14	4	34	2.33	..
German Democratic Republic	74	34	3	43	1.88	..
Hungary	63	13	3	22	2.02	..
Poland..................	70 [h]	20	10	35	2.27	..
Romania	70 [i]	9	..	..	2.54	..
USSR	75 [j]	23 [g]	3 [j]	48 [j]	2.28	..
Southern Europe						
Greece	33 [e]	14	20	27	2.29	4 520
Spain	32	19	17	31	2.52	5 350
Yugoslavia	46 [h]	19	12	25	2.16	2 620

Source: L. Paukert, "Personal preference, social change or economic necessity? Why women work", *Labour and Society,* vol. 7, No. 4, October-December 1982 (International Institute for Labour Studies) (Geneva, ILO, 1982).

[a] Gross enrolment ratio: total third-level enrolment of women as percentage of female population aged 20–24. Third level: anyone who undertook post-secondary studies, whether or not they completed the full course.

[b] Female third-level students registered in humanities and arts as percentage of total number of female third-level students, excluding non-specified.

[c] Female third-level students registered in the groups of subjects consisting of: natural sciences, mathematics, medicine and health-related sciences, engineering, architecture and industrial programmes, as percentage of total number of third-level female students, excluding non-specified.

[d] Average number of children that would be born to each woman of the population if each were to live through her childbearing lifetime (15–49) having children at the same rate as women of those ages who actually did, in a given year.

[e] 1979.

[f] England and Wales only.

[g] 1975.

[h] 1978.

[i] 1977.

[j] Estimate.

While such conclusions may be historically correct, their relevance to the most recent recessions is questionable. In any case, there may be significant differences between age cohorts (see below). Calculations based on aggregate data for the female labour force may therefore be misleading. Some indication that women remain in the labour force rather than withdrawing when employment opportunities decline, is reflected by their unemployment rates which, in most of the countries of the region, were higher than those of males in 1984, more than double in some cases.

The apparently weak influence of the discouraged-worker effect among women supports the hypothesis of a stronger labour force attachment than was evident in the past. One explanation for this change is the fact that, in many cases, families now depend on the earnings of both husband and wife. Also, the increasing incidence of female-headed single-parent families means that more women work, or would if they could find a job.

It has been pointed out [13] that the impact of the added-worker effect tends to be limited by the fact that the non-working population able to take employment is declining in relative importance. In the United States in mid-1981, there were about 600,000 non-active wives of unemployed husbands, a low figure in comparison with a total female labour force of more than 46 million. It was estimated that, even if 50% of the wives with unemployed husbands had become economically active, the rate of female labour force participation would have increased by only 0.3%.

---

[13] L. Paukert, *op. cit.*

TABLE III.12

Labour force participation by level of education and sex, selected countries, selected years

(Percentages)

Country, year, level of education	Males	Females
Belgium, 1977		
Primary education or incomplete secondary ..	83	30
General education, lower	94	55
General education, higher	96	66
Technical or vocational school, lower	97	60
Technical or vocational school, higher	98	70
Lower teachers' training	93	79
Higher, below university level	98	79
University	98	82
Canada, 1983		
0–8 years	58	26
High school	79	54
Some post-secondary	80	63
Post-secondary certificate or diploma	88	68
University degree........................	91	76
Finland, 1978		
No education after comprehensive school....	60	47
Education on secondary level, lower	86	74
Education on secondary level, upper	71	63
Higher education........................	87	79
France, 1975		
No general certificate indicated.............	..	29
CEP (*Certificat d'Etudes primaires*)	..	46
BEPC (*Brevet d'Etudes du 1er Cycle*)	..	61
Baccalauréat............................	..	66
More advanced than *Baccalauréat*	..	75
Norway, 1980		
Primary school	69	43
Secondary school I	85	61
Secondary school II	82	65
University..............................	90	77
Spain, 1975		
Less than primary education	74	13
Primary education	84	22
Secondary general education	58	28
Vocational training.......................	76	46
Technical/engineering school	87	53
University..............................	87	66
United States, 1979		
0–8 years	..	23
High school 1-3 years	..	42
High school 4 years.......................	..	57
College 1–3 years	..	60
College 4 years or more	..	67

Sources: Belgium: INS, *Socio-economic Survey* (Brussels, 1977). Finland: *Labour Force Survey*, statistics on educational and occupational structure in 1978; "Position of Women", *Statistical Report TY 1979: 9*; *Statistical Survey*, No. 65, Central Statistical Office of Finland. France: "*Population Census*", *Institut national de la statistique et des études économiques, Les collections de l'Insee*, No. 86 (1975). Norway: *Labour market statistics 1980*, Central Bureau of Statistics (Oslo, 1981). Spain: *Instituto Nacional de Estadística, Características de la población española deducidas del padrón municipal de habitantes, 1975*, vol. II (Madrid, 1979). Canada: Statistics Canada, *Labour Force Annual Averages, 1975–1983*. United States: *Perspectives on Working Women: A Databook*, U.S. Department of Labor (Bureau of Labor Statistics, October 1980), Bulletin 2080.

Note: Data are not strictly comparable between countries because of differences in age coverage as follows:
Belgium: population and labour force aged 14–64;
Canada: population and labour force aged 15 and above;
Finland: population and labour force aged 15–74;
France: aged 17 and above, activities relating to the female population not at school;
Norway: population and labour force aged 16–74;
Spain: population aged 14 and over and total labour force;
United States: population and labour force aged 15 and above.

2. PROBLEMS OF COMBINING HOUSEHOLD DUTIES WITH PAID WORK

The employed woman's double burden of combining household duties and child care with paid work has been universally recognized. It has also been acknowledged that, although each individual family should seek a solution to this problem, social policies should complement their efforts. However, the necessary changes in attitude are only slowly coming about.

Surveys conducted by the European Economic Community (EEC) in 1975 and 1978 provided some insight into societal expectations and attitudes on this subject. According to the Commission of the European Communities, the first of these surveys showed, *inter alia*, that men "overestimate the positive attitude of women to housework and underestimate women's desire for paid employment". It was also concluded from the surveys that "women's desire for gainful employment is far greater than the readiness of men to perform household duties, in which connection it should be pointed out that men have a tendency to claim to be more helpful in the home than they really are".[14] In order to assess the division of tasks within the household, a section in the Commission's survey on housework and paid employment asked both wives and husbands about help with housework. The results are shown in table III.13.

The impact of policies on women's participation in the labour force should not be overlooked. Paid parental leave, which makes child-care leave and benefits available to either fathers or mothers, makes it possible for domestic labour to be shared between parents, so that women can participate in the labour force on a more equitable basis. Such child-care measures help each parent to combine work and family responsibilities. Benefits paid only to mothers, including paid leave designed to encourage them to stay at home with young children, set up barriers to women's full and permanent integration into the labour market.

An important recent development with respect to women's participation in the labour force has been the weakening of the negative relation between fertility and participation in the labour force. The increased labour force participation of women with young children has caused a rapidly growing need for day-care facilities for children. Such facilities are still inadequate in many countries. Thus, women with young children face a further obstacle regarding their integration into the labour market.

3. OCCUPATIONAL STATUS OF WOMEN IN THE LABOUR MARKET

The changing occupational status of female labour provides further evidence of women's increasing role in the economy. In almost all countries of the ECE region, the vast majority of women in the labour force are wage or salary earners (see table III.14). With one or two exceptions, the percentage of women who are family helpers has declined and, in the latest census (1981 in most countries), not more than 8% of women workers in any of the western countries were classified as unpaid family

[14] European Parliament, *Working Documents 1980–1981*, Report on the Position of Women in the European Community, drawn up on behalf of the *Ad Hoc* Committee on Women's Rights (Brussels, 11 January 1981), Part II, Document I–289/80.

TABLE III.13

Contribution of men to housework

(*Percentages*)

	Belgium	Denmark	France	Germany, Federal Republic of	Ireland	Italy	Luxem-bourg	Nether-lands	United Kingdom
MEN									
"I help my wife"									
Often	38	37	39	28	32	15	32	41	48
Sometimes	44	46	45	57	51	54	51	52	39
Never	17	11	11	13	16	30	15	6	12
Don't know	1	6	5	2	1	1	2	1	1
Total	100	100	100	100	100	100	100	100	100
WOMEN									
"My husband helps me"									
Often	28	37	28	22	25	13	15	27	32
Sometimes	40	41	44	54	50	35	49	54	45
Never	31	18	27	23	24	49	32	18	22
Don't know	1	4	1	1	1	3	4	1	1
Total	100	100	100	100	100	100	100	100	100

Source: Commission of the European Communities, *European Men and Women in 1978:* A Comparison of their Attitudes to Some of the Problems Facing Society (Brussels, February 1979).

workers. However, in all countries, from two thirds to more than three quarters of family helpers are female. The percentage of women who are self-employed has also shown a long-term tendency to decline almost everywhere, although recent data (1980 or 1981) are available for only eight countries in the region.

4. EMPLOYMENT IN THE SERVICE SECTOR

The high percentage of women employed in the service sector has had an important effect on women's participation. Employment growth in most of the ECE countries is concentrated in services. It has been noted that, over the period 1975–1979, the service sector was overwhelmingly the major source of new jobs and that this trend has become even more evident since the second oil-price shock in 1979.[15]

5. PART-TIME EMPLOYMENT

The service sector appears to have been less affected by cyclical influences than other sectors and has therefore continued to be an important source of employment opportunities. There is evidence that this relatively strong performance of the service sector in job creation, despite worsening economic conditions, has been possible largely because of an expansion of part-time employment (see also section E below). In several of the west European countries, although full-time employment declined during the most recent recession, part-time employment continued to increase, in some cases quite considerably (see table III.16).[16] In most countries for which data are available, the share of women in part-time employment

---

[15] OECD, *op. cit.*

[16] Comparisons of part-time employment between countries must be approached with care, because definitions of part-time work may differ significantly from one country to another. In these comparisons, the concept refers to weekly working time, seasonal or part-year workers being excluded, except in the case of Canada and the United States. For a more extensive discussion of the problem of definition, see OECD, *op. cit.*, Technical Annex, Note D.

increased between 1973 and 1981. The data indicating large increases in women's labour force participation in many countries thus obscure the fact that these were due largely to a rise in part-time employment.

The availability of part-time employment may have had some influence on the participation of women in the labour force, although there is apparently no clear pattern across countries in the region. Despite the fact that married women currently contribute to the financial support of their families in most of the ECE countries, they are nevertheless expected to retain responsibility for household duties. Also, in many countries there is a serious shortage of affordable child-care facilities, so that many women are able to engage in paid work only on a part-time basis. In some countries, however, "family responsibilities" do not explain why women work part time.

In Canada, for example, women in the 25–44 age group have the lowest percentage of part-time employment of any age group of employed women. There are also indications that an increasing number of married women would prefer full-time employment if it were available. In Canada in 1981, 25% of married women who worked part time said that they did so because of personal or family responsibilities, and another 14% said they could only find part-time work.[17] In 1983, the corresponding figures were 19% and 24%.

D. Employment and unemployment of women

As indicated above, throughout most of the United Nations Decade for Women, the countries of the ECE region experienced slow or negative economic growth and most of the market-economy countries were faced with the longest and deepest recession since the depression of the 1930s. Employment stagnated or even declined in many countries, while unemployment increased sharply,

---

[17] Statistics Canada, *Labour Force Annual Averages, 1975–1983.*

TABLE III.14

Occupational status of women workers

(*Percentages*)

Region and country	Year	Employers and own-account workers	Employees	Unpaid family workers	Unpaid family workers who are female
Western Europe and North America					
Austria	1961	11	63	26	76
	1971	10	75	15	76
Belgium	1970	..	..	..	..
	1977	11	83	6	79
Denmark	1976	5	86	9	..
	1981	..	..	..	..
Finland	1975	6	85	9	72
	1980	5	87	8	82
France	1975	8	84	8	78
	1982	7	85	8	85
Germany, Federal Republic of	1970	6	92	2	31
	1981	5	87	8	87
Ireland	1961	56	26	19	14
	1971	12	86	3	14
Italy	1971	16	74	10	61
	1981	15	79	6	61
Norway	1970	4	88	8	73
	1980	4	92	4	75
Sweden	1970	3	92	5	74
	1975	3	95	2	84
Switzerland	1960	8	91	1	5
	1970	4	87	9	66
United Kingdom	1971	4	94	1	82
	1981	..	..	..	..
United States	1970	4	95	1	71
	1980	4	95	1	69
Southern Europe					
Greece	1961	14	27	59	65
	1971	16	38	46	69
Portugal	1960	10	87	3	8
Spain	1970	11	78	11	31
	1975	9	81	10	40
Yugoslavia	1961	16	32	52	62
	1971	14	45	41	63

Sources: National population census statistics.

reaching the highest levels of the post-war period. These developments affected the employment of both men and women although, on the whole, the repercussions of the economic slow-down and recession were more severe for men.

According to available estimates, the total number of those employed in the market-economy countries of the region and in Yugoslavia increased by 8% between 1975 and 1984, from under 260 million to nearly 280 million. More than four fifths of the 21.5 million additional jobs were filled by women. Women's employment rose by over 18 million, compared with less than 3.5 million for men. In percentage terms, women's employment increased by 20%, which represented nearly ten times the increase in male employment. Employment decreased for men in more than half of the countries; only in the case of the Federal Republic of Germany was the number of employed women lower in 1984 than in 1975. Even in this

case, the decrease was marginal. As a result of these trends, the share of women in total employment rose from 36% in 1975 to nearly 40% in 1984.

Data for individual countries show that, although women's employment in the recent past has increased at a considerably faster pace than that of men, the employment of women also stagnated or increased only marginally in several countries (see table III.17). Apart from the Federal Republic of Germany, where women's employment actually declined, only small increases occurred in Belgium and Switzerland and only slightly higher ones in Austria, France, Spain, Turkey and the United Kingdom. However, there were large increases in employment in other cases: in both Canada and the United States, the number of employed females rose by more than one third. In western Europe, only the Netherlands and Norway and, in southern Europe, only Portugal, came close to North America in this regard. There were relative changes

TABLE III.15

Changes in employment in industry and services, selected countries, 1970–1980

Country	Average annual percentage change	
	Industry	Services
Austria	0.2	2.4
Belgium[a]	−1.9	2.0
Canada[a]	2.4	4.4
Finland	0.1	3.1
France[a]	−0.6	2.2
Germany, Federal Republic of[a]	−1.1	1.0
Netherlands[b]	−1.7	1.7
Sweden	−0.8	2.8
Switzerland	−1.7	1.3
United Kingdom[a]	−1.5	1.3
United States[a]	1.2	3.2

Source: Economic Survey of Europe in 1982 (United Nations publication, Sales No. E.83.II.E.1), p. 67.

[a] Includes armed forces.

[b] Man-years.

of between 10% and 20% in Denmark, Finland, Greece, Ireland, Italy and Sweden, which placed these countries between the two above-mentioned groups of countries.

In assessing the significance of these trends, two factors should be considered: in the first place, even though the employment of women rose more rapidly in all countries than that of men, in the large majority of countries the female labour supply has, for some time, been more dynamic than that of males. In many cases, the growth of employment opportunities for women has not kept pace with the dynamic nature of female labour supply. In the second place, the data for the period 1975–1984 may not be representative of longer-term trends. In particular, the data for 1984 may be distorted because they refer to the period in the cycle, at least in the case of western and southern Europe, when unemployment was at a very high level. It is well known that, in general, male employment is affected by recessions earlier and to a greater extent

than female employment. Even though 1975 was also a recession year, the mid-1970s recession was much less severe than that of the early 1980s. Thus, the full effect of the most recent recession on women's employment may not yet be fully evident and as occurred in past recessions the employment of men may start to rise considerably more rapidly than that of women if the recovery continues.

In more general terms, data on employment should be considered in conjunction with those on unemployment. Despite the substantial expansion of employment opportunities for women in the past few years, women's share in unemployment also increased in many market-economy countries. Moreover, because the increase of female employment did not keep pace with rapid growth of the female labour force, women's unemployment rates increased.

It was pointed out in the 1980 study that the growing number of women in the labour force had been accompanied, in a number of market-economy countries, by a considerable rise both in female unemployment and in women's share in total unemployment. The study also pointed out that, in many countries, this share was higher than the proportion of women in the labour force and that, consequently, the rate of unemployment among women was higher than among men.

The more rapid increase in female than in male unemployment in the mid-1970s, also noted in the 1980 study, has subsequently continued. Women's share of unemployment increased in 13 of the 20 countries for which data are available (see table III.18). Moreover, in the majority of countries, women continue to account for a disproportionate share in unemployment compared with their share in the labour force. Exceptions to this trend are Austria, Ireland, the Netherlands, Turkey and the United Kingdom. In Belgium, Denmark, France, Italy, Portugal and Yugoslavia, more than half of those without work in 1984 were women. In these same countries, women accounted for between 35% and 45% of the total labour force. The same data, used to calculate the

TABLE III.16

Full-time and part-time employment since the first oil shock, 1973–1981

(Average annual growth rates)

	1973–1975		1975–1979		1979–1981	
	Full-time	Part-time	Full-time	Part-time	Full-time	Part-time
Belgium	−0.1	22.1	−0.4	8.7	−0.9	5.0
Canada	2.6	6.8	2.0	7.0	2.1	6.6
Denmark	..	..	1.7	5.8	−2.1	2.2
Finland	..	..	−0.4	2.3[a]	2.4	5.9
France	0.5	15.3	0.4	2.6	−0.1	1.8
Germany, Federal Republic of	−2.4	6.2	0.3	1.8	1.2	5.4
Ireland	..	..	2.9	−3.3	..	..
Italy	2.2	11.3	1.4	−12.7	1.1	3.4
Luxembourg	2.3	8.0	−0.9	3.4	..	..
Netherlands	0.7	14.5	0.8	9.1	..	..
Norway	..	..	1.0	6.2	1.1	3.5
Sweden	1.7	5.2	−0.9	6.9	−0.1	2.6
United Kingdom	−0.5	5.5	0.9	−1.9	−2.8	−2.6
United States	0.8	2.3	4.1	3.8	0.5	0.6

Source: OECD, Employment Outlook (September 1983).

[a] 1976–1979.

TABLE III.17

Changes in employment, by sex, 1975–1984 and share of women in total employment, 1975 and 1984

(Percentages)

Country	Change in employment			Women's share in total employment	
	Both sexes	Males	Females	1975	1984
Austria.........	0.3	−1.9	3.6	39.4	40.7
Belgium........	−4.2	−7.3	1.9	33.6	35.7
Canada.........	18.3	7.6	36.9	36.1	41.9
Denmark.......	3.8	−1.9	12.2	41.1	44.3
Finland.........	9.0	6.6	11.7	46.6	47.7
France	−0.1	−2.8	4.9	36.0	37.8
Germany, Federal Republic of ...	−2.8	−4.2	−0.3	37.2	38.1
Greece	7.2	5.8	10.5	29.1	30.0
Ireland	2.6	−1.9	14.7	27.2	30.4
Italy	4.9	−0.3	17.7	28.6	32.1
Netherlands.....	7.3	−3.2	33.3	28.6	35.6
Norway	15.4	5.5	31.8	37.6	42.9
Portugal........	14.3	3.6	31.8	38.0	39.8
Spain	−12.2	−21.2	21.3	21.2	29.3
Sweden.........	4.8	−3.5	15.9	42.3	46.9
Switzerland	−1.2	−2.9	2.1	34.2	35.3
Turkey	4.1	2.4	6.9	37.9	38.9
United Kingdom .	−4.3	−9.8	4.8	37.9	41.5
United States....	22.1	13.5	35.7	38.7	43.0
Yugoslavia......	5.4	4.5	7.1	36.5	37.1

Sources: National data and secretariat estimates.

ratio of female to male unemployed show that, in Belgium, France, Italy and Yugoslavia, unemployed women outnumber men by 25% or more.[18]

The prevalence of higher unemployment rates for women than for men can be inferred from the larger share of women in total unemployment than in the total labour force. Although the interpretation of recent trends in this regard is complicated by the fact that it is difficult to assess the role of cyclical versus structural trends in unemployment, on the whole it can be affirmed that, in the ECE region, unemployment levels of men tend to be lower than those of women. An analysis of the evolution of unemployment rates in ten west European countries and in Canada and the United States showed that, in general, unemployment rates for men were lower than for women and that the difference between the rates for women and men had increased during the 1970s.[19] Data for 1975 and 1984 confirm this evolution. Whereas women's unemployment rates in 1975 were still lower than those of men in seven countries, by 1984 this was true for only five countries (see table III.19), in spite of the fact that, during recessions, male unemployment

[18] Some caution must be exercised in interpreting these data, in particular when unemployment levels are low. Under such conditions, a comparatively small change in the absolute number of unemployed men and/or women can cause a large difference in percentages or ratios.

[19] *Economic Survey of Europe in 1981* (United Nations publication, Sales Number E.82.II.E.1), pp. 23–25.

TABLE III.18

Female shares in unemployment and ratio of female to male unemployed, 1975–1984

	Women as a percentage of				Female/male unemployment ratio	
	Labour force		Unemployed			
Region and country	1975	1984	1975	1984	1975	1984
Western Europe						
Austria..............	40	41	54	38	65	62
Belgium	34	38	52	55	51	124
Denmark	41	45	43	53	70	112
Finland	47	48	43	48	88	94
France	37	39	57	56	56	125
Germany, Federal Republic of ..	37	39	42	44	59	77
Ireland	27	29	19	24	37	31
Italy	30	35	55	56	40	125
Netherlands..........	28	35	22	33	40	48
Norway	38	43	48	46	60	85
Sweden	43	47	54	49	73	97
Switzerland	34	35	20	40	52	67
United Kingdom.......	38	40	26	31	61	44
North America						
Canada	37	42	43	44	57	74
United States	39	43	44	45	63	80
Southern Europe						
Greece	30	31	50	42	41	73
Portugal	38	43	42	62	61	164
Spain	21	30	25	34	27	52
Turkey	36	35	25	18	61	22
Yugoslavia	38	39	54	57	58	133

Sources: National data and secretariat estimates.

TABLE III.19

Unemployment rates, by sex, 1975 and 1984

(*Percentages*)

	1975			1984		
Region and country	*Both sexes*	*Males*	*Females*	*Both sexes*	*Males*	*Females*
Western Europe						
Austria	1.7	1.3	2.3	3.9	4.1	3.7
Belgium	4.2	3.1	6.3	13.0	9.4	18.8
Denmark	4.9	4.7	5.1	10.2	8.8	12.0
Finland	2.2	2.4	2.1	6.1	6.0	6.2
France	4.1	2.8	6.3	9.1	6.7	12.8
Germany, Federal Republic of	4.0	3.7	4.5	8.3	7.6	9.4
Ireland	6.0	6.6	4.3	16.2	17.5	13.0
Italy	5.8	3.7	10.5	10.7	7.3	17.2
Netherlands	4.5	4.9	3.5	13.7	14.3	12.7
Norway	2.3	1.9	2.9	3.0	2.8	3.2
Sweden	1.6	1.3	2.1	3.1	3.0	3.3
Switzerland	0.3	0.4	0.2	1.2	1.1	1.3
United Kingdom	3.1	3.6	2.1	11.6	13.5	8.8
North America						
Canada	6.9	6.1	8.1	11.2	11.1	11.4
United States	8.3	7.6	9.3	7.2	7.0	7.4
Southern Europe						
Greece	1.8	1.2	3.0	8.3	6.9	11.3
Portugal	5.5	5.1	6.1	10.8	6.4	15.3
Spain	5.0	4.8	5.7	20.4	19.3	23.1
Turkey	12.9	15.2	8.9	21.0	26.3	11.0
Yugoslavia	1.2	4.6	8.8	9.5	6.7	13.9

Sources: National data and secretariat estimates.

generally tends to rise to a greater extent and more rapidly than female unemployment.

Women's unemployment rates reached over 10% in more than half of the countries in 1984. In comparison, similarly high unemployment levels for men were found only in one third of the countries. There was, however, considerable variation between countries as regards women's unemployment rates: they were comparatively low in Austria, Norway, Sweden and Switzerland (between 1% and 5%) and between 5% and 10% in Finland, the Federal Republic of Germany, the United Kingdom and the United States. In all other countries, more than 10% of the female labour force was unemployed, and the proportions were approximately one fifth in Belgium, Italy and Spain.

There are significant differences in the unemployment rates of the different age groups (see table III.20). As noted in the 1980 study, unemployment rates among young people are frequently much higher than those of older men and women. In most countries, the highest male and female unemployment rates are found in the 15–19 age group, and they are only slightly lower in the 20–24 age group. Furthermore, unemployment rates for young women are significantly higher than those for young men in a number of countries. In France, for example, 22% of men aged 15–19 and 14% of those aged 20–24 were unemployed in 1982. Corresponding rates for young women in these age groups were 44% and 21%. The relevant rates in other countries were as follows: Italy: males 28% and 19%, females 42% and 27%; Portugal: males 10% and 6%, females 28% and 22%; Spain: males 44% and 27%, females 53% and 37%.

However, the situation is reversed in Canada, Finland, the Netherlands, Turkey, the United Kingdom and the United States, where unemployment rates for men in the 15–19 and 20–24 age groups are higher than the corresponding rates for women.

While unemployment rates are generally lower in the central age groups, women's unemployment rates in these ages are often higher than those of men. In eight of the fourteen countries for which data are available, women's unemployment rates in the 25–34 age group are higher than those of men. In seven of the countries, women aged between 35 and 44 have higher unemployment rates than men in the same age group.

A comparison of the distribution of the female labour force in general with the distribution of female unemployment by age group further confirms the concentration of high female unemployment among younger women. In the west European countries, women aged between 20 and 24 account for 10%–20% of the female labour force, but also for 17%–30% of female unemployment (see table III.21). By contrast, women aged between 30 and 34 represent about 10%–15% of the labour force and about 10%–13% of the unemployed. In most countries, women in the older age groups (40–54 years) are underrepresented among the unemployed in comparison with their share in the labour force.

As regards the duration of unemployment, data for Austria and Canada are presented in table III.22 (p. 31). The average duration of unemployment has increased for men and women in both countries since 1980. In Austria, women who were unemployed in 1982/83 were, on the average, without work for 112 days and men for 110 days.

TABLE III.20

Unemployment rates, by age and sex, in selected countries, 1981–1982

(Percentages)

Country	Year	Total		15–19		20–24		25–34		35–44		45–54		55–64		65 and over	
		Males	*Females*	*Males*	*Females*	*Males*	*Females*	*Males*	*Females*	*Males*	*Females*	*Males*	*Females*	*Males*	*Females*	*Males*	*Females*
Canada	1982	11.1	10.8	24.6	18.9	19.0	14.3	10.3	10.5	7.4	8.6	6.7	7.4	7.0	6.5	–	–
Denmark	1981	8.3	8.5	5.5	9.7	15.5	17.2	10.5	9.9	6.7	5.7	6.9	5.5	7.7	6.1	2.5	1.5
Finland	1982	6.3	6.0	20.0	17.7	9.5	8.6	4.4	4.1	3.4	3.0	5.3	4.3	12.6	13.8	–	–
France	1982	5.8	10.5	21.5	44.4	13.5	20.6	5.2	9.5	3.3	6.5	3.8	6.0	5.4	6.4	0.4	0.5
Germany, Federal Republic of	1981	3.7	6.2	6.4	9.2	5.7	8.0	3.9	7.5	2.6	4.3	2.6	4.3	5.2	6.5	–	–
Italy	1981	5.4	14.4	28.3 a	41.9 a	19.4	26.9	3.0 b	10.2 b	1.0 c	5.1 c	1.2 d	4.2 d	2.3 e	6.9 e	7.4	27.3
Netherlands	1981	6.1	6.1	13.1 f	11.3 f	..	4.3	5.8 b	4.4 b	3.9 c	2.6 c	3.0 g	2.2 g	3.9	2.4	..	..
Norway	1981	1.4	2.7	8.3 h	9.3 h	3.8	4.3	0.7 i	2.2 i	..	..	..	..	..	..	0.7 j	–
Portugal	1981	3.5	12.2	9.7	27.6	6.4	22.0	3.1	12.7	0.7	5.0	1.1	2.7	1.1	2.1	–	–
Spain	1982	15.1	19.9	44.4 h	52.6 h	26.8	36.5	15.3	17.8	8.6	7.5	8.5	3.5	8.9	1.1	1.5	–
Sweden	1982	3.0	3.4	9.6 h	11.6 h	6.3	5.8	2.9	3.3	1.5	2.0	1.6	1.7	3.1	3.0	–	–
Turkey	1980	5.4	2.4	11.0	6.1	7.8	4.4	4.5	1.4	3.2	0.6	3.1	0.3	2.8	0.3	1.8	0.2
United Kingdom	1981	12.5	8.0	26.2 h	23.9 h	17.7	13.1	11.1	7.6	8.5	3.5	8.2	3.7	14.8	4.7 k	1.4	0.5 j
United States	1982	9.6	9.4	23.1 h	21.7 h	15.0	13.0	9.7	9.3	6.7	7.0	5.6	5.8	5.5	5.2	3.7	4.4

Source: OECD, *Labour Force Statistics, 1970–1981,* except for Denmark (census); and Turkey (census).

a 14–19.   b 25–39.   c 40–49.   d 50–59.   e 60–64.   f 15–24.   g 50–54.   h 16–19.   i 25–59.   j 60 and over.   k 55–69.

TABLE III.21

Distribution of female labour force and female unemployment, by age group

(*Percentages*)

Region and country	Year	15–19 A	B	20–24 A	B	25–29 A	B	30–34 A	B	35–39 A	B	40–44 A	B	45–49 A	B	50–54 A	B	55–59 A	B	60–64 A	B	65 and over A	B
Western Europe																							
Austria	1981	12.6	..	16.2	..	12.3	..	11.5	..	10.8	..	10.9	..	8.3	..	8.7	..	6.2	..	1.3	..	1.2	..
Belgium	1977	7.7[a]	13.5[a]	20.2	29.1	18.4	20.6	13.2	9.8	10.1	6.8	9.2	6.3	8.5	6.0	7.0	5.3	3.6	2.6	1.1	0.0	0.8	0.0
Denmark	1981	8.5[a]	9.2	12.6	25.7	13.0	18.3	13.5	12.8	13.7	9.6	10.2	6.4	8.7	5.4	7.6	5.1	6.6	5.4	3.4	1.9	2.1	0.4
Finland	1980	2.9	10.9	10.9	17.2	14.0	14.8	16.2	12.3	12.4	7.4	11.5	7.1	10.3	7.7	9.9	9.8	7.5	8.0	3.4	4.5	0.9	0.4
France	1982	3.7	14.3	14.7	29.2	15.4	15.7	15.0	11.2	12.0	7.2	9.1	4.9	9.3	4.8	9.2	5.2	7.4	5.4	3.1	1.9	1.0	0.2
Germany, Fed. Rep. of	1981	9.7	11.6	15.1	20.2	12.5	17.0	10.8	11.5	10.3	7.9	12.7	8.1	9.6	6.3	8.5	6.5	7.4	8.9	1.8	2.1	1.7	0.0
Ireland	1981	16.0	..	26.8	..	15.7	..	8.6	..	6.3	..	5.7	..	5.3	..	5.0	..	4.3	..	3.3	..	3.0	..
Italy	1981	12.9[a]	47.8[a]	16.0	29.7	14.6	13.0	13.5	5.1	10.7	2.3	10.3	1.7	8.6	0.4	7.2	0.1	3.9	0.0	1.3	0.0	0.8	0.0
Netherlands	1981	9.5	..	23.1	..	15.5	..	13.4	..	10.9	..	9.1	..	7.1	..	5.4	..	4.0	..	1.5	..	0.5	..
Norway	1980	8.9[b]	..	13.4	..	11.6	..	22.7[c]	..			17.3[d]	..			16.4[e]	..			8.7[f]	..	0.9[g]	..
Sweden	1980	4.3[b]	..	11.3	..	11.9	..	13.3	..	13.1	..	10.9	..	10.1	..	10.0	..	9.2	..	5.2	..	0.7	..
Switzerland	1980	11.4	..	16.2	..	12.3	..	10.9	..	10.6	..	9.5	..	8.9	..	7.9	..	6.7	..	3.3	..	2.2	..
United Kingdom	1981	10.0[b]	23.5[b]	13.7	21.4	10.1	21.2[h]	10.8	..	10.7	13.1[i]	10.6	..	10.3	13.0[j]	10.0	..	8.6	6.4	3.3	0.8	1.8	0.7
North America																							
Canada	1981	10.3	19.1	18.4	24.5	15.1	15.0	13.1	11.2	10.6	8.0	8.7	6.3	7.5	5.3	6.6	4.5	5.2	3.6	3.0	1.9	1.5	0.8
United States	1980	8.6	17.6	16.2	21.5	27.2[h]	51.4[k]			18.9[i]				15.5[j]				10.8[l]	7.1[l]			2.8	2.4
Southern Europe																							
Spain	1981	15.2[b]	37.8[b]	22.8	34.0	15.0	12.6	10.0	4.9	7.2	2.6	6.0	1.8	6.8	2.1	6.6	1.9	5.4	1.4	3.3	0.6	1.6	0.3
Turkey	1980	28.3[m]	55.3[m]	14.1	25.6	10.5	7.6	8.5	3.3	7.5	1.9	7.7	1.8	7.2	1.1	6.2	0.8	3.6	0.5	2.4	0.3	3.7	0.3

Sources: National population census statistics.

A = Labour force.   B = Unemployment.

[a] 14–19.   [b] 16–19.   [c] 30–39.   [d] 40–49.   [e] 50–59.   [f] 60–69.   [g] 70 and over.   [h] 25–34.   [i] 35–44.   [j] 45–54.   [k] 25–54.   [l] 55–64.   [m] 12–19.

TABLE III.22

Austria and Canada: duration of unemployment, around 1980

Country, years, duration of unemployment	Percentage of total unemployed		Average duration in days	
	Male	Female	Male	Female
Austria				
1979–1980			83	100
For less than 90 days	37.1	25.3		
For more than 180 days	23.5	30.0		
1982–1983			110	112
For less than 90 days	21.8	20.4		
For more than 180 days	37.8	36.2		

	4 weeks or less		5–13 weeks		14 weeks and over		Average duration in weeks	
	1980	1983	1980	1983	1980	1983	1980	1983
Canada								
Men								
15–24 years	36	26	32	28	29	45	12.3	19.3
25–44 years	29	19	30	24	38	55	16.5	25.0
45 years and over	26	17	28	21	43	59	19.7	27.5
Married	29	19	30	25	37	54	15.8	23.9
Single	34	24	32	27	32	48	13.9	21.5
Other	26	16	26	20	48	61	20.4	30.4
Women								
15–24 years	36	29	32	29	28	39	12.6	17.1
25–44 years	33	24	27	27	35	47	15.1	20.5
45 years and over	28	21	27	21	42	54	17.8	25.2
Married	32	24	28	25	35	48	14.8	20.4
Single	36	29	33	30	28	40	13.0	17.9
Other	29	22	29	26	39	51	16.7	23.5

Sources: Statistics Canada, *Labour Force Annual Average, 1975–1983* (Ottawa, February 1984); and G. Fischer, *Employment Policies in Austria,* Austrian Federal Ministry of Social Affairs (May 1984).

Note: The table does not include those who had work which was due to start within four weeks of the reference week, who had not actively looked for work in the previous four weeks, but who were available for employment in the reference week. Thus percentages may not total 100.

In Canada, in 1983, the corresponding average periods were 17–25 weeks for women (depending on age), and 19–28 weeks for men (also according to age). In both countries, long-term unemployment appears to be more prevalent among men than women. In Canada, 55% of unemployed men aged 25–44 years had been out of work for 14 weeks or longer in 1983, while 47% of unemployed women in that age group had been unemployed for the same duration. In Austria in 1982/83, 36% of unemployed women and 38% of unemployed men had been out of work for more than six months. On the basis of marital status, unemployed married women in Canada had almost the shortest average duration of unemployment of any group: in 1983 this averaged 20.5 weeks, compared with 23.9 weeks for married men, 21.5 weeks for single men and 30.4 weeks for men who were separated, widowed or divorced.

The data relating to the United Kingdom (table III.23) shed some light on the duration of male and female unemployment according to age. It can be seen that, compared with men, the much higher proportion of women unemployed for up to six months is balanced by a similarly higher proportion of men who are unemployed for more than a year. The data for individual age groups, however, indicate that the major difference in the duration of unemployment by sex is in the central age group, i.e.

those between 25 and 54 years old. Nearly half of the men in this age group are unemployed for over one year whereas, the corresponding proportion for women is only slightly over 25%. With regard to those under 25 years old, a higher proportion of men than of women is also unemployed for a longer duration, but the difference in this respect is smaller than in the central ages. On the other hand, unemployment of longer duration at a later age seems to be higher for women than for men.

Information on the flows into unemployment for Canada and the United States also reveals some interesting patterns. Table III.24 shows that, in both countries, the majority of women who were unemployed in 1979 had been re-entrants to the labour force whereas, in 1981, the majority were without work because they had lost their jobs. In Canada, that trend continued until 1983, when 44% of all unemployed women were without work because of losing their jobs. About one-third of unemployed women and 10%–15% of unemployed men in these countries are re-entrants to the labour force. In Canada, relatively low percentages of the unemployed of both sexes are new entrants to the labour force but, in the United States, new entrants accounted for a higher percentage of unemployment than those who had left their jobs voluntarily.

TABLE III.23

United Kingdom: distribution of unemployment, by sex, age and duration, third quarter of 1983

(Percentages)

	Total unemployed and duration															
	Under 25				25–54				55 years and over				All ages			
	Up to 26 weeks	27–52 weeks	Over 52 weeks	All	Up to 26 weeks	27–52 weeks	Over 52 weeks	All	Up to 26 weeks	27–52 weeks	Over 52 weeks	All	Up to 26 weeks	27–52 weeks	Over 52 weeks	All
Men	47.5	22.0	30.5	100.0	34.0	19.0	47.0	100.0	33.0	23.2	43.8	100.0	38.5	20.7	40.8	100.0
Women	55.1	23.9	21.0	100.0	48.0	24.2	27.8	100.0	25.5	20.0	54.5	100.0	50.2	23.8	25.9	100.0

Source: Employment Gazette, vol. 92, No. 10 (October 1984), p. 531.

TABLE III.24

North America: flows into unemployment; unemployed persons, by reason and sex, selected years

(Percentages)

Country, sex and year		Job losers	Job leavers	New entrants	Re- entrants
Canada					
1979	Men	60	19	4	16
	Women	35	21	8	36
1981	Men	61	18	4	17
	Women	37	20	7	36
1983	Men	69	12	4	15
	Women	44	16	6	33
United States					
1979	Men	53	14	11	22
	Women	32	15	15	38
1981	Men	62	10	19	10
	Women	39	13	14	34

Sources: U.S. Bureau of Labor Statistics, Employment and Earnings, monthly, and unpublished data; and Statistics Canada, Labour Force Annual Averages, 1975–83 (Ottawa, February 1984).

Note: Percentages may not add to 100 because of rounding.

The 1980 study noted some of the factors which may account for the fact that women are disproportionately affected by unemployment. It observed that certain characteristics of female employment are likely to make women more likely to be laid off than men. Temporary part-time workers, for example, may be more exposed to unemployment but this phenomenon should not be over-estimated because, in most countries, the majority of employed women have full-time jobs. Women who have re-entered the labour market, or who have high mobility as a result of frequent job changes, may also be more vulnerable to lay-offs because they lack seniority in comparison with male workers so that lay-offs conducted on a seniority basis will naturally tend to increase women's unemployment. It has also been suggested that improved unemployment protection schemes in some countries may have encouraged women, especially married women, to register as unemployed, or to enter the labour force for the purpose of qualifying for unemployment benefits, both of which would play a part in increasing female unemployment rates.

The 1980 study pointed out that, although in several countries during the recession of 1974–75, the activity rates of married women did not show a net decline, as had been the case in previous recessions, the rates increased less than they would have done had there been better job prospects. This points to the possible existence of hidden unemployment in this group of the population. The possibility that women's employment and unemployment might be affected during a recession by the phenomena of the "discouraged worker" and the "added worker" has already been discussed.[20] In this connection, it has been noted that there is a tendency for unemployment to be concentrated in certain families. In particular, rather than support their families by working when a husband has lost his job, the wives of unemployed husbands are more likely to be unemployed as well.[21] United States data indicate that the wives of unemployed husbands

[20] See section C.1 above.

[21] L. Paukert, op. cit.

have above-average unemployment rates, just as husbands of unemployed wives have particularly high unemployment records.[22] One possible explanation of this is that partners in marriage often have a similar educational background and that unemployment rates tend to vary according to the level of education, the more highly-educated generally having lower unemployment rates.

Studies in the United Kingdom indicate that the incidence of unemployment among both partners in marriage is surprisingly high. In one study, the unemployment rate, both registered and unregistered, among the economically active wives of unemployed men was found to be 17%, compared with 4% for all wives.[23] However, a large proportion of unemployed men, 60% of those newly-registering as unemployed and 85%–90% who had been unemployed for over a year, had non-working wives. The study also found that social class and cultural factors play an important part in a wife's decision to supplement, or take over, the male breadwinner role.

Sectoral and geographical factors are also found to be strong influences in this regard. All members of families living in economically-depressed areas are more likely to become unemployed than those in areas with a higher level of activity. In addition, when recession sets in, the high incidence of unemployment in the manufacturing sector is likely to have a marked impact on industrial or manual workers who are frequently members of the same family.[24]

E. The growth of part-time employment

One of the most significant aspects of the increased employment of women over the past decade has been the impressive rise in part-time work. Unfortunately, it is difficult to make detailed comparisons between countries because of the varying definitions of part-time work. The International Labour Organisation defines part-time employment as work on a regular and voluntary basis for a daily or weekly period of substantially shorter duration than current or normal statutory hours of work.[25] However, there is no consensus on what constitutes working hours which are substantially shorter than normal. As the 1980 study noted, part-time work is normally measured in terms of hours usually worked per week, the cut-off point between full-time and part-time employment varying between 30 and 35 hours per week.[26] The definitions applicable to the tables in this section are those used by each country.[27]

TABLE III.25

Part-time employment in selected ECE countries, around 1981

Country	Part-time workers as a percentage of total employment		Women as a percentage of	
	Males	Females	Total employment	Part-time employment
Austria	2	18	40	87
Belgium	1	16	36	86
Canada	7	32	40	72
Denmark	3	44	45	92
Germany, Federal Republic of	1	26	38	94
Finland	2	8	48	80
France	2	16	38	85
Greece	1	4	31	63
Ireland (1979)	1	8	28	69
Italy	1	6	32	64
Luxembourg (1979)	1	17	30	88
Netherlands	8	45	31	68
Norway	11	54	41	78
Poland	5	6	43	50
Sweden	7	46	46	85
United Kingdom ..	1	37	41	94
United States	8	24	43	70

Sources: OECD, *Employment Outlook* (Paris, September 1983) except for Austria: E. Bartunek, C. Böhm and I. Gross, *The Economic Role of Women in Austria* (Austrian Federal Ministry of Social Affairs, Vienna, 1984); and Poland: *Rocznik Statystyczny*, 1983, p. 57. Percentage of total employment calculated from OECD, *Labour Force Statistics 1970–1981*.

Although data on part-time employment are available for only 16 countries in the region, it is possible to make some observations on its importance and recent evolution (see table III.25). The data on the proportions of male and female part-time workers provide clear evidence that, as already observed in the 1980 study, part-time work is a distinctive feature of female employment. The percentage of those working part time is much higher for women than for men in all countries for which information is available. Part-time employment for men represents only one or two per cent of total male employment in most countries, although it is between 5% and 11% in Canada, the Netherlands, Norway, Poland, Sweden and the United States.

However, there is also considerable variation in the distribution of female employment between full-time and part-time jobs, even if allowance is made for differences in definition. In Denmark, the Netherlands, Norway and Sweden, the proportion of women employed in part-time jobs ranges from 44% to 54%, whereas in Canada, the

[22] United States Department of Labor, *Employment and Earnings*, various issues.

[23] See C. Hakim, "The social consequences of high unemployment", *Journal of Social Policy*, Vol. II, Part 4 (Cambridge University Press, October 1982).

[24] L. Paukert, *op. cit.*

[25] ILO, *Part-time Employment: An International Survey* (Geneva, 1973), p. 3.

[26] *The Economic Role of Women ...*, p. 23.

[27] The diversity in national definitions is considerable. For instance, although, for the purposes of the national labour force surveys carried out by EEC member countries, part-time workers are generally those who so declared themselves, there are many national variations. In Belgium, one criterion used is that the hours must have been reduced at the wish of the individual. In Canada, part-time workers are those who usually work less than 30 hours (35 hours up to 1974) per week. Those who work less than 30 hours but consider themselves to be full-time

workers, are classified as employed full time. In Finland, part-time workers are those who normally work less than 30 hours a week in their main job. In France, all working hours less than 30 hours are counted as part time. In the Federal Republic of Germany, reference may be made to the usual contractual working time in the enterprise concerned. In Italy, the usual hours worked should be less than those normally worked in the same enterprise. In the Netherlands, part-time workers in the surveys up to and including 1979 were defined as those who usually worked both less than the normal hours of work and less than 40 hours a week. In the 1981 survey, the latter definition was applied. In Norway, those who actually worked less than 35 hours during the survey week are considered as working part time. This also applies to Sweden except that those who did so for economic reasons were, until 1975, excluded from coverage. In the United States, those who worked between 1 and 34 hours in the survey week were classified as part-time workers. For a full discussion of problems of definition, see also OECD, *Employment Outlook* (Paris, September 1983), Technical Annex, Note D.

United Kingdom and the United States it varies between 24% and 37%. The percentage is much lower in some other countries of the region: in Finland, Greece, Ireland and Italy, part-time women workers account for between 5% and 9% of total women's employment. The importance of female part-time workers compared with male part-time workers is illustrated by the fact that, while women accounted for between 28% and 48% of total employment in 1981, they represented between 63% and 94% of all those employed part time, except in Poland, where 50% of part-time workers were women.

Since part-time workers have generally been found to work for about half of the normal hours of full-time workers, it may be assumed, in order to calculate the extent of women's employment on the basis of "full-time equivalent" jobs, that two part-time workers are the equivalent of one full-time worker. In general, the effect of expressing employment in full-time equivalents is to reduce the differences between countries in comparison with unweighted data. Nevertheless, the variation between countries remains considerable, even in terms of full-time equivalents (see table III.26). In general, account should be taken of the fact that, although part-time employment for women has increased in many of the countries for which data are available, full-time employment has also increased in almost all countries.

While a high percentage of women work part time in some of the Nordic countries, a high percentage also works full time. In Denmark, for example, where 72% of women participate in the labour force and 44% of women's employment is part time, half of the female population aged 15 to 64 is employed on a full-time equivalent basis. In Sweden, 75% of adult women participate in the work force and 46% of employed women work part time, but 56% of the working age female population is employed on a full-time equivalent basis. Of those countries for which data are available, Finland has the highest female employment rate, with 62% of all women aged 15 to 64 years employed on a full-time equivalent basis. Rates in other countries range from as low as 25% in the Netherlands to as high as 49% in the United States.

TABLE III.26

Full-time and part-time female employment rates, around 1981

(*Percentages*)

Country	Female population aged 15–64		
	Working full time	Working part time	Equivalent full time[a]
Belgium	35	7	38
Canada..................	36	17	45
Denmark	36	28	50
Finland..................	60	5	62
France	39	7	43
Germany, Fed. Rep. of	35	12	41
Ireland (1979)	30	3	32
Italy	33	2	34
Luxembourg (1980)	31	6	35
Netherlands..............	18	15	25
Norway	29	34	46
Sweden..................	40	34	56
United Kingdom..........	34	20	44
United States.............	42	13	49

Sources: Calculated from data in OECD, *Labour Force Statistics 1970–1981*; OECD, *Historical Statistics, 1960–1981*; and OECD, *Employment Outlook* (Paris, September 1983).

[a] Assuming two part-time workers equal one full-time worker.

As regards trends in part-time employment, there are also large differences in the distribution of the increase in employment between full-time and part-time workers. In North America, where female employment increased by about 30% between 1973 and 1981, most of the increase (80%) was accounted for by full-time jobs. On the other hand, in Norway and Sweden, where female employment increased by 22% and 25% respectively, 80% of the increase was accounted for by part-time jobs. In Ireland, Italy and the United Kingdom, part-time employment of women actually declined during the period, while female full-time employment increased (see table III.27). When increases in employment are expressed in terms of full-time equivalents, differences in the growth of female employment between countries are even more marked, with female employment (on a full-time equivalent basis) increasing by less than 2% in Belgium, the Netherlands and Poland, and by between 20% and 32% in Canada, Italy, Norway and the United States. In any event, in 11 out of the 15 countries for which data are available, part-time workers accounted for a higher percentage of female employment in 1981 than in 1973. In five of the countries, however, the percentage of men who work part time has also increased. Between 1977 and 1981, for instance, the part-time employment of men rose from 6% to 7% in Canada, from 1% to 2% in Finland, from 3% to 8% in the Netherlands, from 5% to 11% in Norway, and from 6% to 7% in Sweden.

There is little specific information on the reasons for the part-time employment of women or men, although there are clearly differences between various age groups. In North America, for example, many young people combine higher education with part-time employment. The high rates of part-time employment among young people are thus among the reasons for the higher rates of part-time employment of men in Canada and the United States, and perhaps also in some of the west European countries. Information on the reasons for part-time employment is collected by Canada as part of its monthly *Labour Force Survey*. The reasons given by women for working part time, based on annual averages for 1976 and 1983, are shown in table III.28.

The data clearly show that the majority of younger women (in the 15 to 24 age group) are employed part time because they are still continuing their education. In the 25–54 age group, most women were not interested in full-time employment, although there was a significant change between 1976 and 1983. In the earlier year, 58% of women in this age group stated that they did not want to work full-time while, in 1983, only 49% gave this as a reason for their part-time employment. In the same period, the percentage of women in the 25–54 year age group who said they were employed part time because they could not find full-time work, increased from 10% to 27%. With respect to marital status, the majority of married women who worked part-time in both 1976 and 1983 stated that they were not interested in full-time work. However, the percentage of these women has declined: only 19% of married women who worked part-time in 1983 said they did so because of family responsibilities, compared with 26% in the earlier year. On the other hand, the percentage of married women who would have preferred to work full time, had such jobs been available, increased from 10% in 1976 to 24% in 1983. In Canada, where unemployment in 1983 was 12% compared with 7% in 1976, regardless of marital status, the

TABLE III.27

Growth in women's part-time employment, in selected countries, around 1973 and 1981

Country	Part-time workers as a percentage of total female employment		Percentage distribution of increase in female employment		Percentage increase in	
	Around 1973	Around 1981	Part-time	Full-time	Female employment	Female full-time equivalent workers [a]
Belgium	8	16	95	5	5	1
Canada [b]	20	32	37	63	30	22
Denmark [b]	40	44	60	40	9	7
Finland [c]	7	8	22	78	5	5
France	11	16	59	41	7	4
Germany, Federal Republic of	20	26	120	−20	−1	−4
Ireland [d]	10	8	−9 [e]	109 [e]	..	..
Italy	9	6	−3	103	22	24
Luxembourg [d]	14	17	40	60	..	..
Netherlands [f]	16	45	51 [d]	49 [d]	20 [b]	1 [b]
Norway [b]	48	54	80	20	25	20
Poland [b]	5	6	51	49	3	2
Sweden	39	46	80	20	22	17
United Kingdom	38	37	−7	107	4	5
United States	25	24	20	80	31	32

Sources: Calculated from data in OECD, *Employment Outlook* (Paris, September 1983) except for Poland: *Rocznik Statystyczny* (1983), p. 57.

[a] Assuming two part-time workers equal one full-time worker.

[b] 1975 and 1981.

[c] 1976 and 1981.

[d] 1973 and 1979.

[e] 1975 and 1979.

[f] 1981 data are not comparable with 1973 data because of a change in the definition of part-time workers.

percentage of part-time women workers who could not find full-time work increased significantly, reflecting the severity of economic conditions.

The 1980 study pointed out the difficulty of determining how much of the expansion of part-time employment is a result of supply factors and how much can be attributed to the demand side. As regards the latter, a number of factors have emerged. Part-time employment is used extensively by employers to deal with peak periods of business, particularly in service-sector activities, such as retail trade and banking. This is also one of the major reasons for the high proportion of female part-time

employment, as working women are mostly concentrated in these sectors. However, it has also been noted that another explanation for the growth of part-time employment stems from employers' desire for more flexibility in the work force in the face of uncertain economic prospects and increasing job protection. A 1982 study revealed a fairly widespread shift in policy on the use of human resources at the enterprise level aimed at securing greater flexibility of the work force, in the wake of the severe recession following the first oil shock.[28] It may well

[28] OECD, *The Challenge of Unemployment: A Report to Labour Ministers* (Paris, 1982).

TABLE III.28

Canada: reasons for part-time employment of women, 1976 and 1983

(Percentages)

Year, age and marital status	Personal or family responsibilities	Continuing education	Could find only part-time work	Did not want full-time work	Other reasons
1976					
15–24 years	5	63	15	16	2
25–54 years	26	1	10	58	4
55 years and over	15	–	8	68	8
Married	26	2	10	60	3
Single	2	68	14	13	3
Other	15	–	17	57	9
1983					
15–24 years	2	52	33	12	1
25–54 years	20	2	27	49	3
55 years and over	7	–	16	69	7
Married	19	1	24	53	3
Single	–	55	32	10	2
Other	9	–	41	43	5

Source: Statistics Canada, *Labour Force Annual Averages, 1975–1983* (Ottawa, February 1984).

Note: Totals may not add to 100 because of rounding.

be that employers who had retained full-time workers or staff at the beginning of the recession, despite a shortage of work—the so-called "labour hoarding" practice—eventually dismissed these workers, replacing them with part-time employees.

It has also been argued that changes in operating conditions, including the use of new technology, have led many enterprises to restructure activities and to redistribute the work tasks.[29] Certain jobs which previously required a full-time employee can now be carried out on a part-time basis. Even where hourly earnings of part-time workers are the same as those of full-time workers, the availability of part-time workers enables the employer to save money by more closely adjusting the number of employees to the volume of business. It has also been suggested that part-time work, especially of women, has been used in the United Kingdom as a substitute for other types of labour power to cope with short-lived booms in a declining manufacturing sector.[30] Employers can also use part-time employment as a way of avoiding fixed employment costs in industries which face greater economic uncertainty.[31]

It has, in fact, been found that hourly wage rates for part-time workers are often lower than for full-time workers, thus creating incentives for employers to engage the former. It has been argued, in this context, that employers hire part-time workers not because their hourly rate is low, but because their hourly rate is much lower than overtime rates.[32] Employers responding to a Commission of Inquiry in Canada[33] claimed that they paid the same hourly wages to part-time and full-time workers doing basically the same jobs. However, the Commission also noted that part-time workers are often not doing the same jobs as full-time workers, and tend to be clustered in occupational categories at the low end of

the full-time pay scale. The Commission also found that employers were generally opposed to the suggestion that they should have to pay prorated fringe benefits to part-time workers.

On the supply side, it has been argued that the availability of increasing numbers of married women who were willing or able to work only on a part-time basis has, to some extent, fuelled the expansion of part-time employment. Part-time work is seen as enabling women to combine work with family responsibilities, as well as providing a degree of flexibility to mothers of young children. However, part-time workers are not infrequently required to work at weekends, during evening hours or even to be available at any time. Such irregular working hours make it difficult to combine employment with household responsibilities, and especially for the working parents to arrange for alternative child care. There are other possible disadvantages of part-time employment: opportunities for training and advancement may be limited or non-existent; there may be little job security; and part-time workers are usually not eligible for employee benefits such as pensions and unemployment insurance.

Finally, the importance of the earnings of part-time women workers to family incomes should not be underestimated. In a survey in the United Kingdom it was found that, even in families where wives' earnings comprised less than 20% of total family income, a majority of wives reported that their families would not be able to manage without their earnings.[34] The report also concluded that husbands of working wives tolerated, in varying degrees, the fact that their wives worked. In many cases, husbands affirmed that they did not want their wives' employment to interfere or conflict with their own work or domestic life. Women's part-time employment, the report notes, may in part be seen as a compromise between paid and unpaid work.[35]

[29] L. Paukert, *op. cit.*

[30] S. Dex and S. M. Perry, "Women's employment changes in the 1970s", *Employment Gazette,* United Kingdom Department of Employment (April 1984).

[31] *Ibid.*

[32] OECD, *Employment Outlook, op. cit.*

[33] *Part-time Work in Canada,* Report of the Commission of Inquiry Into Part-time Work, Labour Canada (Ottawa, April 1983).

[34] J. Martin and C. Roberts, "Women's employment in the 1980s: evidence from the women and employment survey", *Employment Gazette,* United Kingdom Department of Employment (May 1984).

[35] *Ibid.*

CHAPTER IV

SECTORAL AND OCCUPATIONAL DISTRIBUTION

Introduction

The purpose of this chapter is to give an overview of recent trends in the occupational and industrial characteristics of women's employment within the ECE region. The point of departure for this overview is the 1980 study,[1] which presented a broad picture of various aspects of the integration of women in the economy of the region using data from population censuses over the 1950–1970 period. This chapter updates the 1980 study with information, whenever available, from the population censuses around 1980. However, as only limited statistics on occupation and industry from the 1980 round of censuses are generally available, the data for this chapter are also based in part on labour force sample surveys and on national studies. Most of the census data and other statistics currently available are at a high level of aggregation, which severely limits the analysis.

Inter-country and temporal comparisons of occupational and industrial distribution should be carried out with caution. Criteria for classifying economic activities differ between countries and, in many cases over time. Furthermore, it is difficult to compare countries at different levels of industrialization and with different rates of female labour force participation. Finally, allowance must be made for economic developments and changes in trends since the early 1970s. Most of the countries in the region went through periods of recession or economic slow-down during this period. The considerable differences between countries as regards the depth of the recession or economic slow-down further complicate inter-country and temporal comparisons.

A. Aggregate trends in sectoral distribution

The general trends in the sectoral distribution of the female and male labour force in ECE countries between 1950 and 1980 are given in table IV.1.[2] In broad terms, changes in sectoral distribution during the 1970s, in coun-

tries for which data around 1980 are available, can be summarized as follows: decreases in the percentage of the economically active in the agricultural sector; increases in the percentage working in the service sector; and a mixed pattern in the share of industrial employment in conformity with the trends observed in the 1980 study.[3] Industrial labour continued to expand rapidly in those countries where its initial share was low. By contrast, in the most industrialized countries, the share of employment in industry declined. Also, in several of these countries, the share in agriculture, which was already very low, decreased further. Even allowing for the lack of comparability over time of some of the data, the broad changes were significant and affected both the male and the female labour force.

In general, the relative increase in the number of women working in the service sector was stronger than that of men. This conforms with the trends observed for the preceding decades, indicated in the 1980 study. As a result of these trends, an increasing percentage of the female labour force is employed in the service sector in nearly all countries of the region (see table IV.1). This is especially the case in western Europe and North America, where about three fifths to four fifths of all female workers are employed in services. In Belgium, Canada, the Netherlands, Norway and the United States, this sector accounts for 80% or more of all women in the labour force, compared with between approximately 45% and 60% for men. The proportion of women in the service sector is relatively low (between 55% and 65%) in Austria, the Federal Republic of Germany and Italy. Service sector employment accounts for 40%–45% of the male labour force in these countries. The most recent data available for the east European countries suggest that employment in the service sector represents between 40% and 55% of total female employment, except in Romania. The corresponding proportions for males are between approximately 25% and 35%. In the countries of southern Europe, with the notable exception of Turkey, between 25% and 65% of women in the labour force and between 35% and 45% of men work in the service sector. The percentage of women working in the agricultural sector is low (less than 5%) in almost the whole of western Europe. The proportion of women working in industry in western Europe and North America varies between approximately 15% and 30%, and has shown a tendency, as in the case of men, to decline. The share of women in industry in most countries of eastern Europe is significant (about 40%) and, on the whole, has not yet shown a tendency to fall. Data for southern Europe do not reveal a consistent pattern in this respect, probably due in part to a lack of comparable data.

---

[1] *The Economic Role of Women in the ECE Region* (United Nations publication, Sales No. E.80.II.E.6).

[2] For most of the countries this implies a change in the data source for the years around 1980, compared with the information for the years around 1950, 1960 and 1970. The sources for the latter were the population censuses of each year, whereas the data for years around 1980 are mostly derived from labour force sample surveys. Information from the recent population censuses around 1980 is in general not yet available. Data from sample surveys are usually subject to sampling error. The distribution given in table IV.1 may thus differ from distributions given in the census publications of each country. In addition, the general precautions set out in Chapter III, note 1 of the 1980 study with respect to inter-country and temporal comparisons should also be noted, especially in respect of the criteria for counting the number of active people in farm activities (in particular unpaid family helpers), which vary between countries and, in some cases, within countries over time.

[3] *The Economic Role of Women ...*, Chapter III, section 1.

TABLE IV.1

Percentage distribution of economically active men and women, by major economic sectors in ECE countries, for years around 1950, 1960, 1970 and 1980

Region, country and year	Men			Women		
	Agriculture	Industry	Services	Agriculture	Industry	Services
Western Europe						
Austria[a]						
1951	26	47	27	45	21	34
1961	18	53	28	30	37	32
1971	12	51	37	17	29	53
1981	9	31	40	13	24	64
Belgium						
1947	14	54	33	8	40	53
1961	9	53	38	4	32	64
1970	5	51	44	3	30	67
1981	4	42	54	2	17	81
Denmark						
1950	29	39	31	18	22	60
1960	23	43	34	5	25	70
1970	13	44	43	7	23	71
1981	10	43	47	3	18	79
Finland						
1950	47	33	20	46	21	33
1960	38	38	24	32	22	46
1970	24	42	34	16	24	60
1980	14	44	41	10	23	67
France						
1962	21	46	33	20	27	54
1968	16	48	36	15	26	60
1975	11	46	42	8	25	66
1982	9	43	48	7	22	72
Germany, Federal Republic of						
1950	16	53	31	35	26	39
1961	10	58	33	20	34	47
1970	6	55	39	10	35	55
1981	5	53	42	8	30	63
Ireland						
1951	47	26	27	21	20	59
1961	43	27	31	15	22	63
1971	32	33	35	9	25	66
1979	25	37	38	7	24	69
Italy						
1951	42	34	24	41	28	31
1961	28	43	28	31	32	38
1971	17	49	35	19	33	49
1980	13[a]	43	44	16	28	56
Luxembourg						
1947	22	51	28	37	13	50
1960	14	56	30	18	12	70
1970	10	49	42	11	16	72
1980	..	..	..	..	..	..
Netherlands						
1947	20	40	40	18	17	64
1960	13	48	39	4	23	73
1971	7	43	49	3	18	79
1979	7	42	51	3	14	83
Norway						
1950	32	40	28	8	26	66
1960	24	41	35	4	22	74
1970	13	44	42	7	19	74
1981	10	41	48	6	14	80

TABLE IV.1 (continued)

Region, country and year	Men			Women		
	Agriculture	Industry	Services	Agriculture	Industry	Services
Sweden						
1950	26	47	28	7	26	68
1960	18	53	29	4	27	69
1970	10	51	39	5	21	74
1981	8	45	47	3	15	82
Switzerland						
1950	22	51	27	5	36	59
1960	15	56	29	4	27	69
1970	10	51	39	5	21	73
United Kingdom [b]						
1951	6	54	40	2	40	59
1961	5	53	42	1	36	63
1971	4	53	43	1	30	69
1980	4	48	48	1	23	76
North America						
Canada [c]						
1951	23	35	42	3	24	73
1961	15	35	50	5	18	78
1971	8	34	58	4	15	81
1982	6	35	59	3	14	83
United States						
1960	10	47	44	2	25	73
1970	5	42	53	1	21	78
1982	5	38	56	2	18	80
Eastern Europe and USSR						
Bulgaria						
1956	55	25	20	78	10	12
1965	36	41	23	55	23	22
1975	21	48	31	26	37	37
1980	26	46	28	24	37	39
Czechoslovakia						
1947	30	43	27	53	27	30
1961	21	54	25	30	37	33
1970	17	54	29	17	40	43
1980	15	57	28	12	40	48
German Democratic Republic						
1964	15	53	32	15	37	49
1971	12	57	31	11	39	49
1980	14	64	23	9	37	54
Hungary						
1949	55	27	18	61	18	21
1960	39	40	21	42	29	29
1970 [c]	26	49	25	23	40	37
1980	22	46	32	15	41	44
Poland						
1950	46	29	25	68	14	18
1960	37	37	26	59	17	24
1970	32	44	24	46	24	30
1980	12	59	29	6	43	51
Romania						
1956	59	24	16	83	7	9
1966	45	35	20	72	12	16
1970	8	57	35	3	43	54
1980	9	57	34	3	49	48
USSR						
1959	35	35	30	53	22	25
1970	25	45	30	27	31	42
1980	..	..	..	..	..	..

TABLE IV.1 (concluded)

Region, country and year	Men			Women		
	Agriculture	Industry	Services	Agriculture	Industry	Services
Southern Europe						
Cyprus						
1976	21	29	51	42	23	35
1980	17	37	46	33	44	24
Greece[a]						
1951	53	20	28	45	26	29
1961	50	23	28	69	14	17
1971	36	30	34	54	17	29
1977	27	34	39	48	18	33
1981	25	34	40	40	19	40
Portugal						
1950	54	25	21	33	24	43
1960	50	29	21	18	29	53
1981	20	45	35	32	26	41
Spain						
1950	54	26	20	25	25	50
1960	40	34	26	18	28	53
1970	28	39	33	14	31	56
1982	18	42	39	16	21	63
Turkey						
1970	56	17	27	90	5	4
1980	43	23	34	88	5	7
Yugoslavia						
1953	65	21	14	82	8	10
1961	54	28	18	69	14	17
1971	44	35	21	57	20	23
1980	6	58	36	3	41	57

Sources: For 1950, 1960 and 1970, *The Economic Role of Women in the ECE Region* (United Nations publication, Sales No. E.80.II.E.6), table III.1; for years around 1980, International Labour Office, *Yearbook of Labour Statistics* (Geneva, 1982, 1983); national statistics.

Note: Totals exclude "unclassified", except for Canada and Hungary.

[a] Because of changes in definition, data for different census years are not comparable.

[b] Data refer to Great Britain.

[c] Services include "unclassified".

Table IV.2 provides data on the shares of women in the total labour force, as well as by major economic sectors, in the various countries. It shows that the female share of the total labour force, as well as in the non-farm sectors, increased in most of the countries of the region for which 1980 data were available. The increase was particularly strong in some of the countries where the female share of the labour force was fairly low around 1970, such as Belgium (with an increase of 30% to 38%), Italy (from 27% to 33%) and Norway (from 28% to 42%).[4] The table also confirms, as already suggested by the data in table IV.1, that the feminization of the service sector increased over the decade. The number of countries where women account for at least half of total service sector employment increased considerably in industrial western Europe and North America. By 1980, Canada, the United Kingdom, the United States and the four Nordic countries (Denmark, Finland, Norway and Sweden) were in

this group, in addition to most of the east European countries, many of which had more women than men in service activities as early as 1970. In several of the remaining countries of western Europe for which data for 1980 are available (Austria, Belgium, France and the Federal Republic of Germany), the number of women and men in the service sector was nearly equal. In Switzerland, the percentage of women in the service sector had reached nearly 50% by as early as 1970, and a further increase may be expected to be shown by more detailed data for 1980, when they become available.

The increase of women in the service sector does not necessarily reflect only increases in the female share of the non-farm sectors in general. In effect, some countries (Belgium, the Netherlands and the United Kingdom) with an increase in the female share of the service sector, experienced a decline in the female share of the industrial sector. This indicates that a stronger polarization of economic activity by sex, as measured at the sectoral level, had taken place in these countries. The general trends in industrial segregation by sex in the various countries cannot, however, be fully ascertained from the sectoral distribution shown in tables IV.1 and IV.2, as the general trends in the distribution move, to a large extent, in the same direction for both the male and female labour force. A summary measure of these relative changes is the

---

[4] In the case of Norway, it should be noted, however, that the rather dramatic increase is partly caused by a change in the definition of the labour force. The percentage for 1980 includes all persons economically active for at least one hour per week. The figure for 1970 is based on the number of people working for at least 1,000 hours over the 12-month period preceding the census date. The corresponding Norwegian figure for 1980 is 32% (census data). Similar changes in the definition of the labour force may apply to other countries.

TABLE IV.2

The share of women in the total labour force, by major economic sectors, in ECE countries, around 1960, 1970 and 1980

(*Percentages*)

Region, country and year	All sectors	Non-farm sectors	Industry	Services
Western Europe				
Austria				
1961	40.3	36.5	32.1	43.4
1971	38.6	37.2	26.6	47.7
1981	38.6	37.5	28.7	49.7
Belgium				
1961	27.0	27.9	18.1	38.3
1970	29.5	30.1	20.0	39.0
1981	37.7	43.4	18.3	45.6
Denmark				
1960	21.2	36.0	20.8	48.5
1970	36.6	38.3	22.9	48.8
1981	44.4	46.5	24.8	57.8
Finland				
1960	39.4	41.7	27.5	55.4
1970	42.4	44.8	29.4	56.6
1980	46.3	47.5	30.8	58.3
France				
1968	34.6	35.1	22.2	46.7
1975	36.6	37.4	24.1	47.4
1982	39.4	34.9	25.1	49.7
Germany, Federal Republic of				
1961	37.0	34.3	25.5	45.6
1970	35.8	34.8	26.2	44.1
1981	38.4	38.0	26.4	48.8
Ireland				
1961	25.9	33.6	23.9	38.9
1971	26.3	32.4	21.1	40.3
1979	27.7	31.2	19.4	40.5
Italy				
1961	25.1	24.5	19.7	30.8
1971	27.0	26.6	20.0	34.1
1980	33.2	30.8[a]	23.4[a]	37.2
Netherlands				
1960	22.3	23.9	12.0	34.6
1971	25.9	26.8	12.4	35.9
1979	29.7	30.0	11.4	40.0
Norway				
1960	22.9	27.3	13.9	38.7
1970	27.6	28.9	13.9	39.9
1981	41.7	42.4	18.7	53.9
Sweden				
1960	29.8	33.2	17.9	50.7
1970	35.4	36.7	18.9	50.7
1981	45.9	47.0	22.3	54.3
Switzerland				
1960	30.1	32.8	22.1	47.0
1970	34.3	35.2	23.9	47.7
1980	34.4	..	..	..
United Kingdom[b]				
1961	32.5	33.3	24.3	42.2
1971	36.5	37.1	24.5	47.8
1980	39.1	40.6	23.6	51.5
North America				
Canada[c]				
1961	27.3	29.5	16.1	36.6
1971	34.3	35.4	18.5	42.5
1982	41.2	42.2	22.0	50.0

TABLE IV.2 (*continued*)

Region, country and year	All sectors	Non-farm sectors	Industry	Services
United States				
1960	32.7	34.5	20.8	44.8
1970	37.8	38.7	23.4	47.1
1981	42.2	48.3	26.1	52.6
Eastern Europe and USSR				
Bulgaria[c]				
1965	44.0	35.5	30.9	42.4
1975	46.8	45.1	40.4	51.0
1980	47.1	47.7	41.6	55.5
Czechoslovakia[c]				
1961	41.0	38.2	32.3	48.2
1970	44.7	44.6	37.4	54.4
1980	46.6	47.4	38.3	59.4
German Democratic Republic[c]				
1964	44.2	43.3	33.8	54.4
1971	46.3	46.5	37.3	57.7
1980	52.4	53.7	38.9	66.6
Hungary[c]				
1960	35.1	33.6	28.5	40.3
1970	41.2	42.1	36.6	50.3
1981	44.9	46.6	39.4	54.5[d]
Poland				
1960	43.3	33.4	26.0	41.6
1970	46.0	40.5	31.5	51.9
1980	42.7	44.4	34.8	54.8
Romania				
1956	45.3	26.4	20.2	33.9
1966	45.2	29.2	21.3	39.9
1970	32.7	33.9	26.7	42.8
1980	38.7	40.2	35.1	46.9
USSR				
1959	51.9	44.2	40.6	47.9
1970	50.4	49.8	41.3	58.7
Southern Europe				
Yugoslavia				
1961	36.6	27.9	22.3	35.4
1971	36.8	31.2	25.4	39.0
1980	35.5	36.3	28.1	41.2

Sources: For 1960 and 1970, national population censuses; for years around 1980, see table IV.1.

Note: Totals exclude "unclassified", except for Canada and Hungary.

[a] Mining and quarrying not included.

[b] Data refer to Great Britain.

[c] Services include "unclassified".

[d] Group 0 (not adequately defined) included in services.

index of dissimilarity (DI index).[5] This measure was applied to the sectoral distribution of table IV.1 for each country and year. The results are shown in table IV.3.

The general trend during the decade 1970 to 1980 has been towards an increased or stable level of sectoral segregation, rather than towards a lower level. The only excep-

[5] The index of dissimilarity (DI index) provides a measure of the level of sectoral segregation by sex. The higher the value of the index, the greater the dissimilarity of the sectoral distributions of the male and the female labour force. It should be kept in mind, however, that the figures in table IV.3 cannot be used as a general measure of the level of industrial segregation in each of the countries, considering that the sectoral distributions of table IV.1 are given at a very aggregate level. As pointed out in all studies of industrial and occupational segregation by sex, the relative level of segregation depends heavily on the level of aggregation in the distributions. In general, the level of segregation will increase as the level of disaggregation increases. As mentioned earlier, too much importance should not be attached to inter-country and temporal com-

parisons, especially for the earlier censuses, because the classification of economic activity, in particular in agriculture, may vary from one country to another and from period to period. Despite these reservations, table IV.3 gives a useful summary measure of the general trends of sectoral segregation as presented in table IV.1. For more details see C. Hakim, *Occupational Segregation*: A comparative study of the degree and pattern of the differentiation between men's and women's work in Britain, the United States and other countries. Research Paper No. 9, Department of Employment (London, Her Majesty's Stationery Office, 1979); OECD, *Women and Their Integration in the Economy,* (Paris, 1984).

TABLE IV.3

Dissimilarity (DI) index [a]

Country	1950	1960	1970	1980
Western Europe				
Austria....................	26.0	16.0	21.5	27.5
Belgium	20.0	26.0	23.0	27.0
Denmark	28.5	36.0	27.5	28.5
Finland	13.0	22.0	26.0	25.5
France	30.5	23.5	24.0	23.0
Germany, Federal Republic of	27.0	24.0	17.5	23.5
Ireland	32.0	32.5	31.0	31.0
Italy	7.0	12.0	16.0	15.0
Luxembourg	37.0	44.0	32.0	..
Netherlands...............	24.5	34.0	29.5	32.0
Norway	38.0	39.0	31.5	31.5
Sweden	40.0	40.0	35.0	35.0
Switzerland	32.0	40.0	34.5	..
United Kingdom	18.5	21.0	26.0	28.0
North America				
Canada	30.0	27.5	23.0	24.0
United States	..	29.5	25.0	23.5
Eastern Europe and USSR				
Bulgaria..................	23.0	19.0	11.0	11.0
Czechoslovakia............	23.0	17.0	14.0	20.0
German Democratic Republic	..	16.5	18.5	31.0
Hungary	9.0	11.0	12.0	12.0
Poland...................	22.0	22.0	20.0	22.0
Romania	..	24.0	27.0	14.0
USSR	..	18.0	14.0	..
Southern Europe				
Cyprus...................	..	..	..	22.5
Greece	7.5	19.5	18.0	15.5
Portugal	22.0	32.0	..	18.5
Spain	30.0	27.5	22.5	23.5
Turkey	..	..	34.5	45.0
Yugoslavia	17.0	15.0	15.0	20.5
M_t* [b]	23.3	24.2	22.2	23.8
S_t* [b]	9.1	8.2	6.7	6.4
Coefficient of variation (%)	39.0	38.0	30.2	26.9

[a] Calculated on the basis of the sectoral distribution (3 sectors) given in table V.1.

[b] Mean (M_t*) and standard deviation (S_t*) calculated for the DI indices of each year for the 20 countries represented in all four years.

tions are Greece and the United States, both of which show a slight reduction in the value of the index over the decade. In general, table IV.3 also indicates a tendency towards greater equality in the levels of sectoral segregation at the country level over the last decade. The inter-country differences in sectoral segregation decreased slightly over the period. The coefficient of variation with respect to the DI indices for each year, for the twenty countries which provided data for all four years, decreased from 37% in 1950 to 27% in 1980. This reinforces the general impression from table IV.1 that the trend is towards smaller inter-country differences in sectoral distributions. However, as information for the years around both 1980 and 1950 is lacking for several countries in the region, caution should be exercised in generalizing that this tendency applies to the ECE region as a whole.

B. Trends in industrial distribution in individual sectors

The 1980 study also covered the more detailed industrial distribution by branches, including developments in some countries during the period after the 1970 round of censuses. This section focuses more explicitly on recent developments in industrial segregation by sex at a more detailed level than represented by the broad sectoral categories dealt with above. Table IV.4 shows the female share of employment in selected west European countries over the period 1958/1960 to 1981, in all non-farm sectors combined, and in eight selected industrial and service sectors separately. [6] The results do not show a clear trend with respect to developments in the countries represented in the table. In some of the countries, such as Finland and the United Kingdom, the industrial distribution was relatively stable from 1974/1976 to 1980, as regards both women's share of total employment in the non-farm sectors, and their shares in each of the industrial branches. In other countries, women's share of total employment increased, but developments with respect to their shares in each of the industrial sectors were somewhat different. In the Federal Republic of Germany and Italy, there was an increase in women's shares in the manufacturing and service sectors, whereas in Belgium, Norway and Sweden most of the increase in female employment took place in the service sectors, with stable or declining female shares in manufacturing.

All the countries in table IV.4 show a high female share of total employment in community, social and private services. Women constitute the majority in these sectors in all the countries included in the table, with the exception of Italy, where the share in 1980 was close to 50%. In three of the Nordic countries (Finland, Norway and Sweden) in particular, the share of female employment was very high in these sectors and, as will be seen, this is a general characteristic of the employment of women, which may be linked to both the industrial and the occupational segregation of the labour market.

Table IV.5 shows the development of female employment in the major sectors of economic activity for six east European countries, from 1970 to the beginning of the 1980s. However, the classification into major industrial sectors does not directly correspond to the categories of the International Standard Industrial Classification of all economic activities (ISIC) used in table IV.4. A comparison between the countries in the two tables with regard to the structure and trends in female employment is therefore possible only in general terms. On the whole, as in west European countries, the female share of the service sector also increased in the east European countries over the period considered. In addition, the female share of employment in the manufacturing sectors is generally considerably higher in the countries of eastern Europe than in those represented in table IV.4. Nevertheless, the data in table IV.5 also show considerable differences between the countries, with respect both to the

---

[6] The limitations as regards inter-country and temporal comparisons referred to earlier should be kept in mind. In particular, it should be noted that the percentage shares of women in all non-farm sectors for the period 1968–1970 differ for some of the countries, especially Norway and Sweden, in tables III.2 and III.4 of the 1980 study. This inconsistency is probably due to different definitions of total employment. While census data were used for table III.2, table III.4 was based on current statistics, which include all part-time work. However, as most of the data for recent years are from labour force sample surveys, they should be fairly comparable with those for earlier periods.

TABLE IV.4

Share of women in total employment in non-farm sectors, in seven west-European countries, selected periods between 1958 and 1981

(Percentages)

Sector	Belgium				Finland				Germany, Federal Republic of				Italy			
	1958–1960	1968–1970	1974–1976	1981	1959–1960	1968–1970	1974–1976	1980	1958–1959	1968–1970	1974–1976	1981	1959–1960	1968–1970	1974–1976	1980
All non-farm sectors	31	33	35	43	42	44	47	48	34	34	36	38	29	26	27	31
of which:																
Mining, quarrying	1	2	3	2	..	..	..	12	..	..	..	6	..	..	..	..
Manufacturing	26	26	26	23	36	35	36	38	31	30	29	32	34	28	27	32
Electricity, gas, water	7	6	6	..	..	..	..	21	5a	8a	8a	14	5a	4a	5a	9
Construction	2	3	3	4	6	7	9	9	4	6	7	8	1	1	1	3
Wholesale and retail trade, hotels, restaurants	41	48	44	46	60	59	62	60	54	54	54	56	30	35	37	33
Transport and communications	6	8	12	13	24	23	27	25	14	17	19	20	7	7	7	11
Finance, insurance, real estate	..	47	45	39	..	..	..	60	42	45	45	46	..	..	..	29
Community, social and private services	58b	53b	53b	53	68	70	66	68	50b	47b	48b	52	45	39	42	49

Sector	Norway				Sweden			United Kingdom			
	1958–1960	1968–1970	1974–1976	1981	1968–1969	1974–1976	1981	1959–1960	1968–1970	1974–1976	1980
All non-farm sectors	31	32	39	42	40	43	47	35	38	41	41
of which:											
Mining, quarrying	–	12	..	..	5	10	7	3	4	4	5
Manufacturing	22	20	22c	23	25	26	27	32	30	30	29
Electricity, gas, water	8c	7c	..	..	14c	12	19	11	14	19	20
Construction	2	2	5	6	6	6	8	4	6	8	7
Wholesale and retail trade, hotels, restaurants	43d	46	53	56	53d	52	52	51	54	56	55
Transport and communications	13	16	20	23	22	26	27	14	16	17	18
Finance, insurance, real estate	..d	47	45	45	..d	47	47	44	50	51	52
Community, social and private services	61b	59	62	64	67b	68	71	53b	54b	58b	57

a Including mining and quarrying.

b Including hotels and restaurants.

c Including sanitary services.

d Finance, insurance and real estate are included in wholesale and retail trade.

Sources: The Economic Role of Women in the ECE Region (United Nations publication, Sales No. E.80.II.E.6), table III.4; International Labour Office, Yearbook of Labour Statistics (Geneva, 1982, 1983).

TABLE IV.5

Share of women in total employment, by sector, in six east-European countries, for years around 1970, 1980 and 1983

(*Percentages*)

Sector	Bulgaria			Czechoslovakia			German Democratic Republic	
	1970[a]	1980	1983	1970	1980[b]	1982[b]	1970	1980
All sectors	44	47	49	47	45	45	48	52
of which:								
Agriculture and forestry	51	45	48	48	42	41	46	42[c]
Mining, quarrying, manufacturing, electricity, gas and water.............	45	48	49	44	41	41	42	43[d]
Construction........................	14	18	20	15	14	14	13	16
Commerce..........................	54	63	64	72	69	72	36	71
Transport, storage and communication ..	20	23	25	31	31	31	69	73
Services	65	66	68	60	63	64	70	73
Other	35	48	51	55	39	4	54	55

Sector	Hungary		Poland			Romania		
	1970	1980	1975	1980	1982[e]	1970	1980	1982
All sectors	41	43	42	43	43	33	39	40
of which:								
Agriculture and forestry	39	36	25	27	25	15	16	19
Mining, quarrying, manufacturing, electricity, gas and water.............	42	44[f]	39	39	37	32	40	41
Construction........................	16	18	18	19	18	8	12	12
Commerce..........................	61	63	72	71	71	47	58	60
Transport, storage and communication ..	22	24	24	26	28	16	15	16
Services	57	60	64	64	65	48	55	56
Other	41	23	80	83	84	43	39	43

Sources: National statistics.

[a] Without employees in co-operative State collective farms.

[b] Excluding those on child-care leave.

[c] Excluding apprentices.

[d] Excluding building draft.

[e] Figures are for full-time employees.

[f] Excluding water supply.

overall level of female employment and to the changes in the female share of the manufacturing sectors. In Czechoslovakia, the women's share both in total employment and in manufacturing sectors declined over the period. Poland experienced a rather stable level in the former and a decrease in the latter while, in the other countries, there were increases in both cases.

The analysis of the broad sectoral distributions in table IV.1 can be extended by focusing on the more detailed breakdown of industrial sectors provided by the first-digit ISIC level.[7] Table IV.6 depicts the industrial distribution of both the female and the male labour forces for the years around 1970 and 1980 in those countries for which data were available. The table also shows, for each of the countries, the contribution of each industrial sector to the general DI index for the years 1970 and 1980 respectively.[8] Table IV.7 sums up the changes in the magnitude

of the DI index over the period 1970-1980 for each country. Compared with the DI indices for the most aggregated level of sectoral distribution given in table IV.3, the index is higher for both years and for all countries. This illustrates the point, mentioned earlier, that all measures of occupational and industrial segregation are dependent upon the level of aggregation used in the classification. However, for a number of the countries listed in table IV.7, the changes in the level of industrial segregation, as measured by the index at the one-digit ISIC level, are the opposite of the changes in the index applied to the broad sectoral distributions of table IV.1. This indicates another disadvantage of the index with respect to measuring temporal changes: even the direction of change, towards greater or lesser segregation, is dependent on the level of disaggregation of the industrial (or occupational) classification.[9]

The general tendency towards less inter-country variation in the level of industrial segregation also applies to the changes in the DI indices given in table IV.7. The value of the coefficient of variation for the indices decreased slightly from 1970 to 1980. This is also confirmed by the graphical presentation of the changes at

[7] It should be noted that even the one-digit level classification presents the industrial distributions at a very aggregated level. Nevertheless, female employment in most countries is rather heavily concentrated in the service sector and even a division within this sector into broad categories offers insight into the different structures of female and male employment.

[8] As the index is an unweighted sum of the numerical value of the differences between an industrial sector's share of the male and the female labour force respectively, these differences (or more correctly, half of the difference) also represent a measure for the (additive) contribution of each sector to the overall value of the index.

[9] Account should also be taken of the fact that, for some of the countries, the 1970 distributions given in table IV.6 are not identical to the broad sectoral distributions of table IV.1. Relatively minor differences may account for part of this lack of consistency at country level.

TABLE IV.6

Distribution of men and women, by sector, in selected ECE countries, 1970 and 1980

(Percentages)

Austria / Belgium

Industry (one-digit ISIC level)	Austria 1970 Men	Women	Contribution to DI index	Austria 1980 Men	Women	Contribution to DI index	Belgium 1970 Men	Women	Contribution to DI index	Belgium 1980 Men	Women	Contribution to DI index
1. Agriculture, hunting, forestry and fishing	12.2	17.0	4.8	8.6	12.6	4.0	5.5	2.7	2.6	3.6	1.7	1.9
2. Mining and quarrying	1.2	0.2	1.1	0.8	0.1	0.7	2.0	0.1	1.9	1.1	0.0	1.1
3. Manufacturing	34.8	27.6	7.3	35.1	21.5	13.6	35.8	29.0	6.8	29.0	15.8	13.2
4. Electricity, gas and water	1.7	0.4	1.3	1.5	0.5	1.0	1.3	0.2	1.1	0.2	1.3	1.1
5. Construction	13.3	1.4	11.8	13.4	1.6	11.8	11.6	0.9	10.8	10.5	0.7	9.7
6. Wholesale/retail trade, restaurants and hotels	11.5	23.3	11.8	12.1	27.1	15.0	14.1	25.2	11.1	15.9	23.8	7.8
7. Transport, storage and communication	8.9	2.4	6.5	8.6	2.9	5.7	8.7	2.7	6.4	10.1	2.3	7.3
8. Financing, insurance, real estate and business services	3.3	4.6	1.3	4.5	6.3	1.8	4.3	5.5	1.3	6.5	7.4	0.9
9. Community social and personal services	13.1	23.1	10.1	15.4	27.4	12.1	16.7	33.7	17.1	22.0	47.6	25.6
Total	100.0	100.0	56.1 [a]	100.0	100.0	65.6 [a]	100.0	100.0	59.1 [a]	100.0	100.0	68.7 [a]

Denmark / Finland

Industry (one-digit ISIC level)	Denmark 1970 Men	Women	Contribution to DI index	Denmark 1980 Men	Women	Contribution to DI index	Finland 1970 Men	Women	Contribution to DI index	Finland 1980 Men	Women	Contribution to DI index
1. Agriculture, hunting, forestry and fishing	13.3	7.5	5.8	10.0	3.2	6.8	23.0	16.0	7.0	14.3	10.4	3.9
2. Mining and quarrying	0.2	0.0	0.2	0.2	0.0	0.2	0.5	0.1	0.4	0.8	0.1	0.7
3. Manufacturing	29.9	24.0	5.9	28.3	15.6	12.7	27.2	22.2	5.0	29.5	20.8	8.7
4. Electricity, gas and water	0.8	0.1	0.7	1.0	0.2	0.8	1.3	0.3	1.0	1.7	0.5	1.2
5. Construction	14.0	1.6	12.4	13.6	1.7	11.9	13.6	1.4	12.2	12.3	1.4	10.9
6. Wholesale/retail trade, restaurants and hotels	13.0	21.7	8.7	12.7	16.7	4.0	10.0	23.5	13.5	10.5	18.4	7.4
7. Transport, storage and communication	8.7	3.9	5.8	9.3	3.5	5.8	9.6	3.9	5.7	11.4	4.3	7.1
8. Financing, insurance, real estate and business services	4.5	7.4	0.5	6.1	6.6	0.5	2.3	5.0	2.7	4.1	7.0	2.9
9. Community social and personal services	15.2	33.3	18.1	18.5	52.2	33.7	11.8	25.4	13.6	15.3	37.0	21.7
Total	100.0	100.0	59.5 [a]	100.0	100.0	76.4 [a]	100.0	100.0	61.2 [a]	100.0	100.0	65.0 [a]

TABLE IV.6 (continued)

Germany, Federal Republic of / Ireland

Industry (one-digit ISIC level)	Germany, Federal Republic of						Ireland					
	1970			1980			1970			1980		
	Men	Women	Contribution to DI index	Men	Women	Contribution to DI index	Men	Women	Contribution to DI index	Men	Women	Contribution to DI index
1. Agriculture, hunting, forestry and fishing	6.0	10.2	4.2	4.7	7.5	2.8	31.4	8.9	22.5	24.9	6.4	18.5
2. Mining and quarrying	1.8	0.1	1.7	2.1	0.2	1.9	1.4	0.1	1.3	1.5	0.2	1.3
3. Manufacturing	40.6	33.2	7.4	38.6	27.8	10.8	19.1	23.6	4.5	21.7	20.8	0.9
4. Electricity, gas and water	1.1	0.3	0.8	1.2	0.3	0.9	1.7	0.4	1.3	1.5	0.6	0.9
5. Construction	11.9	1.6	10.3	11.4	1.6	9.8	11.9	0.6	11.3	12.1	1.0	11.1
6. Wholesale/retail trade, restaurants and hotels	10.8	23.2	12.4	10.6	21.0	10.4	14.2	22.0	7.8	14.7	21.2	6.4
7. Transport, storage and communication	7.0	2.7	4.3	7.7	3.0	4.7	6.5	3.4	3.2	7.0	3.8	3.2
8. Financing, insurance, real estate and business services	4.0	5.8	1.8	5.0	6.9	1.9	2.7	5.0	2.2	2.4	5.3	2.9
9. Community social and personal services	16.9	22.8	5.9	18.5	31.6	13.1	11.1	36.0	24.9	14.2	40.9	26.6
Total	100.0	100.0	48.8[a]	100.0	100.0	56.3[a]	100.0	100.0	78.9[a]	100.0	100.0	71.9[a]

Italy / Norway

Industry (one-digit ISIC level)	Italy						Norway					
	1970			1980			1970			1980		
	Men	Women	Contribution to DI index	Men	Women	Contribution to DI index	Men	Women	Contribution to DI index	Men	Women	Contribution to DI index
1. Agriculture, hunting, forestry and fishing	49.7	50.5	0.8	40.5	43.0	2.5	13.2	7.5	5.7	10.3	6.0	4.2
2. Mining and quarrying	(combined)						32.5	18.1	14.4	28.8	12.4	16.4
3. Manufacturing							(combined)					
4. Electricity, gas and water	1.1	0.2	0.9	1.5	0.3	1.2		0.8				
5. Construction	14.3	0.7	13.8	14.3	1.1	13.3	11.9		11.1	12.5	1.1	11.3
6. Wholesale/retail trade, restaurants and hotels	11.8	17.8	6.0	18.4	19.6	1.2	11.8	26.2	14.4	13.2	23.4	10.2
7. Transport, storage and communication	6.6	1.7	4.9	7.3	2.0	5.3	12.5	6.1	6.5	12.1	5.2	7.0
8. Financing, insurance, real estate and business services	1.7	1.1	0.6	2.7	2.4	0.3	3.4	6.2	2.8	4.9	5.8	0.9
9. Community social and personal services	14.7	28.0	13.3	15.3	31.7	16.4	14.6	35.0	20.4	18.2	46.1	27.9
Total	100.0	100.0	40.2[a]	100.0	100.0	40.1[a]	100.0	100.0	75.1[a]	100.0	100.0	77.9[a]

Note: For Italy, rows 1–2 (Agriculture, hunting, forestry and fishing; Mining and quarrying) are combined by a brace; for Norway, rows 2–3 (Mining and quarrying; Manufacturing) are combined by a brace.

TABLE IV.6 (continued)

Sweden / Canada

Industry (one-digit ISIC level)	Sweden 1970 Men	Women	Contribution to DI index	Sweden 1980 Men	Women	Contribution to DI index	Canada 1970 Men	Women	Contribution to DI index	Canada 1980 Men	Women	Contribution to DI index
1. Agriculture, hunting, forestry and fishing	10.0	4.6	5.4	7.6	3.1	4.5	8.5	2.9	5.6	6.2	2.8	3.4
2. Mining and quarrying	0.8	0.1	0.7	0.5	0.0	0.5	2.1	0.3	1.8	2.3	0.5	1.7
3. Manufacturing	34.1	20.0	14.1	31.4	13.6	17.8	24.6	14.1	10.6	23.3	11.9	11.4
4. Electricity, gas and water	1.0	0.2	0.8	1.3	0.3	1.0	1.4	0.4	0.9	1.5	0.5	1.0
5. Construction	14.4	1.1	13.3	11.5	1.2	10.3	9.3	1.0	8.2	8.1	1.3	6.8
6. Wholesale/retail trade, restaurants and hotels	11.0	0.4	9.4	12.1	15.7	3.6	16.8	18.8	2.0	17.3	17.9	0.6
7. Transport, storage and communication	9.0	3.9	5.1	9.3	4.0	5.3	9.4	3.8	5.5	9.2	4.1	5.1
8. Financing, insurance, real estate and business services	4.4	5.9	1.5	6.5	6.8	0.3	3.3	8.4	5.1	4.0	8.9	5.0
9. Community social and personal services	14.7	43.3	28.6	19.3	54.9	35.6	24.8	50.2	25.4	28.1	52.2	24.1
Total	100.0	100.0	79.9[a]	100.0	100.0	78.9[a]	100.0	100.0	65.1[a]	100.0	100.0	59.1[a]

United States / Czechoslovakia

Industry (one-digit ISIC level)	United States 1970 Men	Women	Contribution to DI index	United States 1980 Men	Women	Contribution to DI index	Czechoslovakia 1970 Men	Women	Contribution to DI index	Czechoslovakia 1980 Men	Women	Contribution to DI index
1. Agriculture, hunting, forestry and fishing	5.6	1.8	3.8	4.9	1.6	3.2	16.6	16.3	0.3	14.5	11.7	2.8
2. Mining and quarrying	1.1	0.2	0.9	1.6	0.4	1.3						
3. Manufacturing	28.3	18.6	9.7	26.1	16.7	9.3	41.7	37.3	4.4	42.5	36.7	5.8
4. Electricity, gas and water	2.0	0.4	1.6	1.9	0.6	1.4						
5. Construction	10.3	1.0	9.3	10.4	1.2	9.2	13.1	3.1	9.9	14.5	3.9	10.7
6. Wholesale/retail trade, restaurants and hotels	18.7	22.7	4.0	19.0	22.7	3.7	5.1	14.1	9.0	5.5	14.8	9.3
7. Transport, storage and communication	6.5	3.1	3.4	6.4	3.4	3.1	9.0	4.8	4.2	8.0	4.6	3.4
8. Financing, insurance, real estate and business services	4.2	7.1	2.9	6.7	10.8	4.1	0.7	1.3	0.6	0.8	1.6	0.8
9. Community social and personal services	23.3	45.1	21.8	22.9	42.6	19.7	13.8	23.0	9.2	14.1	26.7	12.6
Total	100.0	100.0	57.4[a]	100.0	100.0	55.0[a]	100.0	100.0	37.8[a]	100.0	100.0	45.2[a]

(For Czechoslovakia, rows 2 to 4 — mining and quarrying, manufacturing, and electricity, gas and water — are combined under manufacturing as indicated by the brace in the original table.)

TABLE IV.6 (continued)

Hungary

Industry (one-digit ISIC level)	1970 Men	1970 Women	1970 Contribution to DI index	1980 Men	1980 Women	1980 Contribution to DI index
1. Agriculture, hunting, forestry and fishing	25.6	22.9	2.7	20.9	15.4	5.5
2. Mining and quarrying	4.8	1.0	3.8	3.0	0.9	2.1
3. Manufacturing	30.6	35.4	4.8	28.9	32.7	3.8
4. Electricity, gas and water	2.9	1.1	1.8	3.3	1.5	1.9
5. Construction	10.7	2.8	7.9	11.8	3.4	8.5
6. Wholesale/retail trade, restaurants and hotels [b]	5.5	2.6	7.1	7.1	10.0	18.59
7. Transport, storage and communication	9.1	3.8	5.3	10.8	4.6	6.24
8. Financing, insurance, real estate and business services	..	..	..	..	..	..
9. Community social and personal services	10.8	20.4	9.6	10.5	22.9	12.42
Total	100.0	100.0	42.8 [a]	100.0	100.0	49.02 [a]

Greece

Industry (one-digit ISIC level)	1970 Men	1970 Women	1970 Contribution to DI index	1980 Men	1980 Women	1980 Contribution to DI index
1. Agriculture, hunting, forestry and fishing	36.2	55.2	18.9	26.8	48.1	19.0
2. Mining and quarrying	0.8	0.2	0.7	0.8	0.1	0.7
3. Manufacturing	17.5	17.3	0.2	20.1	17.7	2.4
4. Electricity, gas and water	1.0	0.3	0.7	1.0	0.3	0.7
5. Construction	11.1	0.2	10.9	11.9	0.3	11.6
6. Wholesale/retail trade, restaurants and hotels [b]	12.3	8.9	3.4	13.8	11.0	2.8
7. Transport, storage and communication	8.6	1.5	7.1	11.1	1.8	9.3
8. Financing, insurance, real estate and business services	2.5	2.4	0.1	2.9	3.2	0.3
9. Community social and personal services	9.9	14.0	4.1	11.8	17.5	5.7
Total	100.0	100.0	54.8 [a]	100.0	100.0	46.0 [a]

Spain

Industry (one-digit ISIC level)	1970 Men	1970 Women	1970 Contribution to DI index	1980 Men	1980 Women	1980 Contribution to DI index
1. Agriculture, hunting, forestry and fishing	28.0	13.6	14.4	17.7	15.5	2.4
2. Mining and quarrying	1.3	0.1	1.2	1.1	0.1	1.0
3. Manufacturing	24.6	30.3	5.7	26.1	28.3	5.8
4. Electricity, gas and water	0.9	0.2	0.7	1.0	0.1	0.9
5. Construction	12.7	0.9	11.7	14.4	0.7	13.7
6. Wholesale/retail trade, restaurants and hotels [b]	11.7	18.1	6.4	17.4	25.1	7.7
7. Transport, storage and communication	6.4	2.3	4.1	7.2	1.8	5.4
8. Financing, insurance, real estate and business services	2.5	2.2	0.4	4.0	3.1	0.8
9. Community social and personal services	11.9	32.3	20.4	11.1	33.4	22.3
Total	100.0	100.0	64.9 [a]	100.0	100.0	48.7 [a]

Bulgaria

Industry (one-digit ISIC level)	1970 Men	1970 Women	1970 Contribution to DI index	1980 Men	1980 Women	1980 Contribution to DI index
1. Agriculture, hunting, forestry and fishing	11.4	14.5	3.1	26.0	24.2	1.8
2. Mining and quarrying	}	}	}	}	}	}
3. Manufacturing	41.4	42.3	1.0	33.2	33.9	0.7
4. Electricity, gas and water	}	}	}	}	}	}
5. Construction	17.7	3.6	14.1	13.1	3.2	9.9
6. Wholesale/retail trade, restaurants and hotels [b]	7.4	10.8	3.4	5.8	10.9	5.2
7. Transport, storage and communication	11.8	3.8	8.0	10.8	3.6	7.2
8. Financing, insurance, real estate and business services	}	}	}	}	}	}
9. Community social and personal services	10.4	25.0	14.6	11.1	24.2	13.1
Total	100.0	100.0	44.1 [a]	100.0	100.0	37.9 [a]

TABLE IV.6 (concluded)

Industry (one-digit ISIC level)	German Democratic Republic 1970 Men	Women	Contribution to DI index	1980 Men	Women	Contribution to DI index	Romania 1970 Men	Women	Contribution to DI index	1980 Men	Women	Contribution to DI index
1. Agriculture, hunting, forestry and fishing	13.7	12.5	1.3	13.5	8.7	4.8	8.0	2.9	5.1	8.9	2.7	6.1
2. Mining and quarrying ⎱ 3. Manufacturing ⎰	47.9	37.7	10.3	51.0	34.8	16.1	40.5	40.1	0.4	42.7	46.1	3.3
4. Electricity, gas and water												
5. Construction	11.9	2.0	9.9	12.9	2.2	10.7	16.8	3.2	13.6	14.1	2.9	11.2
6. Wholesale/retail trade, restaurants and hotels	9.5	5.6	1.7	4.7	10.4	5.7	6.4	11.8	5.5	5.4	11.7	6.3
7. Transport, storage and communication	6.7	16.2	9.5	6.1	14.9	8.8	9.3	3.0	6.3	12.0	3.4	8.6
8. Financing, insurance, real estate and business services ⎱ 9. Community social and personal services ⎰	10.3	26.0	15.8	11.8	29.0	17.1	19.0	39.0	20.0	16.9	33.2	16.3
Total	100.0	100.0	48.4[a]	100.0	100.0	63.1[a]	100.0	100.0	50.9[a]	100.0	100.0	51.8[a]

Sources: International Labour Office, Yearbook of Labour Statistics (Geneva 1975 and 1982); and national sources.

[a] Contribution to DI index/2 = DI.

[b] Includes category 8 in the case of Hungary.

TABLE IV.7

Decomposition of changes in the index of dissimilarity (DI), 1970–1980

Country	1970	1980	Change			
				Due to		
			Total	Sex repre-sentation	Employment structure	Interaction
Austria..............	28.0[a]	32.8[b]	4.8	4.0	0.5	0.3
Belgium..............	29.5	34.3[b]	4.8	2.9	−0.1	1.9
Canada.............	32.6[c]	29.5[d]	−3.0	−3.0	−0.3	0.3
Czechoslovakia.......	18.9	22.6[b]	3.7	2.4	1.1	0.2
Denmark...........	29.8	38.2[b]	8.5	6.3	0.9	1.3
Finland	30.6	32.5	1.9	1.6	1.1	−0.8
Germany, Federal Republic of........	24.4[a]	28.2[b]	3.8	3.8	0.7	−0.7
Greece	27.4[a]	23.0[e]	4.4	4.6	−0.8	0.6
Hungary	21.4	24.5	3.1	0.6	1.5	1.0
Ireland..............	39.5[a]	35.9[f]	−3.5	−4.1	−0.1	0.7
Italy	20.1[a]	20.1[b]	−0.1	−2.0	0.7	1.3
Norway	37.6	39.0	1.4	−1.0	0.5	1.9
Spain	32.5	24.4[b]	−8.1	−8.4	1.1	−0.8
Sweden	40.0	39.5[b]	−0.5	−1.9	−0.4	1.8
United States	28.7[g]	27.5	−1.2	−1.2	0.1	0.1
Mean	29.4	30.1				
Standard deviation....	6.3	6.2				
Coefficient of variation	21.4	20.6				

[a] 1971.   [b] 1981.   [c] 1975.   [d] 1982.   [e] 1977.   [f] 1979.   [g] 1974.

country level in the index, in relation to changes in the female share of the total labour force over the period in question (figure IV.1). Apparently there is no clear relationship at country level between changes in women's share of the total labour force and changes in the level of industrial segregation, as measured by the DI indices of tables IV.6 and IV.7. There are examples of reduced as well as increased segregation in countries with considerable increases in the female share of the labour force. Generally speaking, however, the changes over the period implied a stronger concentration with respect to both the level of industrial segregation and the female share of the labour force, as the 1980 points tend to be less scattered than the 1970 points.

The change in the value of the DI index between two separate years may be decomposed into three parts: one part is due to the change in the representation rates according to sex within employment categories (industry or occupation). A second part may be due to changes in the total employment structure. Thirdly, there may be interaction between the two other variables, which cannot be attributed to either. Given the structural change at broad sectoral levels towards a greater concentration in the service sector and a decrease in the manufacturing sector over the last decade, it is reasonable to expect that changes both in employment structure and in the representation rates of each sex (percentages male and female) within each sector will have affected the index. The shifts in the broad sectoral distribution towards an increase in employment in the service sector have clearly caused an increase in women's employment. On the other hand, the actual increase in women's share of the total labour force may have been larger or smaller than could

be expected by their initial representation within each of the sectors. Table IV.7 also shows the breakdown of the changes in the DI index for each country. In general, the effects of changes in the female representation rates seem to have been stronger than those in the total employment structure. Most frequently, the structural and compositional effects work in the same direction.[10] In general, however, the changes which took place have worked towards both reduced and increased segregation at country level. It may therefore be concluded that this analysis offers no clear picture with respect to the general trends, apart from the tendencies mentioned above, towards a larger degree of similarity at country level as regards industrial segregation.

C. Female concentration in community, social and private services

There is, however, one clear trend in industrial segregation by sex: the female labour force is strongly concentrated in one branch of the tertiary sector, i.e. "community, social and private services". The calculation of the contribution of each industrial sector to the overall value of the DI index shows that this sector is, in general, the largest single contributor to the numerical value of the index for each country and year. Moreover, the relative contribution of this sector to industrial segregation increased from 1970 to 1980, even in some of the countries which experienced a reduction in the overall value of the index (Ireland and Sweden). The industrial distribu-

[10] See also OECD, *op. cit.*

Figure IV. 1

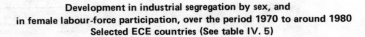

Figure IV. 1

**Development in industrial segregation by sex, and
in female labour-force participation, over the period 1970 to around 1980
Selected ECE countries (See table IV. 5)**

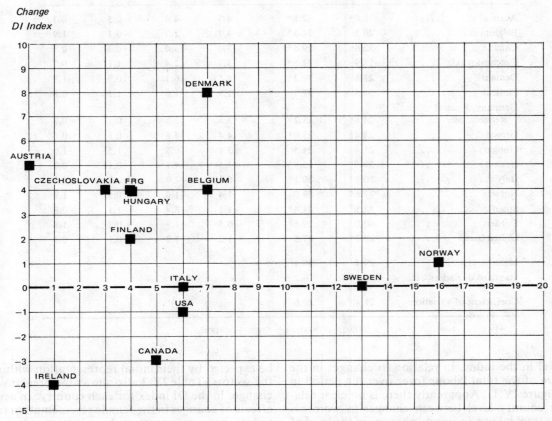

tions of table IV.6 show that, in all countries, a very substantial part of the female labour force is employed in this sector; in some of the countries the proportion even exceeds 50%. The percentages for men are much lower, indicating that industrial segregation by sex within the service sector is an important factor in overall industrial segregation.

The structural differences with respect to male and female employment within the service sector are shown in figure IV.2. The figure gives, for the years around 1980, the percentage of the female and the male labour force in the total tertiary sector, and the percentage employed in community, social and private services. Also included in the figure are some countries for which data on industrial distribution could be obtained for the years around 1980, but where corresponding data for those around 1970 were not available (see note to table IV.5). The data indicate that differences according to sex in the employment structure within the community, social and private services are larger than those in respect of the rest of the service sector. With the exception of Greece, this is true of all countries, regardless of whether the service sector has a large or a comparatively small share of the total labour force. This finding implies an important linkage between occupational and industrial segregation by sex.

The occupations frequently found in the community and social service sector are, to a very large extent, also those which constitute the most predominant female occupations within each of the countries, i.e. health, education and social services.[11] These employment sectors experienced significant growth over the decade in most countries of the region. The growth was particularly strong in countries where these services are publicly run and where the expansion in public services is associated with an institutionalized social welfare State containing a large public sector. This is the case in the Scandinavian countries and in the Netherlands, where the philosophy and structures of the social welfare State have been developed over the decades following the Second World War. However, the expansion in education, health and social services also took place in countries where these services are, to a larger extent, part of the private sector.

The expansion in health care and social services also implies a partial transfer of work which was formerly performed without remuneration within the family to paid work within the formal sectors of the economy. Research

[11] Female predominance in the majority of occupations within these fields was clearly illustrated in the 1980 study, *The Economic Role of Women ...*, Chapter III, sections 2 and 3, in particular chart III.1.

Figure IV. 2

**Female and male share of labour force,
economically active in service (total), and in community,
social and private services, around 1980**

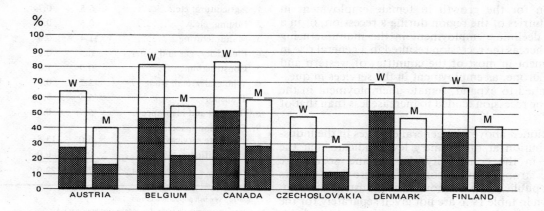

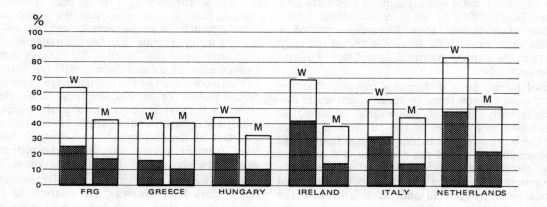

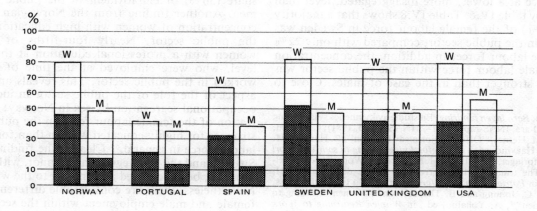

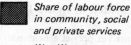

Share of labour force
in community, social
and private services

W = Women
M = Men

from several countries of the region indicates that such a "transfer of family functions to the public sphere" is a very important factor behind the large increase in female employment and an important characteristic of the employment structure of the modern welfare State.[12] The expansion of the traditionally female occupations in health, community and social services also provides an explanation for the growth in female employment in several countries of the region during a recession, or in a period of declining employment in the manufacturing sectors. Whereas the recession resulted in a general rise in unemployment in most of the countries of western and southern Europe, as employment in the services in question continued to expand, female unemployment in the course of the recession tended to increase less than that of men.[13]

As mentioned above, the general changes in the industrial distribution at the country level indicate that the expansion in the community, health and social-care sectors was strongest in the countries where these sectors are mostly publicly run. Although the industrial distributions shown in table IV.6 are not given separately for the public and private sector, the strong expansion of this sector in the Scandinavian countries may be taken as an indication of this. As shown in figure IV.2, by 1980 the community, health and social-care services comprised over 50% of total female employment in Denmark and Sweden and nearly 50% in the case of Norway. This sector's share of the female labour force also equalled or exceeded the share in the total service sector of the male labour force in these three countries, as well as in Finland and the Netherlands.

In general terms, such differences indicate that the female and male labour force in these countries is distributed differently, not only according to industrial sectors, but also at the level of the public and private sectors of the economy. The extent to which female and male employment in each of the countries is distributed among the public and private sectors of the economy cannot, in general, be assessed directly from the industrial classification given by conventional classifications at the one-digit level. In the case of Sweden, however, a supplementary classification was brought into use in the 1980 population census. Data from this census may be taken as an illustration of the segregation of the female and male labour force at a lower, more disaggregated, level than provided by table IV.6. Table IV.8 shows that a majority (nearly 52%) of the female labour force in Sweden was employed in the public sector, compared with only 22% of the male labour force. In addition, the concentration of the female labour force within the public sector was also much stronger than in the case of males. Close to

[12] K. Bjoru, *Barn ingen hindring*. En studie av kvinnenes sysselsetting i Norge i 1970-ara, INAS-rapport 81–2 (INAS) (Oslo, 1981); C. Hakim, *op. cit.*; H. M. Hernes, "Offentliggjoring av familien", R. Haukaa, M. Hoel and H. Haavind, eds., *Kvinneforskning, bidrag til samfunnsteori* (Universitetsforlaget, Oslo, 1982); H. M. Hernes, "Women and the welfare state: The transition from private to public dependence", H. Holter, ed., in *Patriarchy in a Welfare Society* (Oslo University Press, Oslo, 1984); C. Jonung and B. Thordarsson, "Women returning to work, "Sweden"", A. Yohalun, ed., in *Women Returning to Work* (Allenheld Osmun, Montclair, N.J., 1980); C. Jonung, *Patterns of Occupational Segregation by Sex in the Labour Market*, Report 1983:89 (Sweden, University of Lund, 1983); also in G. Schmid, ed., *Discrimination and Equalization in the Labour Market: Employment Policies for Women in Selected Countries* (Wissenschaftszentrum, Berlin), forthcoming.

[13] See also chapter III, section D.

TABLE IV.8

Sweden: percentage distribution of economically active[a] men and women, by private and public sector, and industry, 1980

Industry	Men		Women	
	Private	Public	Private	Public
1. Agriculture, etc.	6.5	0.7	3.4	0.2
2. Mining, etc.	0.6	0.0	0.1	0.0
3. Manufacturing.........	31.4	0.6	13.9	0.2
4. Electricity, gas and water	0.5	0.8	0.1	0.2
5. Construction	10.0	1.4	1.1	0.3
6. Wholesale/retail trade ..	12.2	0.0	15.7	0.0
7. Transport	5.5	3.8	1.7	2.6
8. Banking and insurance..	5.7	0.9	5.2	2.3
9. Community, social and private services	5.0	13.8	6.6	46.0
0. Unclassified	0.3	0.0	0.2	0.0
TOTAL	77.7	22.0	48.0	51.8

Source: Swedish population census, 1980.

[a] People economically active for at least one hour per week.

90% of the women employed in the public sector worked in the community, health care and social services, while this was so for only 63% of the men. These data clearly indicate that, at least in Sweden, the public sector constitutes a much more important segment of the labour market for the female than for the male population. Further analysis of the Swedish data shows that, by 1980, women also constituted the majority (close to two thirds) of those employed in the public sector. The feminization of the public sector was strongest at the decentralized levels of the public sector (local and municipal government, administration and supply of services), where three quarters of the employees were women. At the central level (central government and administration), male employees were still in the majority, comprising 60%.

The Swedish data can be supplemented with some recent data from Norway. An analysis of employment data from the 1980 census and recent labour force sample surveys showed that, by 1980, close to 43% of the female labour force worked in the public sector. As in the case of Sweden, Norwegian women also account for a larger share (56%) of employment in the public sector than men. Another finding from the Norwegian data was a concentration of women with high educational levels in the public sector. Nearly four-fifths of Norwegian women with a professional education at the university level, who were employed at the time of the census, worked in the public sector. This reveals an interesting aspect of the role of the public sector in industrial and occupational segregation by sex in Norway: the concentration of the female labour force in the public sector is stronger for highly-educated women than for the female labour force in general.[14] Clearly, the findings from the Swedish and the Norwegian data cannot, without further research, be generalized as applying to the whole region. Nevertheless, there are considerable differences between female and male employment within the sector of community, health care and social services in practically all the countries represented in figure IV.2.

[14] K. Skrede, "Kvinner i et presset arbeidsmarked", Foredrag: AF-konferansen Sandefjord 27.1.1984 (som stensil fra Institutt for anvendt sosialvitenskapelig forskning (INAS) (Oslo, 1984).

D. Aggregate trends in occupational distribution

Whereas occupational segregation is of special interest, it is unfortunately difficult to obtain data for the decade 1970–1980 on changes in occupational distribution for the female and the male labour force, even at the highest level of aggregation. Consequently, the information on recent trends in occupational segregation by sex is very fragmented for countries in the ECE region. Table IV.9 gives the coefficients of female representation (CFR) for the main occupational groups (one-digit ISCO [15] level) for 1970 and 1980 for those countries in the region where occupational data could be obtained at this level. [16]

Changes in the CFR value give an indication as to whether the representation of women in each particular occupational group has moved towards a more equal

---

[15] International Standard Classification of Occupations.

[16] A CFR value greater than 1 indicates that women are over-represented in the occupational group, relative to their share in the total labour force. Correspondingly, a CFR value below 1 indicates an under-representation of women.

---

representation of men and women. However, changes with respect to over- and under-representation frequently take place in opposite directions for different occupational groups. Hence, it is impossible to conclude anything from the table alone, with respect to the aggregate trends of occupational segregation at country level. As mentioned above, the DI index offers a summary measure of the structural differences of male and female employment (at the level of aggregation given by the occupational distributions).

Table IV.10 provides the corresponding DI indices for the occupational distribution (one-digit ISCO level) of the male and female labour force. The table includes those countries in table IV.9 for which occupational data were obtained for years around 1970 and 1980. As a summary measure, the DI index has its disadvantages, the most important being that it does not reflect the level of female employment and the relative size of each occupational category. As shown above, whereas some of the countries of the region experienced substantial increases in the female share of the labour force over the period, in other countries the level of female employment changed

TABLE IV.9

Degree of over- or under-representation of women in main occupational groups, years around 1970 and 1980

(In percentages; share of women in total non-farm occupations = 1)

Region and country	Share of women in total non-farm occupations		Ratio of the share of women in main groups to their share in the total											
			ISCO 0, 1		ISCO 2		ISCO 3		ISCO 4		ISCO 5		ISCO 7, 8, 9	
	1970	1980	1970	1980	1970	1980	1970	1980	1970	1980	1970	1980	1970	1980
Western Europe														
Austria	37.4	37.7	1.0	0.1ª	0.5	..	1.3	1.2b	1.5	1.4	1.9	1.6	0.5	0.4
Belgium	30.5	32.2	1.4	1.4	0.3	0.4	1.5	1.5	1.5	1.5	2.1	2.0	0.5	0.5
Denmark	36.7	..	1.3	..	0.2	..	1.6	..	1.1	..	1.8	..	0.4	..
Finland	44.4	47.5	1.2	1.1	0.3	0.3	1.7	1.8	1.3	1.2	1.8	1.7	0.5	0.5
France	35.9	38.3	1.1	1.2	0.3	0.4	1.7	1.8	1.4	1.3	2.0	1.8	0.5	0.4
Germany, Fed. Rep. of	32.6	36.8	1.0	1.0	0.4	0.4	1.6	1.6	1.5	1.5	1.5	1.5	0.5	0.4
Ireland	32.0	33.0	1.5	1.4	0.2	0.4	1.9	2.1	1.0	1.0	1.5	1.7	0.4	0.4
Italy	26.7	..	1.6	..	0.3	..	1.3	..	1.4	..	1.5	..	0.6	..
Netherlands	26.5	30.2	1.3	1.2	0.2	0.2	1.6	1.5	1.3	1.2	2.4	2.1	0.3	0.2
Norway	29.7	42.6	1.2	1.2	0.3	0.5	2.0	1.8	1.5	1.3	2.3	1.8	0.3	0.3
Sweden	36.9	47.1	0.9	1.1	0.4	0.4	1.8	1.7	1.3	1.0	2.1	1.6	0.4	0.4
Switzerland	34.8	..	1.0	..	0.1	..	1.5	..	1.6	..	2.0	..	0.5	..
United Kingdom	37.0	..	1.0	..	0.3	..	1.6	..	1.2	..	1.9	..	0.5	..
North America														
Canada	35.7	42.5	1.3	1.2	0.4	0.7	1.9	1.9	0.8	0.9	1.4	1.3	0.3	0.3
United States	38.8	43.5	1.1	1.0	0.4	0.6	1.9	1.8	0.8	1.1	1.5	1.4	0.5	0.4
Eastern Europe and USSR														
Bulgaria	34.0	44.0	1.3	1.3	0.2	0.4	1.4	1.2	1.5	1.5	1.9	1.7	0.8	0.7
Czechoslovakia	44.0	..	1.1	..	0.3	..	1.7	..	1.7	..	1.7	..	0.7	..
Hungary	40.2	..	1.2	..	0.4	..	1.7	..	1.5	..	1.8	..	0.7	..
Poland	40.5	..	1.2	..	0.7	..	1.5	..	2.1	..	1.9	..	0.6	..
Romania	28.6	..	1.6	..	0.4	..	1.7	..	1.4	..	1.8	..	0.6	..
USSR	48.4	..	1.3	..	0.4	..	1.8	..	1.6	..	1.7	..	0.6	..
Southern Europe														
Greece	22.3	..	1.5	..	0.4	..	1.5	..	0.9	..	1.7	..	0.7	..
Portugal	30.3	37.3	1.5	1.5	0.2	0.3	1.1	1.3	0.8	1.2	2.0	1.7	0.8	0.6
Spain	23.4	29.5	1.4	1.2	0.2	0.1	1.3	1.3	1.2	1.5	2.1	2.0	0.6	0.4
Turkey	11.1c	10.6	2.4c	2.5	..	0.4	1.9b, c	2.9	0.3c	0.4	0.6c	0.7	0.7c	0.7
Yugoslavia	33.4	..	1.4	..	0.3	..	1.5	..	1.1	..	2.2	..	0.6	..

Sources: For years around 1970, *Economic Role of Women in the ECE Region* (United Nations publication, Sales No. E.80.II.E.6); for years around 1980, International Labour Office, *Yearbook of Labour Statistics* (Geneva 1982 and 1983); national statistics.

ª Figures for 1980 are not comparable with 1970 owing to changes in occupational classification.

b Includes occupations in ISCO 2.

c 1975.

relatively little. In addition to the DI index, table IV.10 therefore gives another summary measure of the level of occupational segregation by sex, which is more directly related to the level of female employment and to the CFR indices for each occupational group given in table IV.9. This new measure is called the Women Employment (WE) Index.[17]

The indices given in table IV.10 indicate that there have been no dramatic changes in the dissimilarity of the female and male employment structure over the period considered. To a large extent, the values of the DI indices for the years around 1980 are at about the same level as the corresponding indices for the years around 1970. Changes in the WE indices, however, suggest that, in some countries, occupational segregation by sex has somewhat declined. This reflects the effect of the changing female share of employment on the level of occupational segregation, as measured by the WE index. The difference in the changes observed can be related to the substantial increase, during the period, in the female share of the labour force in these countries. Even if the dissimilarity in the male and the female occupational distribution has not changed (or has even increased slightly), female employment has played a more important part in the total occupational structure in recent years, resulting in a decrease in the WE index.

On the whole, however, the figures in table IV.10 indicate a considerable level of occupational segregation by sex, in both 1980 and 1970. Judged by the WE indices, the concentration of the female labour force is very high in all the countries included in the table. Expressed in percentage terms, the WE indices indicate that about 23–30% of the female labour force of the countries of industrialized western Europe and North America would have to change occupations with men in order to achieve a proportionate representation of women in each of the major occupational groups. As in the case of the overall trends in industrial segregation by sex, there is a slight tendency toward smaller inter-country variation, with respect to both the DI and the WE indices. It should be noted, however, that the sample of countries included in table IV.10 is even less representative than that of table IV.6, especially for the countries of eastern Europe. Until data for more countries become available, this tendency should not be considered as applying on the regional level.

E. Vertical and horizontal occupational segregation

In the analysis of the distributional differences between female and male employment, it has become customary

[17] For each of the countries, the index relates directly to the level of female employment and to the CFRs of each occupational group. It can be taken as a measure of the concentration of female employment in relation to the total occupational structure. The advantage of the index lies in its precise interpretation concerning the disproportionate representation of women in the occupational structure. The index may be interpreted as being twice the minimum proportion of women who would theoretically have to exchange occupations with men, in order for all the CFRs to become unity, while maintaining constant the occupational structure. As in the case of the DI index, the WE index has several disadvantages: the most serious, in comparing countries, is that its maximum value (which equals twice the employment share of women) is not constant, but relates directly to the level of female employment in each country. In general, most of the disadvantages in relation to the DI index in the discussion on aggregate trends of industrial segregation by sex, mentioned in section A above, also apply to the WE index, including the fact that the results obtained depend upon the level of aggregation used in the occupational classification. See also OECD, *op. cit.*

TABLE IV.10

Women's employment and DI indices for occupational segregation (ISCO one-digit level), according to sex, selected ECE countries, years around 1970 and 1980

Region and country	Women's employment		DI index	
	1970	1980	1970	1980
Western Europe				
Belgium	56	55[a]	40	40[a]
Finland	46	46	40	43
France	51[b]	49[c]	39[b]	39[c]
Germany, Fed. Rep. of ..	45	46	35	36
Ireland	70	60[d]	46	48[d]
Netherlands...........	67[e]	60[d]	45[e]	43[d]
Norway	70	57[f]	49	49[f]
Sweden	49	47[f]	39	43[f]
North America				
Canada	65	49[g]	49	42[g]
United States	53[h]	47[f]	44[h]	41[f]
Eastern Europe				
Bulgaria...............	28[i]	27[c]	26[i]	27[c]
Southern Europe				
Portugal	32	33[f]	28	29[f]
Spain	53	44[d]	33	31[d]
Mean	52.9	47.7	39.5	39.3
Standard deviation........	46.3	38.3	25.5	23.7
Coefficient of variation....	7.5	80.3	64.6	60.6

Sources: As for table IV.9.

Note: Only countries which use the ISCO one-digit level of occupational categories for both years are included in the table.

[a] 1977.　　[b] 1968.　　[c] 1975.　　[d] 1979.　　[e] 1971.　　[f] 1981.　　[g] 1982.　　[h] 1974.　　[i] 1965.

to distinguish between a horizontal and a vertical component. The former refers to differences in the type of work performed within the occupations and the division of work between occupational categories; the latter is related to the place of occupations within occupational hierarchies. Horizontal occupational segregation by sex refers to the tendency for men and women to be found in different occupational categories and to do different types of work. Vertical occupational segregation may be found both between and within occupational categories. Vertical segregation *between* occupations is present when occupational categories which are predominantly male or female are located at different levels of status or prestige within the occupational structure or within different segments of the labour market. Vertical segregation may also occur *within* occupations. An example of this is where women and men technically occupy the same occupation, but are employed at different levels of responsibility and are allocated different tasks.[18]

It may not always be possible to separate these two components of occupational segregation. Whether or not they can be treated separately in empirical research depends on the classification of occupational categories, and the extent to which the vertical dimension of the occupational structure is reflected in the classification. In some cases, the vertical dimension may be related directly

[18] For a more in-depth discussion of the concepts and measurement of horizontal and vertical segregation see, for instance, C. Hakim, *op. cit.*; and C. Jonung, *Patterns of Occupational Segregation ....*

to specific occupational categories. This is the case with ISCO occupational category 2 (one-digit level) "Administrative work in the private and the public sector". Table IV.9 shows that there was a considerable under-representation of women in these occupations in 1980, as well as in 1970. The CFR, which relates the proportion of women in administrative and managerial positions to their share of the total labour force in non-agricultural occupations in each of the countries, is well below 1, the level of equal representation. In contrast, the CFRs of ISCO occupational category 3, which includes secretarial work and other clerical and office work at lower levels of responsibility, indicate an equally large over-representation of women.

In general, however, it is difficult to treat the vertical dimension symmetrically across the occupational structure, as the different levels of occupational hierarchy may be described in greater detail for some of the occupations than for others. In particular, because men's work is frequently better identified and more carefully categorized than women's, there is a risk of sex-bias in the categorization of occupations.[19] On the whole, it may be concluded that the vertical dimension of occupational segregation may best be treated in a broader empirical context. This permits the conditions of work to be related to the occupational categories, as is done in recent theories and research on labour market segmentation. Several empirical studies carried out in this field, both for individual countries and on a cross-national level, indicate that women in the labour force generally tend to be at a disadvantage in terms of skill, status, security and earnings. A large proportion of the labour market segments dominated by women are found in what is often referred to as the "secondary labour market", characterized by low skills, wages and status, and high rates of turnover. In addition, it has been noted that a full grasp of the nature and extent of vertical segregation probably requires small-scale studies of labour organization and division within institutions.[20]

Vertical occupational segregation and labour market segmentation is discussed at greater length in section H, below, where structures and processes of occupational segregation are examined in relation to discrimination theories. However, it is relevant to note here that occupational segregation by sex may be a means of replacing more direct forms of discrimination. This assumes that opportunities for such discrimination are reduced, either through legislation or by collective agreements. One hypothesis is that countries characterized by small wage differentials between men and women display a greater degree of occupational segregation than countries with larger wage differentials. The Swedish case supports this hypothesis: Sweden, in comparison with other industrialized west European countries, has smaller wage differentials between men and women, while having the highest level of occupational segregation.[21]

F. Occupational segregation in the ECE region in a structural perspective

The 1980 study presented an analysis of the structural aspects of female employment in most countries of the ECE region, based on occupational data from the censuses around 1970. The female share of selected non-farm occupations (referring to 2- or 3-digit ISCO level categories) were presented for inter-country and inter-regional comparison.[22] The study revealed a rather complex picture with regard to the inter-region structural variation in female employment. Nevertheless, some characteristics of female employment were observed in virtually all countries, despite the variation in the female share of the labour force.

There were a number of occupations in which the female share was very high in nearly all cases. The highest average representation rates (calculated at the subregional level) were found for secretarial and other clerical work, for nursing and other paramedical professions, and for housekeepers, domestic and related workers. These occupations were followed by several service occupations related to cleaning and laundering, and also salespersons, shop assistants and teachers (other than university). Women were also highly represented in other miscellaneous service occupations, such as restaurant services. As pointed out in the 1980 study,[23] these occupations, with the possible exception of secretarial work, are "typically" female occupations, in the sense that they draw on skills traditionally exercised on an unpaid basis within the home. On the other hand, there were also some occupations in which women were strongly under-represented in nearly all the countries. These occupations included administrative and managerial jobs, most of the academic and scientific professions, and most of the occupations in the industrial production sectors. The exceptions from the latter were production occupations which, to some extent, at least traditionally, may be associated with work related to the household, such as textiles and food and beverage processing.

In general, the countries of industrial western and southern Europe and North America displayed a higher degree of concentration of the female labour force than the countries of eastern Europe and the USSR. The latter countries had, on the whole, a relatively higher representation of women in a number of the highly-skilled professions and in administrative and managerial work, as well as a higher average level of female representation in the production occupations. The study revealed that, in several countries, up to 70%–80% of the female non-farm labour force was concentrated in a group of "typically" female occupations, consisting of paramedical workers (including nurses), teachers (other than university), clerical workers and salespersons, and miscellaneous service workers.[24] The corresponding share of the male, non-farm labour force in these countries was low, ranging from about 15% to 25%. Although in the countries of southern and eastern Europe and in the USSR the concentration of the female labour force in these occupations was lower, the differences between the respective shares of the male and the female labour force were nevertheless considerable.

---

[19] See C. Jonung, *Patterns of Occupational Segregation ...*, page 9, which mentions an attempt in the Swedish census of 1970 to subdivide one female occupation—secretarial work. This proved unsuccessful since, in most such jobs, the different work tasks merged. The author suggests that men's work traditionally tends to be characterized by a higher degree of specialization than women's, and is therefore easier to categorize.

[20] C. Hakim, *op. cit.*

[21] C. Jonung, *Patterns of Occupational Segregation ...*

---

[22] *The Economic Role of Women ...*, table III.6.

[23] *Ibid*, Chapter III, section 2, p. 39.

[24] *Ibid*, chart III.1.

However, when predominantly female occupations were defined as those where the share of women was larger than their share in the total non-farm labour force, the study revealed that the percentage of the female labour force employed in occupations dominated by women varied relatively little from one country to another. The group of occupations thus identified accounted for about 80% of female employment in nearly all the ECE countries, with the exception of Canada, the United States and the USSR, where the shares were about 65%. However, occupations defined in the same way as being predominantly male generally accounted for only some 20% of all female non-farm employment. The lowest shares (approximately 15%) were found in Ireland, the Netherlands and Norway, and the highest (33%–35%) in Canada, the United States and the USSR.[25]

The 1980 study also reviewed some research on long-term trends in occupational segregation by sex for selected countries (United Kingdom, United States and the USSR). The general conclusion was that the tendency for female workers to be crowded in a relatively small range of occupations had changed relatively little over the last two generations, despite the considerable increase in female labour force participation during that period. On the basis of the examples from studies at country level, the 1980 study concluded: "... it would appear that the concentration or "crowding" of women in occupations where the labour force is predominantly female is a phenomenon which is largely unrelated to differences in levels of economic development, in cultural values, size of country and geographical location, or in economic and social systems. It would seem that throughout the period of industrial development a relatively rigid distribution of jobs and economic roles between the sexes came to be adopted in every country and that this has led to a general categorization of "men's jobs" and "women's jobs", although the set of typical male and female jobs often differs from one country to another. This development has stereotyped certain fields of work as falling within the sphere of women and this has had a significant effect on their employment status".[26]

G. Recent trends in occupational segregation—a review of selected countries

As noted above, the 1980 study reached a rather pessimistic conclusion with regard to female labour market concentration. Meanwhile, in practically all countries of the region, the general increase in the female share of the labour force continued over the decade from 1970 to 1980. In view of the further increase in female labour force participation, it would have been of considerable interest to update the structural description of the situation in the ECE countries at the beginning of the 1970s with recent data on occupational segregation at a correspondingly detailed level. A comparison of occupational distributions at the disaggregated level depends on the availability of detailed data or data from censuses or large-scale sample surveys (micro-censuses). However, if most of the ECE countries carried out a census around 1980, data on occupational distributions at the detailed

level are not yet generally available for the majority of them. In addition, the sample size of the labour force surveys referred to in the preceding sections do not, in general, fulfil the requirements of representativeness. Consequently, comparisons of the female employment structure for 1970 with the corresponding structure in 1980 can be carried out for only a very small number of countries, which cannot be considered as being representative of the region as a whole.[27]

The picture provided by table IV.11 is rather ambiguous. Apparently there has been some increase in the proportion of women in some of the male-dominated occupations; but the increases are slight when adjusted for the rising proportion of women in the labour force. In addition, the female shares in some of the occupations dominated by women have increased considerably. It is impossible to draw any definite conclusions from the data in table IV.11 alone, with respect to the general trends of occupational segregation at the disaggregated level in each of the countries, as data for a number of occupations were not available for both 1970 and 1980. However, the figures provided in the table can, to some extent, be supplemented by the results of recent country studies on occupational segregation at a disaggregated level. Such studies for Austria, Norway and Sweden are considered below.

The concentration of female employment in the Austrian labour market over the 1970 to 1981 period has been the subject of a recent study.[28] It included both industrial sectors and occupations, and used a fairly detailed classification at the two-digit level. The findings indicated a stable level of industrial segregation. Nevertheless, some shifts had taken place in the structure of female employment, with tendencies towards desegregation in some industrial branches (hotel and catering, housekeeping and construction) and towards increased segregation in others (trade, health services, chemical engineering and public services). At the aggregate level, however, these changes offset each other.

With respect to occupations, the findings indicated increased sex segregation for the major groups. Using the more detailed occupational classification, the results revealed that, even if an increase was observed in the female share of some male-dominated occupations, these changes were more than outweighed by the increase of women in the traditionally female-dominated occupations and the share of these occupations in the total employment structure. In 1971, 52% of female wage-earners worked in 6 out of 75 occupational categories (auxiliary administrative work, trade, cleaning, teaching, bookkeeping and health services). The changes over the period were more positive with respect to the vertical dimension of occupational segregation. Women had increasing access to higher occupational positions, mainly for white-collar working women. As far as occupational categories were concerned, a slight polarization was evident between 1972 and 1980. More women were employed as salaried employees and, within this category,

---

[25] The Economic Role of Women ..., table III.13.

[26] Ibid.

[27] In addition, it should be noted that, even for the countries included in the table, the data sets for 1970 and 1980 are not completely comparable, owing to changes in the classification of occupations, in the treatment of part-time workers, etc. (see the notes to table IV.11 for details).

[28] A. Eder and C. Böhm, The Concentration of Female Employment in the Austrian Labour Market: 1970–1980 (Institute for Sociology, University of Vienna, January 1983).

TABLE IV.11

**Share of women in the main non-farm occupations in
some ECE countries, years around 1970 and 1980**

(Percentage of women in employment in each occupational group)

Occupational groups	Finland		Norway			Sweden		United Kingdom [a]	
	1970	1980	1970	1980 [b]	1980 [c]	1970	1980	1971	1981
Professional, technical and related workers (ISCO 0.1) .	51.2	54.9	35.5	51.8	35.9	32.6	51.6	38.3	46.7
of which:									
Architects, engineers, and related technicians	2.4	11.3	3.5	7.0	4.8	7.4	6.3	9.6 }	8.9
Physical and life scientists, and related technicians ...	29.0	50.3	30.0	47.2	37.1	14.3	54.9	9.1 }	
Medical doctors, dentists, veterinarians, pharmacists .	59.1	61.4	19.3	23.3	17.3	19.9	36.3	24.0	–
of which: medical doctors	27.4	34.3	12.1	17.3	14.1	18.3	26.7	19.9	–
Nurses, midwives	94.4	94.1	92.9	92.6	90.3	87.0	91.3	91.3	91.8
Other para-medical workers	95.0	71.1	81.8	81.7	70.9	79.0	83.4	64.9	..
Teachers, university and higher education	21.3	56.6	12.4	35.9	25.9	20.0	24.7	12.3	26.4
Teachers, all other	59.4	61.3	44.8	58.5	45.5	57.7	65.6	57.1	63.2
Social workers	72.0	99.4	61.9	65.9	57.4	67.1	72.0	64.9	65.9
Administrative and managerial workers (ISCO 2)	11.2	16.0	7.5	11.4	9.3	14.9	22.7	9.2 }	
									} 71.7
Clerical and related workers (ISCO 3)..............	74.6	82.9	58.1	69.9	59.8	68.0	75.1	60.3 }	
of which:									
Bookkeepers, cashiers, computing-machine operators	88.8	77.9	53.2	69.2	56.6	74.8	83.1	64.0	
Stenographers, typists, and related workers	96.3	92.3	79.9	84.4	85.1	95.3	88.2	98.9	98.1
Telephone and telegraph operators [b]	85.9	85.6	79.3	80.2	73.7	94.9	94.9	77.5	84.1
Sales workers (ISCO 4)	59.4	57.1	45.2	38.1	37.6	47.7	45.8	44.8	49.4
of which:									
Managers and working proprietors (trade)	43.4	39.1	20.0	30.5	26.5	27.9	34.3	27.6	30.2
Salesmen, shop assistants, and related workers [d]	75.0	60.5	70.7	77.9	64.8	79.5	76.9	80.5	82.7
Service workers (ISCO 5)	81.3	78.9	69.2	77.0	54.8	78.4	73.2	69.3	–
of which:									
Managers and working proprietors (catering, lodging)	..	86.6	..	82.6	43.8	73.3	62.5	58.3	78.4
Waiters, bartenders and related workers............	93.4	87.9	80.9	86.9	77.2	86.7	83.5	80.6	77.9
Cooks	93.1	90.3	59.2	63.4	56.2	78.0	71.3	73.8	62.9
Housekeepers, maids and related workers	100.0	99.2	82.3	98.0	96.8	98.4	97.2	96.3	97.0
Launderers, dry-cleaners, pressers	92.0	90.8	76.8	82.9	76.1	71.8	93.8	77.4	–
Hairdressers, barbers, beauticians, etc..............	96.1	96.6	67.9	81.3	72.4	74.8	79.4	78.2	89.8
Charworkers, cleaners and related workers [d]	96.9	79.9	92.8	79.8	99.8	89.4	65.8	86.0	72.6
Production workers, transport-equipment operators, labourers (ISCO 7, 8, 9)	20.5	21.8	9.0	11.8	7.9	13.3	14.6	17.1	14.9
of which:									
Spinners, weavers, knitters, dyers, etc.	76.8	75.3	48.6	56.3	45.0	54.7	55.9	53.8	–
Tailors, dressmakers, sewers, upholsterers, etc.......	91.3	93.2	79.9	83.6	78.7	76.6	74.7	80.8	79.4
Tanners, fellmongers, shoemakers, leather-goods makers	62.2	67.4	38.5	47.2	38.0	38.9	41.8	50.0	48.7
Paper-product and paperboard-product makers	29.8	..	36.8	73.1	65.4	46.2	..		
								53.6	38.3
Tobacco preparers and tobacco-product makers	77.8	82.9	56.3	57.7	55.7	83.3	70.9	70.6	..
Food and beverage processers.....................	57.0	56.5	26.5	34.6	21.8	33.0	31.3	29.0	18.5
Wood-preparation workers and paper-makers	26.4	13.6	5.2	3.3	2.1	9.8	..	13.1	–
Printers and related workers	40.5	37.6	19.7	22.5	16.1	25.1	27.2	26.4	16.7
Chemical processers and related workers	19.6	24.8	6.5	15.3	12.1	20.9	..		
								9.5	8.8
Rubber and plastics product makers	39.4	42.1	18.9	25.1	18.5	33.0	35.6	31.6 }	
Glass formers, potters and related workers	38.7	39.2	19.8	24.8	11.5	26.0	30.4	31.2 }	18.2
Jewellery and precious-metal workers	17.5	20.5	15.7	22.4	16.5	15.0	27.7	28.6	16.8
Miners, quarrymen, well-drillers, etc...............	2.9	0.3	0.2	1.3	0.7	1.6	0.9	0.2	0.6
Stone cutters and carvers........................	2.2	2.2	–	1.1	0.7	-	2.9	..	..
Bricklayers, carpenters, other construction workers ..	4.1	3 4	0.1	1.2	0.5	0.1	1.4	0.3 }	
Painters (construction)..........................	7.8	7.9	1.2	3.0	1.6	2.4	3.9	3.0 }	0.6
Metal processers	8.7	7.5	1.3	3.0	2.0	6.7	9.9	6.5	5.3
Blacksmiths, toolmakers, machine-tool operators	12.4	10.6	11.4	5.7	3.9	12.5	10.1	21.7	–
Machinery fitters and assemblers, precision instrument makers	0.9	16.7	10.2	19.2	9.4	6.6	18.7	2.3	7.8
Plumbers, welders, sheet and structural metal workers..	1.1	8.2	0.8	3.2	2.1	1.0	0.4	3.0	0.4

TABLE IV.11 (continued)

Occupational groups	Finland		Norway			Sweden		United Kingdom[a]	
	1970	1980	1970	1980[b]	1980[c]	1970	1980	1971	1981
Electrical fitters and related workers	10.1	13.2	6.5	8.1	5.7	12.9	15.1	18.0	2.3
Cabinet makers and related woodworkers	15.3	8.3	1.4	9.8	5.8	6.5	..	8.4	–
Grand total[e]	44.4	47.7	29.7	42.0	28.4	36.9	44.1	37.0	39.1

Sources: For the years around 1970: *The Economic Role of Women in the ECE Region* (United Nations publication, Sales No. E.80.II.E.6) table III. 6; for years around 1980: International Labour Office, *Yearbook of Labour Statistics,* various issues (Geneva); and national population censuses.

[a] Data refer to Great Britain.

[b] Includes all persons who were employed for at least 100 hours during the 12-month period before the census.

[c] Includes all persons who were employed for at least 1,300 hours during the 12-month period before the census.

[d] Country differences in coverage.

[e] Excluding workers in agriculture, forestry, fishing, hunting (ISCO 6), workers not classifiable by occupation (ISCO X) and armed forces.

the proportion of women with medium and high qualifications rose; by contrast, the proportion of women with low qualifications decreased. The trends corresponded to the general shift towards employment at higher levels of qualification which was observed for the work force as a whole. However, the structural changes were relatively stronger for women than for men. It was noted that increased educational qualifications appeared to be an important factor in the changes: the shift towards employment in higher-qualified occupations took place mainly among women with a higher education.

A Norwegian study recently examined the changes in women's share of occupations which normally require educational training at university level.[29] This study, which made use of census data from 1970 and 1980, found that, in most cases, the female share in these occupations had increased over time. However, the female shares of these occupations were generally smaller in Norway than in Sweden (see below). The changes for comparable occupations, however, are more or less in the same direction as in Sweden. For instance, the share of female physicians increased from 12% to 17%, of dentists from 20% to 23%, and of school principals from 9% to 17%. The female share rose between 1970 and 1980 for most of the occupations concerned. There were, however, some important exceptions. Despite the fact that the number of university teachers increased considerably between 1970 and 1980 (from some 3,200 in 1970 to nearly 6,000 in 1980), the share of women in this occupational category decreased from 31% in 1970 to 23% in 1980. There was also another, numerically smaller but symbolically important, exception: the share of women in scientific work in physics fell from 15% to 10%, while the corresponding shares in the other occupations in science and technology increased slightly over the same period. The study also provides an interesting illustration of what may happen when men enter predominantly female occupations, such as nursing. The female share of the nursing profession as a whole decreased from 97% in 1970 to 94% in 1980. However, in both years, the share of women in nursing managerial positions was lower than their share in the nursing profession as a whole (90% in 1970 and 89% in 1980). Even the absolute number of women in nursing managerial positions decreased (from 448 to 246) between the two reference years.

The most extensive study of recent trends in occupational segregation in Sweden is that of Jonung.[30] On the basis of census data for 1960, 1970 and 1975, it analysed occupational segregation by sex at the one-, two- and three-digit levels of the ISCO categories. Using the DI index as a measure, it was found that, in general, occupational segregation by sex had decreased slightly over the periods 1960–1970 and 1970–1975 for all levels of occupational classification. It was pointed out, however, that the reduction in segregation across the major occupational areas, given by the one- and two-digit level, was somewhat larger than that estimated at the three-digit level. Hence, a reduction in segregation across occupational groups was partly outweighed by an increased segregation within these groups. The results also suggested a relative improvement over time: the reduction in the DI index for the most detailed occupational classification was larger for the recent period than for the preceding decade. Jonung found that the changes which had taken place with respect to occupational segregation could be almost equally attributed to men moving into female-dominated occupations as to women moving into male-dominated ones. On the whole, however, the reductions in occupational segregation which did take place were small compared to the potential for change and full equality, had there been a strong move towards equalization. Jonung concluded that the integration of women in the labour force has fallen far short of what could be achieved, even though the trends of the early 1970s are more positive than those of the 1960s. She points out that there is still ample room for policies aimed at influencing occupational choice and employers' recruitment procedures.

On the positive side, Jonung found marked tendencies towards an increased female share in some of the highly skilled and high-status professions in ISCO groups 0 and 1. The share of women in the professional categories increased as follows: physicians from 18% to 23%, dentists from 27% to 30%, veterinarians from 7% to 11%, prosecuting attorneys from 4% to 11%, court lawyers and judges from 12% to 16%, and school principals from 12% to 15%. On the other hand, there were negative signs with respect to female integration within other predominantly male occupations in the professional categories. In the various fields of engineering, women's share increased very little, ranging between 1% and 5%. The latter figures, when compared to the more recent 1980 figures in table IV.11, show that the increase of

---

[29] E. Brandt, *Kvinnedominerte, kjonnsnoytrale og mannsdominerte hoyere utdanninger,* Foredrag ved seminar Kvinnelige akademikere og arbeidsmarkedet mot ar 2000 (Oslo, 30 mars 1984). (Stensil fra NAVFs utredningsinstitutt, Oslo, 1984).

[30] C. Jonung, *Patterns of Occupational Segregation ....*

women in engineering was still very slow between 1975 and 1980. The share of women among university teachers remained the same: 20%. Their share in administrative and managerial jobs in private firms decreased, not only in the early 1970s, but from the 1960s onwards. The data in table IV.11 indicate that the decrease of women in administrative work in the private sector is offset at the occupational-category level by an increase of women in administrative work in the public sector. The female share of all administrative work and managerial jobs rose from 15% in 1970 to almost 23% in 1980.

H. Determinants of occupational segregation

1. THEORIES OF OCCUPATIONAL SEGREGATION—A BRIEF REVIEW

Several economic theories have been put forward to explain the persistence of occupational segregation by sex. These theories can be divided into two broad categories: those which focus on the supply side of the labour market and take the individual worker as the unit of analysis, and those which are based upon a structural analysis of labour market processes, such as various types of discrimination theories and theories of labour market segmentation. Since the theories focus on the supply and demand sides respectively, they may be regarded as complementary rather than mutually exclusive.[31]

The first approach takes the labour supply side of the market as its point of departure. It is based on the human capital theory and focuses upon the division of labour within the home. The main point of the analysis is the assumption that, under the prevailing division of labour within the home (where the responsibilities of household duties and child care fall, to a large extent, on women), the personal investments in human capital (education and training) for women will generally tend to be lower than for men. According to this theory, women know that their future in the labour market is more uncertain than that of men. Home responsibilities may cause them to withdraw from the labour market for shorter or longer periods, choose part-time work, etc. Hence, women's education will tend to be shorter than men's, since it does not pay to spend many years on an education which may not be used in the labour market. The differences regarding educational investments will be strengthened by similar differences with respect to work experience. Women's greater responsibilities at home will generally result in a lower accumulation of work experience than men, because of lower stability in the labour market, part-time work, etc. As a result of lower educational investment and work experience, women will also receive less in-service training, and their prospects for promotion will be more limited.

While human capital theories may provide insight into some of the mechanisms behind vertical occupational

segregation by sex, they do not offer an explanation of horizontal occupational segregation or the concentration of women in a small number of female occupations within each skill category. Attempts have been made to relate the fact that female occupations are largely similar to, or drawn from, skills connected with household duties, to the different sex patterns of human capital investment. It is argued that women choose those occupations because they are thus able to combine work in the home with work in the market. Hence, even when women acquire a specialized education, they will tend to choose a field providing knowledge and skills which can be used both inside and outside the labour market. However, it has been noted that this approach does not take into account the variations in the "sex labelling" of occupations between different industries within the same country, nor can it explain differences between fairly similar countries.[32] Another formulation of the "combination" hypothesis which may represent a better explanation of the concentration of the female labour force than the "skill" version, is the "minimum loss" hypothesis put forward by sociologists.[33] According to this hypothesis, in view of their dual responsibilities, women tend to choose occupations which minimize the risks of future difficulties in combining household duties with paid work outside the home. All things being equal, the risk of future difficulties is lowest in those occupations in which there are already high percentages of female workers.

The structural approach to the causes of occupational segregation by sex relates to the demand side of the labour market and the behaviour of employers. The different levels and areas of women's and men's labour market qualifications will initially place them in different positions and restrict the possibilities of substitution in the market. This will result in a segmented labour market, with low levels of mobility between the segments. According to theories on labour market segmentation,[34] well-qualified workers will find employment in those market segments where jobs are characterized by skill requirements, but where the rewards are also high and the promotion possibilities promising. The less-qualified workers, on the other hand, will have fewer possibilities in the labour market and in general will have to compete in its less favourable segments. These consist of lower-skilled jobs and are characterized by low pay, poor job security and few possibilities of promotion or upward mobility. This theoretical approach explains vertical occupational segregation by sex, by the sex differentials in occupational qualifications.

Labour market segmentation may also be caused by discrimination. Discrimination according to sex can take several forms; discrimination occurs, for instance, where women are paid less than men for the same type of job, or if the job qualifications required for a particular job are higher for women than for men. Direct discrimination may also take the form of restricted promotion possibili-

---

[31] Summary views of economic theories of occupational segregation may be found in C. Hakim, *op. cit.*; and C. Jonung, *Patterns of Occupational Segregation* ... For more detailed discussion of the economic theories of occupational segregation, see for instance OECD, *op. cit.*; F. Blau and C. Jusenius, "Economists' approaches to sex segregation in the labour market: an Appraisal", M. Blaxall, M. and B. Reagan, eds. in *Women and the Workplace: The Implications of Occupational Segregation* (Chicago, 1976); and C. B. Lloyd and B. T. Niemi, *The Economics of Sex Differentials* (Columbia University Press, New York, 1979).

[32] OECD, *op. cit.*

[33] *Ibid*; V. Sapiro, "Sex and games: on oppression and rationality", *British Journal of Political Science,* Vol. 9, No. 4 (1979); and K. Tornes, *Sex Stereotyping and Schooling – An Overview,* Paper presented to the Council for Cultural Co-operation in Europe (Educational Research Workshop on Sex Stereotyping, Klekken, Norway, 4–8 May 1981).

[34] For a review of theories of the dual labour market and the more generalized theories of labour market segmentation, see for example P. Dioringer and B. and M. Piore, *International Labour Market and Manpower Analysis* (Health, Lexington, Mass., 1971); and F. Blau and C. Jusenius, *op. cit.*

ties for women or less access to on-the-job investment and training. Discrimination also exists in indirect forms: one is "statistical discrimination", where a woman seeking a job is not evaluated according to her individual qualifications. Rather, it is assumed that she has the characteristics of the "average" woman worker. Statistical discrimination exists, for example, where women are not given access to jobs at higher levels of responsibility and the promotion possibilities for which they technically qualify, because it is expected that they will have a low level of job stability in the future. Another type of indirect discrimination on the part of the employer may take the form of sex-role stereotyping with respect to the type of work which women can perform in the labour market. This may include an exaggeration of women's comparative advantage in traditionally female work or a prejudice against female employees in work which is deemed not "suitable" for them. As pointed out by Jonung,[35] women are caught in a vicious circle whenever discrimination in the labour market exists. In such cases of discrimination, women who pursue a career receive relatively low gains, and thus the cost of dropping out is also relatively small. Employers can then point to the labour market behaviour of women who do drop out, and continue to discriminate against women.

2. OCCUPATIONAL SEGREGATION AND PART-TIME WORK

Theories and research on labour market segmentation suggest that part-time work is an important factor in sex differences in the labour market as well as in occupational segregation by sex. The 1980 study showed that the proportion of part-time work among the economically active population varied substantially at country level. With respect to the composition of the part-time labour force, however, the picture was the same from country to country: part-time work is dominated by women to a very great extent.[36] As shown in the previous chapter, there have been considerable increases in part-time work during the past decade in most of the ECE countries for which information is available. Moreover, in most countries, the rise in part-time employment was greater for women than for men, thus increasing further the former's share in such employment.[37]

The growing proportion of women in part-time work can be partly related to the changing composition of the female labour force itself. With the increased participation rates of women with family responsibilities, married women and women with young children constitute a large proportion of the female labour force in most ECE countries. Part-time work is a means whereby those women can combine work outside the home with family responsibilities. In this way, the higher participation may itself have thus been associated with the growing importance of part-time work. Some indications to this effect are found in table IV.12, adapted from Sundström.[38] It clearly shows that several of the countries with a high level of labour force participation also have a high percentage of part-time work. All the countries listed in table IV.12 with a high level of part-time work (Denmark, Norway,

TABLE IV.12

Female part-time employment, labour force participation and population working at home, in selected European countries, 1977

(Percentages)

	Female labour force in part-time employment	Female labour force participation	Female population working at home
Belgium	16.1	45.6	35.5
Denmark	42.4	67.3	18.3
Finland	16.0 [a]	58.5	13.0 [a]
France	15.2	50.1	25.0
Germany, Fed. Rep. of	24.4	48.4	26.3
Ireland	9.6	33.3	40.3
Italy	5.9	37.1	38.6
Netherlands	19.9 [b]	32.0	46.5
Norway	50.7 [a]	64.7	31.5 [a]
Sweden	44.3	70.0	20.4
United Kingdom [c]	40.4	57.3	23.4

Sources: Adapted from M. Sundström "Kvinnor och deltidsarbete", M. Lundahl and I. Persson-Tanimura, eds., in *Kvinnan i ekonomien* (Liber, Malmö, 1983), page 71, table 4.1, notes included.

Note: The data for Finland, Norway and Sweden refer to women between 16 and 74 years of age; for the other countries, 14 years and older except labour force participation rates which are defined as the number of women (all ages) in the labour force, divided by the total number of women of 15–64 years of age. Columns 2 and 3 do not add up to 100 because the nominators are different and also because there are women who are not in the labour force who are not working at home either.

[a] The figures refer to 1978.

[b] The low percentage of part-time workers in 1977, compared with recent data, is due to a change in the classification of part-time work.

[c] Refers to Great Britain.

Sweden and the United Kingdom) also have higher levels of female labour force participation rates than all the other countries except Finland. The positive association between higher labour force participation and a high incidence of part-time work does not apply in all cases. Important exceptions are the centrally planned economies where, on the average, female labour force participation rates are high, and the available statistics indicate virtually no differences between the average working hours of the male and the female labour force.[39] There are also important exceptions within the industrialized countries of western Europe and North America. In addition to Finland, both Canada and the United States are examples of countries with a fairly high level of female labour force participation and a lower level of part-time work than is found in the Scandinavian countries and the United Kingdom.

This diversity suggests that the importance of part-time work is also a question of the traditions and norms of the working life environment, as well as the extent to which part-time work is given as an option by employers. The study by Sundström indicated that the substantial increase in part-time employment in Sweden over the decade 1970–1980 was largely due to new entrants into the labour force going into part-time work.[40] The expanding employment opportunities during the decade were found mainly in the service sector, especially in the traditionally female occupations of the public sector, health and social services. Sundström therefore concluded that the extended possibilities of part-time work provided a means by which the employers could adjust their demand for labour to the supply of new recruits to the labour market.[41]

---

[35] C. Jonung, *Patterns of Occupational Segregation ...*, p. 24.

[36] *The Economic Role of Women ...*, chapter VIII.3. See also chapter III above.

[37] See also OECD, *op. cit*.

[38] M. Sundström, "Kvinnor och deltidsarbete", M. Lundahl and I. Persson-Tanimura, eds., *Kvinnan i ekonomien* (Liber, Malmö, 1983).

[39] *The Economic Role of Women ...*, p. 113.

[40] M. Sundström, *op. cit*.

[41] See also OECD, *op. cit*.

The supply side of the labour market is also an important factor in the structure of part-time employment. The age-distributions of those in part-time employment differ for males and females. As discussed in the preceding chapter, male part-time workers tend, in the European countries, to be concentrated in the older age groups, but mostly among the young in North America. Female part-time workers, on the other hand, are frequently found in the prime age groups from 25 to 40 years, corresponding to the phases of the female life cycle with strong family responsibilities.[42] Demand-side factors are also important for part-time employment. Many service activities benefit from the use of part-time workers. The advantages to the employers of part-time, or temporary, labour are such that many enterprises, particularly as the labour shortages of the 1960s and early 1970s disappeared, increasingly adopted policies to this effect.

The evidence clearly indicates that part-time work contributes to an increase in occupational segregation by sex. The countries listed in table IV.12 with a large share of the female labour force in part-time work are also those which rank high with respect to the summary indices of occupational segregation (see table IV.11). Another illustration of how part-time work contributes to increased occupational segregation can be found in the Norwegian data for 1980. In table IV.11, the female shares in the main occupational groups are listed separately for the total economically active population (which includes people who had worked for at least 100 working hours in paid employment during the 12 months preceding the census, and for those with at least 1,300 working hours in paid employment over the same period). When Norwegian data on the lower female share of employment in the latter group were verified, a lower level of occupational segregation by sex was apparent among the full-time and nearly full-time employees than for the economically active population as a whole.

3. Educational qualifications

As already pointed out (see section H.1 above), sex differences in educational qualifications appear to be important factors behind the persistence of occupational segregation by sex. The 1980 study also showed that sex differentials with respect to educational qualifications were considerable in all the countries of the region, despite inter-country variation in the average level of educational qualifications. The disparities according to sex as regards the adult population were large, in terms of both the level of educational attainment and the field of specialization. In every country of the region, the adult female population was concentrated at the lower levels of educational attainment, while this was not true to the same degree for men. At every level of educational attainment, the female population was also much more concentrated in a narrow range of subjects than was the male population. Women were less likely to have a vocational education and, if they did, the fields of specialization

were largely found within occupations where the female shares of employment had already reached significant levels. This illustrates that, even on the (unrealistic) assumption that the restrictions on labour force participation for women were not less than those for men, the occupational opportunities for women workers would still be far more restricted than the opportunities for men.

With respect to the younger population, the 1980 study showed that, in most countries of the region, the enrolment patterns in higher levels of education were much more equal between men and women during the 1970s, as the number of female students expanded rapidly. According to the data presented in the 1980 study,[43] by 1977/78 women participated equally with men at the second level of education (corresponding to secondary school) in most countries of the region (with some exceptions in southern Europe). At the same time, there were still considerable differences in most of the countries in the participation rates at the third level of education, in particular with respect to specialized university degrees.[44] As also noted in the 1980 study, this was to be expected, since there are inevitably some time-lags in the educational system. Even if there is an equal share of women in the number of potential new university recruits, the composition of the university population will still reflect the sex differentials.

The general trends evident at the time of the study, however, indicated positive signs with respect to the educational attainment of young women compared with young men, as far as educational levels were concerned. Sex differences between the younger cohorts of women and men seem to be diminishing in most countries of the region. Unfortunately, this does not imply that employment opportunities for women and men of the younger generations are also rapidly becoming equal. Despite increased female participation in the educational system, women were still found to be concentrated in more narrow ranges of educational specialization at the various levels than men. The 1980 study noted in this context: "The main difference between men's and women's educational patterns, at the present time, is not in the enrolment, or in the study results as shown by the rate of examination success, but in the type of courses followed by men and women particularly at the second and third levels of education".[45]

The more recent educational statistics available from the countries of the region indicate no major changes in the situation described by the 1980 study, which referred to the mid-1970s. Selected country studies with respect to educational levels indicate that the trend towards a more equal participation of women at the various levels of the educational system continued and stabilized over recent years.[46] To the extent that available statistics also include the field of specialization, the signs are much less positive. The presence of a persistent educational segregation by sex, with respect both to vocational education and training and to higher education, has been amply demonstrated. Women remain a minority in the traditionally male-dominated fields. Viewed in a long-run perspective at country level, however, recent trends may be more encouraging. Even the small proportion of female stu-

---

[42] This raises questions both on the extent to which women entering the labour force in part-time employment will be able to increase their working hours when children become older and family responsibilities less demanding, and on the extent to which part-time work is a blind alley or a stepping-stone to permanent full-time employment. To answer these questions, further studies of the working profiles of successive birth cohorts are required.

---

[43] *The Economic Role of Women ...,* table VI.2.
[44] *Ibid,* table VI.6.
[45] *Ibid,* p. 89.
[46] See also OECD, *op. cit.*

dents in science and technology represents an increase over the situation prevailing one or two decades ago. Thus, the long-run trends of sex differentials in the educational system of the United States show some marked tendencies towards less dissimilarity according to sex (table IV.13). Another positive sign of long-term development may be the tendencies observed in the Scandinavian countries towards higher female participation in some of the traditionally male-dominated professional occupations. On the whole, however, the above examples also demonstrate that the tendencies towards higher female participation rates in education and the occupations most notably dominated by men, move at a very slow pace. It would appear that sex differentials in occupational opportunities with respect to educational qualifications are still a major barrier against a desegregated occupational structure. This suggests that educational policies aiming at more equal educational distributions of men and women should have high priority.

I. Occupational segregation in age groups and birth cohorts

There is evidence that occupational segregation may be decreasing with regard to the younger generations. First, as noted by Hakim,[47] the work profiles in younger birth cohorts of women (in this case Great Britain), are different from those of older women. The bi-modal work profile, reflecting a sequence of entry into the labour market, followed by temporary withdrawal and then re-entry, is the traditional and stereotyped notion of the typical woman worker. Survey data from the 1960s suggest that women who exhibited this pattern were becoming a minority among all women workers.[48] It was also pointed out that data at the aggregate level can be used only to a very limited extent in estimating women's working profiles over the life cycle.

Data at the individual level on women's participation in paid work over the life cycle are relatively rare. Nevertheless, some recent retrospective studies on participation in paid work have provided some insight into the problem. In all the countries where such data are available, there is a tendency towards an increased and more continuous participation in paid work over the life cycle for the younger generations of women. Studies from Norway, Sweden and the United States indicate that younger women often continue to work through the childbearing and child-rearing years. For older women, this has mainly occurred among the well-educated; in younger generations the tendency was also found among women with relatively less education (see also chapter III above).[49]

Since more women currently have both paid work and higher education, sex differentials with respect to work

experience and educational attainment are less pronounced for the younger generations. On the assumption that this has increased the interchangeability of women and men in the labour market, less occupational segregation could be expected in younger birth cohorts if there is no discrimination against individual women in the labour market.

Unfortunately, the available occupational data used to survey the aggregate trends in occupational distribution do not include such distribution by age. The more detailed study of occupational segregation by birth cohort and age group will therefore have to await further data from the 1980 censuses. In the meantime, country studies from Norway and Sweden may provide some insight into trends in occupational segregation by sex, within age groups and birth cohorts.

Some calculations on trends in occupational segregation by age in Norway over the period 1970 to 1981 are presented in table IV.14 and may be compared with Swedish results (see below).[50] The table shows that the overall level of occupational segregation, as measured by the DI index, changed very little over the decade, with only a small decrease noted. The table also shows that the dissimilarity levels of the occupational distributions for women and men generally varied relatively little with age. The exception is provided by the very low age groups, where the index is considerably higher than in the higher age groups.[51]

Over the decade, the trends with respect to the general level of dissimilarity developed somewhat differently in the separate age groups. It increased for very young people and for those between 40 and 60 years of age, whereas it decreased for those between 20 and 40 years of age. However, when a birth cohort approach is used, the picture changes towards a relatively stable or increased level of segregation over the decade for the cohorts born before 1940 (over 30 years of age in 1970), while the younger cohorts show a marked decrease in the level of occupational segregation over the decade. This is probably due to the fact that well-educated women and men tend to enter the labour market at a later age than their less-educated contemporaries. The development in Norway is thus consistent with the hypothesis that the notable increase of female educational attainment, relative to that of men, will have a desegregating effect. As in other countries of the ECE region, the gender gap with respect to the levels of educational attainment also decreased markedly in Norway during the 1970s.

Jonung[52] analysed the variation in occupational segregation by age in the occupational data from the Swedish censuses in 1960, 1970 and 1975. Table IV.15 is adapted from that study and shows the calculated DI indices for the occupational distribution of men and women (three-digit level), in various age groups and years. The table compares the development both in separate age groups and over the life cycle, at the aggregate level within birth

[47] C. Hakim, *op. cit.*

[48] *Ibid,* p. 55.

[49] E. Bernhardt, *Arbete och barn. Kvinnors sysselsättning i de barnafödande aldrarna,* Information i prognosfragor 1983:4 (Statistiska Centralbyran, Stockholm, Sweden, 1983), (with English Summary: *Work and Children – Employment Patterns Among Women in the Childbearing Ages* (Statistics, Sweden, Stockholm, 1983); K. Skrede and A. Sorensen, "Pa spor av en ny kvinnerolle – hvilkenbetydning har tidligere livslopstilpasning for kvinners tilknytning til arbeidsmarkedet i ulike livslopsfaser?" K. Skrede and K. Tornes, eds., *Studier i kvinners livslop* (Universitetsforlaget Oslo, 1983); and A. Sorensen, "Women's employment patterns after marriage", *Journal of Marriage and the Family,* Vol. 45, No. 2 (May 1983).

[50] As the calculations in table IV.14 use occupational distributions at the one-digit ISCO level, the results of this table are not directly comparable to the Swedish findings.

[51] A similar result was noted with respect to the Federal Republic of Germany. A study of data from 1960, 1970 and 1980 indicated a significantly lower level of segregation among men and women over 25 years of age than among younger workers (see B. G. Reubens, *Youth at Work: An International Survey* (Allenheld and Osmun, Totowa, N.J., 1983)).

[52] C. Jonung, *Patterns of Occupational Segregation ...*

TABLE IV.13

United States: share of bachelor's, master's and doctoral degrees conferred in 1966–1967 and 1974–1975 which were received by women, in total and selected disciplines [a]

(*Percentages*)

	BA		MA		Ph.D	
	1966–1967	*1974–1975*	*1966–1967*	*1974–1975*	*1966–1967*	*1974–1975*
Total	42.6	45.8	33.8	46.4	11.6	22.9
Business and management . .	8.6	16.6	2.5	8.8	3.9	4.0
Physical sciences	13.6	18.1	9.8	14.3	4.6	9.0
Index of dissimilarity (DI)						
Male and female educational distribution	47.4	41.3	39.6	40.0	33.7	30.1

Sources: United States National Center for Education Statistics, Earned Degrees conferred in 1966–1967 and 1974–1975; and C.B. Lloyd and B.T. Niemi, *The Economics of Sex Differentials* (Columbia University Press, New York, 1979).

[a] Calculated on the basis of total number of degrees in 1966 and 1974; *Equal Employment Opportunity* (United States Government Printing Office, Washington, D.C., 1982); table 17.

TABLE IV.14

Norway: DI index of occupational distributions, male and female labour force, ISCO one-digit level, by age, 1970 and 1980 [a]

	Age group								
	16–19	*20–24*	*25–29*	*30–39*	*40–49*	*50–59*	*60–66*	*67–69*	*Total*
1970	58.4	58.9	50.8	46.7	44.1	46.2	46.7	40.0	48.7
1981	63.7	57.1	48.6	44.4	46.1	47.3	46.0	47.5	47.9
Change	5.3	−1.8	−2.2	−2.3	2.0	1.1	−0.7	7.5	−0.8
of which: [b]									
Sex representation	3.1	−2.1	−2.7	−6.0	−1.0	−3.7	−7.3	3.0	−3.6
Employment structure	−0.7	−0.4	−1.7	−1.4	−1.3	1.1	3.9	2.3	−0.6
Interaction	2.8	1.1	2.2	5.0	4.5	3.7	2.7	2.2	3.4

Sources: Population and Housing Census, 1970, vol. II; *Employment Statistics; Labour Market Statistics, 1981,* No. B 302.

[a] Excludes unclassified occupations and the armed forces; ISCO occupational categories 5, 7 and 8 grouped together.

[b] See annex for the decomposition method.

TABLE IV.15

Sweden: DI index of occupational distribution, male and female labour force, by age, 1960, 1970 and 1975

	Age group								
Year	*16–19*	*20–24*	*25–29*	*30–34*	*35–44*	*45–54*	*55–64*	*65+*	*Total*
1960	75.4	77.5	76.0	74.4	78.7	74.1	73.6	67.5	74.5
1970	73.5	73.8	72.4	71.9	72.8	73.5	73.7	68.8	72.6
1975	70.8	70.2	69.1	70.7	71.0	71.7	72.4	65.4	70.3

Sources: Calculations based on data from the Population and Housing Census 1960, 1970 and 1975 (ISCO three-digit level). The table is adapted from C. Jonung, *Patterns of Occupational Segregation by sex in the Labour Market,* Report 1983:89 (Sweden, University of London, 1983) p. 36, table 7.

‾＼ = Birth-cohort.

cohorts (see the diagonal marks indicating the data on the birth cohort level). The results show a slight decrease in occupational segregation over time both with respect to the fixed age groups and within birth cohorts. As noted by Jonung, the change appears to be somewhat more rapid for the under-35 age groups and especially for the 25–29-year-olds. To the extent that the data make it possible to follow the development within birth cohorts, this trend was less pronounced. The decrease in the segregation level over the decade 1960–1970 was approximately as strong in the ten-year cohort born between 1916 and 1925 (35–44

years old in 1960), as in the five-year cohort born between 1936 and 1940 (20–24 years old in 1960). For the former, the DI index decreased by 5 points over the decade 1960–1970, while the decrease for the latter was nearly 6 points. Within each of the census years, however, table IV.15 shows very little variation with age. Thus, the decrease observed over time in occupational segregation may be attributed more to general trends in the labour market and changes in occupational structure, than to a change in the labour market behaviour of younger women.

CHAPTER V

THE PAY DIFFERENTIAL FOR WOMEN: SOME COMPARISONS FOR SELECTED ECE COUNTRIES

Introduction

Since the completion of the 1980 study,[1] the results of a great deal of additional research on the disparity between men's and women's earnings have become available. New explanatory factors have been suggested, and the scope of the investigations has been considerably enlarged. Although this research has provided new insight into the matter, it has not resolved some of the basic issues. Disagreement still persists, both on the variables to be considered and on the analytical approach to be adopted. It has nevertheless become increasingly clear that there is no one single explanatory variable in respect of the male-female earnings gap, but that a wide range of factors are involved.[2]

A major difficulty in analysing the reasons for the male-female earnings gap appears to be that it is associated with at least three different sets of factors: (i) those related to the personal characteristics of male and female workers and to the type of jobs they tend to occupy; (ii) those related to the structure and functioning of the labour market and to the male and female roles therein; and (iii) those related to men's and women's roles in the family and in society. These three sets of factors not only interact in numerous and complex ways, but are also subject to changes over time and between countries.

The first approach has been to examine differences in the personal characteristics of male and female workers and in the structure of the male and female labour force, so as to assess their impact on the male-female pay gap. The advantage of this method is that it makes it possible to estimate not only the proportion of the male-female pay gap accounted for by measurable factors such as age, education, training and occupation, but also that part of the pay gap which remains unexplained. This unexplained residual has often been taken to measure discrimination against women workers. Another merit of this approach is that it sheds light on the equal-pay-for-equal-work principle, suggesting that it is not inconsistent with differences between average levels of men's and women's pay.

The 1980 study for the most part adopted this "structural" type of approach. Covering 18 market-economy and centrally-planned-economy countries of the region, it showed what proportion of the male-female pay differential could be explained by measurable factors, such as hours worked and similarities in the industrial wage structure throughout the region. It also pointed to the general concentration of women in the lower-paid industries.[3] The analysis also revealed, however, that the differences due to the various structural factors were largely autocorrelated (such as those of age and professional status) and could therefore not be added together, thus limiting the usefulness of the method followed. The study also showed that the influence of structural factors varied between countries, and that inter-country differences in the composition of the female labour force did not go hand in hand with differences in the size of the male-female pay gap. These results suggested the importance of other existing factors.

Many other studies have also demonstrated the limitations of analysing worker characteristics in order to explain the male-female pay gap.[4] As a result of these limitations, increased attention has been focused on the question of how women workers fared in the labour market. Among the relevant issues in this regard is that of occupational segregation, which is discussed in detail in chapter IV.[5] The effects of occupational segregation on female earnings have been examined from various perspectives. One of the findings is that the labour market has tended to assign, more or less systematically, a low value to jobs which are predominantly "female". In order to achieve pay equality, remuneration for jobs in "female" occupations would have to be comparable with that for jobs performed by men, or with men's jobs of "comparable worth". The concept of comparable worth differs from the concept of equal pay for equal work, which implicitly assumes that men and women should receive the same pay for the same work. The concept of comparable worth takes into account differences between men's and women's roles in the labour market, and the fact that women's work is mostly different from that of men. For this reason they receive different pay, as pointed out in the conclusion of the 1980 study.[6] The problem of equal pay for women thus hinges on the value ascribed to work performed in jobs predominantly held by women.

In market economies, levels of pay are determined to a large extent by the labour market which, of course, takes into account not only the demand for labour, but also its supply. The supply of female labour differs from the supply of male labour, owing basically to differences in

[1] *The Economic Role of Women in the ECE Region* (United Nations publication, Sales No. E.80.2.E.6).

[2] See D.J. Treiman and H.I. Hartmann, eds., *Women, Work and Wages: Equal Pay for Jobs of Equal Value* (National Academy Press, Washington D.C., 1981); M.A. Ferber and J.L. Spaeth, "Work characteristics and the male-female earnings gap", *The American Economic Review*, vol. 74, No. 2 (May 1984).

[3] D. Marsden's note on United Nations publication: *The Economic Role of Women in the ECE Region*, in *The Economic Journal*, vol. 93, No. 370 (Cambridge University Press, June 1983).

[4] See D.J. Treiman and H.I. Hartmann, *op.cit.*; and Ferber and Spaeth, *op. cit.*

[5] See also Organisation for Economic Co-operation and Development (OECD), *Women and Employment, Policies for Equal Opportunities* (Paris, 1980); OECD, Working Party No. 6 on the Role of Women in the Economy, *The Concentration of Female Employment: The Example of France* (1982); and other OECD documents on the same subject.

[6] *The Economic Role of Women ...*, pp.118-119.

family roles. In industrialized countries today, a high proportion of working women are married. They thus have the responsibility of running their homes and, in this sense, are mostly "secondary" earners, whereas men with limited, if any, domestic duties are "primary" earners. Women combining household responsibilities with paid employment are thus obliged, for the family's well-being, to try to optimize their dual role. As a result, their labour-supply function differs from that of men, who try to maximize their earnings level, with few constraints. The specific characteristics of women's labour supply affect the level of their relative earnings. For this reason this chapter includes a discussion of male-female earnings differentials within the context of the different roles of the sexes in the labour market, an analysis which did not figure in the 1980 study.

This chapter sets out the latest available statistical evidence on male-female pay differentials on an economy-wide basis, and within the manufacturing and service sectors. It also includes a discussion of recent changes in pay differentials. Subsequent sections are devoted to the impact of various worker and job characteristics on relative female earnings, noting the changes which have occurred in the last few years. After examining differences in hours worked by men and women, the impact of personal characteristics such as age, education and experience on women's relative pay is assessed. The influence of the distribution of the male and female work force by industry and occupation on the male-female earnings gap is then reviewed. Finally, the earnings differentials within the context of the labour market, taking the supply and demand factors into account, and the position of women in the labour market, largely influenced by their specific family roles, are discussed.

A. Survey of statistical evidence

Although, during the last decade, considerable attention has been given to the role of women in the economy, it is still difficult to assemble extensive internationally comparable statistical information on the subject of women's relative earnings. Table V.1 includes, for as many countries as possible, the data currently available on male and female earnings differentials in the total economy, in manufacturing and in those branches of the service sectors for which information is available in most countries: trade, banking, insurance and public administration. It provides a general overview of women's current pay situation in comparison with that of men, particularly in services, where the majority of the female work force is concentrated.

The table was compiled from various sources reflecting widely different national practices which can be summarized under three headings. First, as indicated, the data refer to different years. The second factor reducing comparability concerns differences in coverage: the size of the establishments covered is not the same in all countries, different proportions of smaller establishments in particular being excluded. As women tend to be more concentrated in smaller establishments, a fairly large but varying proportion of them is omitted from official data. Disparities in coverage are also caused by a different approach to the age of employed persons: some countries publish data for adults only (the lower age limit varying between 18 and 21 years); others include juveniles and

apprentices. The third factor reducing comparability is that of the differences in the reported pay periods. In some cases the reference pay period is one hour, in others it is a week, a month or even a year. As the male-female earnings gap is known to increase with the length of the period covered, *ceteris paribus* it is greater on an annual basis than on a weekly or hourly one; comparability is thus reduced by country data being available only for certain different pay periods. A full description of the data coverage and pay periods can be found in the notes accompanying table V.1.

In spite of the limitations to comparability resulting from the lack of homogeneity in the data, some conclusions can nevertheless be drawn from the table. On an economy-wide level, women's earnings lag behind men's least in Sweden and most in the United States of America. In manufacturing, where data are available for a greater number of countries, the earning gaps are again smallest in Sweden and largest in the United States. The male-female wage gap in Sweden is less than 10% for manual workers. Sweden is followed by Denmark, Italy and Norway. These data however, may not be comparable. With respect to Italy, it has been noted that a considerable proportion of women work in small enterprises, where pay tends to be low, or are engaged in undeclared work for even less remuneration.[7] Italy is not the only country where undeclared work, which is not reflected in official statistics, is fairly widespread. Moreover, it can be assumed that the most recent recession has further increased the number of such casual and clandestine workers, a high proportion of whom are women. Qualification is also necessary regarding the data for the United States, which show the largest male-female earnings gap on an economy-wide basis in manufacturing, banking, insurance and real estate. The United States data refer to annual (full-time) earnings; calculated on a weekly or hourly basis, the gap would probably be considerably reduced.

1. PAY DIFFERENTIALS IN MANUFACTURING

As noted in the previous chapter, only a relatively small proportion of the female work force in the countries of the region is employed in manufacturing, particularly in manual jobs. However, for a number of reasons which may be historical, institutional or practical, data on manufacturing earnings are generally the most widely available, especially those for manual workers. All countries of the region regularly publish such statistics, in most cases broken down by sex. Because of the scarcity of other statistical information on women's earnings, they merit attention, even though they cover only a relatively small proportion of the female labour force.

Table V.1 shows that the male-female pay differential is generally wider in the case of non-manual workers than for manual workers. The United States is a notable exception in this respect. The larger pay gap for non-manual workers may of course be partly attributable to the fact that manual workers' earnings are normally expressed on an hourly basis while, for non-manual workers, they are usually calculated on a monthly basis. However, even in the United Kingdom, where both manual and non-manual earnings are expressed on a weekly basis, the

---

[7] R. De Grazia, "Clandestine employment: a problem of our times", *International Labour Review*, vol. 119, No. 5 (Geneva, ILO, September-October 1980).

TABLE V.1

Women's earnings as a percentage of those of men, in selected sectors, in 17 market-economy countries

Country	Year	All sectors			Manufacturing		Trade		Banking (8)	Insurance (9)	Public administration (10)
		Total (1)	Manual (2)	Non-manual (3)	Manual (4)	Non-manual (5)	Wholesale (6)	Retail (7)			
Austria	1983	77.6	72.1	75.7	..	..	74.2 (Trade, combined)		79.2 (Banking & insurance, combined)		82.2
Belgium	1982	63.3	..	..	72.6	59.3	65.0	71.1	71.2	68.4	..
Canada	1979	..	..	73.8	..	..	74.4	75.5	76.4	68.1	..
Denmark	1983	..	..	..	88.6	71.4	69.4	87.3	78.6	68.5	74.0
Finland	1981	75.0	..	83.1	76.8	76.1	69.7	67.5	74.5	66.1	83.9
France	1982	..	75.5	64.8	77.7	61.7	68.3	65.9	77.4	76.8	..
Germany, Federal Republic of	1982	..	..	..	72.7	66.7	56.4	70.0	..	..	..
Greece	1980	..	..	..	67.4	57.0	79.0	58.5	67.1	58.9	..
Ireland	1982	..	..	..	68.5	..	61.1	85.8	79.5	71.1	..
Italy	1982	..	..	..	86.7	..	..	61.2	56.6	60.4	..
Netherlands	1981	76.8	75.2	..	74.7	65.3	70.5	80.6	77.5	65.5	82.9
Norway	1982	75.6	..	..	83.2	74.6	79.4	79.2	81.8	84.6	..
Portugal	1980	80.7	..	..	72.0	72.7	72.5	95.0	76.9	71.7	88.3
Sweden	1982	..	..	66.9	90.3	..	..	63.0	78.2	72.6	78.8
Switzerland	1980	..	..	..	67.7	66.4	74.7	..	..	..	..
United Kingdom	1980	65.7	61.9	61.2	60.3	53.2	54.1	56.1	49.9 (Banking & insurance, combined)		60.9
United States	1981	59.1	61.2	52.8	57.6	60.1	58.3	59.7	47.8 (Banking & insurance, combined)		67.0

Note: All weekly, monthly and yearly earning data refer to full-time workers.

Austria. Median monthly earnings of wage and salary earners, standardized for number of working hours. Col. (10) refers to total public service employment.
Source: Data supplied by the Government of Austria.

Belgium. Col. (4): hourly earnings of manual workers in manufacturing (ISIC 2-5). Cols. (6)-(9): average monthly earnings of employees, in 1974. In 1982 (2nd quarter), percentages of earnings differentials of male and female "intellectual workers", in the private sector only were: wholesale trade: 58.4; retail trade: 61.8; banking: 67.0; insurance: 66.2.
Sources: Data compiled from *Statistiques Sociales*, No. 3, 1983, Institut National de Statistique (Brussels); EUROSTAT, *The Structure of Earnings in Distribution, Banking and Insurance, 1974* (Brussels).

Canada. Col. (1): annual average earnings of full-time workers (persons who worked mostly full-time, 50 or 52 weeks in the reference year).
Sources: Data compiled from "Earnings of men and women", selected years, Catalogue 13 577, occasional, quoted in *The Current Employment Situation of Women*, paper presented at the Federal Provincial Meeting of Ministers responsible for the status of women, 31 May-1 June 1983, by the Hon. Judy Erola.

Denmark. Col. (4): hourly earnings of unskilled workers in manufacturing. Col. (5): monthly earnings of employees in manufacturing (estimate based on the weighted average of data for nine major manufacturing branches). Cols. (6)-(9): average monthly earnings of employees.
Source: Data compiled from Statistiske Efterretninger, Danmarks Statistik, *Indkomst, Forbrug og Priser* (Copenhagen, 1984-7).

Finland. Cols. (4) and (5): industry = mining, quarrying, manufacturing and public utilities. Col. (4): hourly earnings of manual workers in manufacturing. Col. (5): average monthly earnings of office staff in industrial establishments. Col. (6): office staff in trade sector workers. Col. (7): salespersons and shop assistants.
Source: Data compiled from *Statistical Yearbook of Finland 1982*, Central Statistical Office of Finland (Helsinki, 1983).

France. Col. (1): average net yearly earnings of full-time workers. Col. (2): average net yearly earnings of manual workers. Col. (4): hourly earnings of manual workers in manufacturing. Cols. (5)-(9) refer to 1978. Cols. (5)-(9): average monthly earnings of full-time employees. Col. (10): average yearly earnings of State employees (*agents de l'Etat*).
Sources: F. Bourit, P. Hernu, M. Perrot, "Les salaires en 1982", *Economie et Statistique*, No. 154, April 1983 (Paris); *Les Collections de l'INSEE*, series M, No. 90-91; F. Vlassenko, *La Structure des Salaires dans l'Industrie et les Services en 1978*, No. 98 (1981); D. Quarre and A. Minczeles, *Les Salaires des Agents de l'Etat en 1978* (INSEE, Paris); and EUROSTAT, *Structure of Earnings, 1978/79*, Volume 2—France (Luxembourg/Brussels, 1983).

Italy. Col. (4): hourly earnings of manual workers in manufacturing. Cols. (6)-(9): average monthly earnings of full-time employees.
Sources: EUROSTAT, *Wages and Incomes*, Statistical Bulletin, various issues; EUROSTAT, *The Structure of Earnings in Distribution, Banking and Insurance, 1974* (Brussels).

Netherlands. Col. (1): average weekly earnings of wage and salary earners in non-agricultural activities. Adults. Col. (2): average weekly earnings of wage earners (manual workers) in non-agricultural activities. Adults. Col. (4): hourly earnings of manual workers in manufacturing. Cols. (6)-(9): average monthly earnings of employees, in 1974.
Sources: Data supplied by the ILO Bureau of Statistics; EUROSTAT, *The Structure of Earnings in Distribution, Banking and Insurance, 1974* (Brussels).

Norway. Data refer to adult workers. Col. (4): hourly earnings of workers in manufacturing. Col. (5): average monthly earnings of office staff in manufacturing. Col. (6): average monthly earnings of office staff in wholesale and retail trade. Col. (7): shop personnel in wholesale and retail trade.
Source: Data compiled from Norges Offisielle Statistikk, Central Bureau of Statistics of Norway, *Lonns-Statistikk 1982* (Wage Statistics 1982) (Oslo, 1983).

Portugal. Basic pay of male and female workers. Col. (1): all non-agricultural activities.
Source: Commission of European Communities, *L'Emploi des Femmes au Portugal*, Document V/2139/82-FR (Brussels, 1982).

Sweden. Col. (1): income from work of full-year, full-time economically active persons, in 1980. Col. (4): hourly earnings of manual workers in manufacturing. Col. (5): average monthly earnings of full-time employees in manufacturing, mining and quarrying. Col. (6): average monthly earnings of full-time employees in wholesale trade. Col. (7): hourly earnings of salespersons and shop assistants. Col. (8): average monthly earnings of full-time employees in banking. Col. (9): average monthly earnings of full-time employees in insurance companies. Col. (10): state employees in 1981.
Sources: Data compiled from Official Statistics of Sweden, Statistics Sweden, *Löner 1982*, part 1 and 2 (Stockholm, 1983); and *Arbetsmarknads Statistik Arsbok* (1982-83).

Switzerland. Col. (3): average monthly earnings of (non-manual) employees. Col. (4): hourly earnings of manual workers in manufacturing, including family allowances. Cols. (5)-(10): public administration.
Sources: Data compiled from *Annuaire Statistique de la Suisse*, 1981, Office Fédéral de Statistique (Berne, 1981); and ILO, *Yearbook of Labour Statistics*, 1983.

United Kingdom. Average gross weekly earnings of workers whose pay was not affected by absence. Cols. (1)–(3): adult workers aged 21 and over. Cols. (4)–(10): men aged 21 and over, and women aged 18 and over. Cols. (8)–(9): banking, finance, insurance and business services.

Source: Data compiled from *New Earnings Survey, 1980*, United Kingdom Department of Employment (London, Her Majesty's Stationery Office, 1981).

United States. Average money earnings of year-round, full-time workers. Col. (2): blue-collar workers in the total economy. Col. (3): white-collar workers in the total economy. Col. (4): craft workers and operatives in manufacturing. Col. (5): clerical and sales workers in manufacturing. Cols. (8)–(9): finance, insurance and real estate. Col. (10): public administration.

Source: Data compiled from Current Population Reports, *Money Income of Households, Families and Persons in the United States: 1981*, U.S. Department of Commerce, Bureau of the Census (Washington, D.C.).

Germany, Federal Republic of. Col. (3): monthly earnings of administrative, clerical and technical employees in industry, commerce, financial institutions and insurance. Col. (4): hourly earnings of manual workers in total industry (ISIC 2–5) = mining and quarrying, manufacturing, electricity, gas and water and construction. Col. (5): average monthly earnings of full-time employees in industry, (ISIC 2–5).

Sources: Data compiled from *Statistisches Bundesamt Wiesbaden*, Fachserie 16, Reihe 2.1; *Löhne in der Industrie*; Reihe 2.2; *Angestelltenverdienste in Industrie und Handel*, various issues; *Statistical Yearbook of the Federal Republic of Germany, 1983*.

Greece. Col. (4): hourly earnings of manual workers in manufacturing. Cols. (5) and (7): average monthly earnings of full-time employees.

Sources: ILO, *Yearbook of Labour Statistics, 1983*; and data supplied by the Government of Greece.

Ireland. Col. (4): hourly earnings of manual workers in manufacturing. Cols. (6)–(9): average monthly earnings of full-time employees.

Sources: EUROSTAT, *Wages and Incomes*, Statistical Bulletin, various issues; EUROSTAT, *The Structure of Earnings in Distribution, Banking and Insurance, 1974* (Brussels).

male-female pay gap is considerably wider in the latter category. As shown in table V.2, in the United Kingdom the male-female pay gap is larger for non-manual than for manual workers, not only in manufacturing but in all sectors for which information is available, with the excep-

tion of "professional and scientific services". This was already the case in the early 1970s. Although relative female pay has increased for all categories of workers, particularly in manufacturing, the manual to non-manual ratio has, on the whole, remained unchanged.

TABLE V.2

United Kingdom: average gross weekly earnings of full-time adult women workers, as a percentage of those of men, by sector, 1971–1980

Sector	1971		1980	
	Manual	Non-manual	Manual	Non-manual
Total (weighted average)	52.0	50.6	60.9	58.5
Mining	–	–	–	–
Manufacturing........................	50.5	44.3	60.3	53.2
Construction	–	41.8	–	51.5
Electricity, gas, water.................	–	51.2	–	54.0
Transport and communication	67.0	51.5	75.1	58.2
Distributive trades	52.7	44.2	64.4	53.6
Insurance, banking, finance, business services	–	46.0	–	49.9
Professional and scientific services......	58.0	58.7	65.1	68.1
Miscellaneous services	54.2	52.7	65.4	64.4
Public administration.................	66.1	56.7	72.8	60.9

Source: Data compiled from the *New Earnings Survey,* United Kingdom Department of Employment (London, Her Majesty's Stationery Office, 1971 and 1980).

TABLE V.3

France: average annual earnings of full-time manual and non-manual women workers, as a percentage of those of men, by sector, 1978

Sector	All workers	Manual workers	Non-manual workers
All activities..............................	71.9	72.7	62.5
Industry[a]	64.8	72.2	60.7
Coal mining............................		83.5	62.8
Oil refining		77.8	59.1
Nuclear fuel production.................		85.4	65.5
Electricity, gas, steam		84.5	71.1
Water distribution		83.2	66.4
Ore extraction		63.6	64.9
Basic metal industry		74.6	58.5
Chemical industry......................		75.4	60.6
Artificial fibres		76.2	73.2
Machine building (heavy machinery)......		77.5	58.7
Computer and office machinery..........		80.3	61.7
Electrical machinery and electronics		80.3	63.4
Automobile industry		76.1	61.8
Precision instruments		75.5	54.5
Food, drink and tobacco		74.3	56.7
Textile industry		78.9	56.8
Leather industry		79.7	57.0
Footwear and clothing industry		76.6	57.9
Paper, printing and publishing...........		66.7	58.1
Construction and public works.............	97.2	78.4	58.6
Transport and communications	80.1	..	..
Distribution	67.0	..	64.6
Wholesale trade	..	..	68.0
Retail trade	..	..	63.1
Banking	..	..	71.9
Insurance	..	..	62.0

Sources: Data compiled from *Les Collections de l'INSEE,* series M, No. 90–91 (Paris, 1981); and E. Vlassenko, *La Structure des Salaires dans l'Industrie et les Services en 1978,* No. 98 (1981).

Note: Full-time data.

[a] Excluding construction and public works. Selected branches only.

TABLE V.4

Federal Republic of Germany: average full-time earnings of manual and non-manual women workers as a percentage of those of men, by sector, 1982

Sector	Manual workers		Non-manual workers, monthly
	Hourly	Weekly	
Industry, commerce, banking and insurance..........	..	..	64.8
Industry [a]	72.7	69.2	66.7
Mining.....................................	..	..	61.2
Basic materials industry	77.3	74.0	70.6
of which:			
Iron and steel	75.7	73.2	66.0
Oil processing...............................	71.6	70.3	70.3
Chemicals...................................	74.0	71.4	72.0
Artificial fibres	76.6	75.2	72.9
Investment goods industry	75.9	72.6	65.8
of which:			
Machine building............................	76.5	73.0	65.4
Automobile and vehicle industry	82.8	79.7	65.6
Electro-technical industry.....................	77.9	74.9	67.1
Precision instruments	78.6	77.0	68.2
Office equipment, data-processing			
equipment.................................	82.9	80.6	65.9
Consumer goods industry	72.6	68.5	66.4
of which:			
Paper and cardboard	72.8	67.2	64.7
Printing and publishing	69.7	67.2	66.1
Footwear...................................	80.6	78.1	63.9
Textiles	81.1	76.2	69.1
Clothing	76.6	73.4	70.3
Food, drink and tobacco	70.3	63.9	69.5
Construction	..	..	62.6
Wholesale trade..................................	..	..	68.3
Retail trade......................................	..	..	65.0
Banking...	..	..	77.4
Insurance	..	..	76.8

Source: Data compiled from Statistisches Bundesamt, *Statistical Yearbook of the Federal Republic of Germany, 1983* (Wiesbaden).

[a] Industrial construction.

A larger difference in pay between men and women non-manual workers than for manual workers in industry is also observed in the case of France. Table V.3 shows annual full-time relative female earnings for both manual and non-manual workers. A graphic illustration of the absolute differences in male and female manual and non-manual earnings in France is provided in figure V.1. Non-manual women workers earn only slightly more than male manual workers in most sectors, while the pay difference between manual and non-manual women workers is much less pronounced than in the case of men. In France, the pay advantage of non-manual over manual male workers, as well as over manual and non-manual women workers, is particularly large in certain high-technology industries, such as oil-refining or the computer and data-processing sectors. In these sectors the top grades of managers and technicians can bargain for high salaries, while female employees tend to remain concentrated in lower-grade, mostly clerical, occupations where they are paid on average only slightly more than in sectors with lower profits and pay possibilities. It should be noted that, in the traditional "women's" sectors such as textiles, footwear and clothing, manual and non-manual pay is lower than in other sectors. The pay gap in respect of non-manual workers is, curiously enough, larger than in industry as a whole, while the pay gap concerning manual workers is slightly narrower, because all wages in these sectors, including men's, are very low.

Tables V.4 and V.5 show the differences between male and female pay for manual and non-manual workers in the Federal Republic of Germany and Sweden. In both countries, women manual workers seem to be doing relatively better in "male" industries than in traditionally "female" ones. In the Federal Republic of Germany, the pay gap is considerably wider in the consumer-goods sector (particularly in food, drink and tobacco) rather than in the investment-goods sector and in basic materials. In Sweden, female manual workers earn on average 95% or more of men's pay in the wood and furniture industry, basic metals, metal products, transport equipment and precision instruments, all traditionally "male" industries. Women do relatively less well in food, beverages and tobacco or in textiles, clothing and leather, where they comprise the majority of the work-force. As far as non-manual women workers are concerned, in the Federal Republic of Germany they receive the highest relative pay in chemicals and in artificial fibres while they

Figure V. 1

France, 1978.
Average annual earnings of manual and non-manual
full-time male and female workers in selected industries
(Thousands of francs)

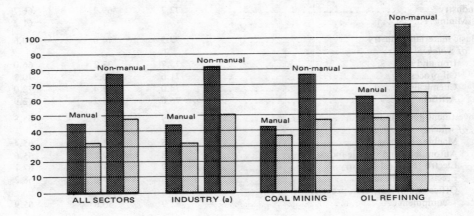

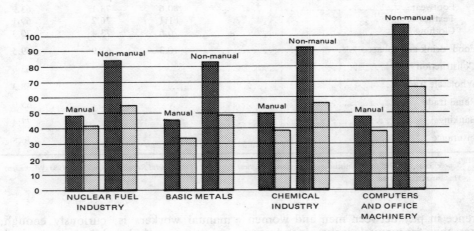

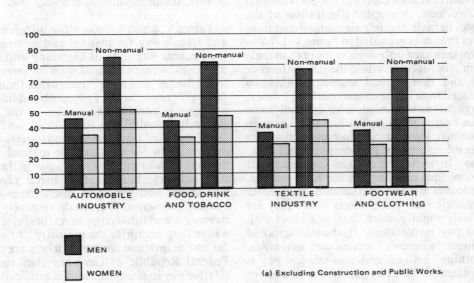

MEN

WOMEN

(a) Excluding Construction and Public Works.

TABLE V.5

**Sweden: average hourly and monthly earnings of manual and non-manual
male and female workers, by sector of activity, 1982**

(Kronor)

Sector	Hourly earnings of manual workers			Monthly earnings of full-time, non-manual workers		
	Males	*Females*	*Female earnings as percentage of male earnings*	*Males*	*Females*	*Female earnings as percentage of male earnings*
Mining and quarrying	51.5	46.3	89.8	9 589	7 160	74.7
Manufacturing	46.6	42.1	90.3	9 501	6 905	72.7
Food, beverages, tobacco	46.5	41.6	89.4	9 084	6 750	74.3
Textiles, clothing, leather	42.0	38.5	91.6	8 967	6 612	73.7
Wood, wood products and furniture	42.7	40.5	94.8	8 637	6 271	72.6
Paper and paper products	52.4	44.5	84.9	9 909	6 750	68.1
Printing and publishing	52.3	45.7	87.4	9 626	7 516	78.1
Chemical industry	46.8	41.3	88.3	9 929	7 250	73.0
Non-metallic mineral products	46.4	41.8	90.1	9 206	6 735	73.2
Basic metal industry..............	49.7	47.0	94.7	9 782	7 064	72.2
Metal products	45.7	42.7	95.8	9 494	6 766	71.3
Fabricated metal products	44.5	41.0	92.0	9 090	6 572	72.3
Machinery (non-electrical)	45.5	42.5	93.5	9 608	6 774	70.5
Electrical machinery.............	45.3	42.5	94.0	9 589	6 708	70.0
Transport equipment	47.4	45.8	96.6	9 469	6 905	72.9
Precision instruments............	43.6	42.1	96.5	9 734	7 186	73.8
Other manufacturing	41.9	39.0	93.0	8 797	6 274	71.3
Construction	51.7	40.0	77.3	9 377	6 465	68.9
Wholesale trade	36.4 [a]	35.1	96.4	9 170	6 645	72.5
Retail trade	36.5 [b]	34.7	95.0	8 297	6 495	78.3
Banking	..	..	..	9 127	7 020	76.9
Insurance......................	..	..	..	10 285	7 375	71.7

Source: Data compiled from Statistics Sweden, *Löner 1982* (Stockholm, 1983).

[a] Storepersons and drivers.

[b] Salespersons and shop assistants.

do poorly in footwear, a "female" branch. However, women's earnings are comparatively low in paper and cardboard and in the mechanical industries, which are "male-dominated". In Sweden, non-manual women workers seem to be paid most equitably in printing and publishing, and earn the least compared to men in the paper and paper-product industry. It is likely that, for non-manual women workers, the organizational side of the industry, the size of the firm and its location play a considerable role as regards the relative level of their pay.

In this respect, table V.6 shows that, in Switzerland, the food sector, which is dominated by a large multinational corporation, pays non-manual men workers much higher salaries than non-manual women. Moreover, the male-female pay gap is considerably larger in food processing than in industry taken as a whole. However, in the chemical industry, which is also operated by large companies, relative earnings of non-manual women workers are comparatively high. As noted in section D.1 below, non-manual female workers are paid less than non-manual male workers as they reach a certain pay ceiling at an earlier age (see figures V.2 and V.3 relating to Sweden and the United Kingdom).

2. PAY DIFFERENTIALS IN THE SERVICE SECTOR

Data on the male-female earnings gap are generally not available for the service sector as a whole (with a few exceptions, such as Switzerland). However, tables V.1– V.7 provide information on the pay differences in a number of service industries. The data indicate that the pay gap between non-manual men and women workers tends to be wider in manufacturing than in the four service sectors for which data are published in most countries: wholesale trade, retail trade, banking and insurance. The reason is not, it seems, that non-manual female employees earn less in manufacturing but that the average pay of non-manual men workers tends to rise with age more in industry than in services. This may be partly due to a weighting effect. Most workers in the service sectors, even those with low qualifications, are counted as non-manual, which lowers the average pay of non-manual male workers. It also seems, however, that manufacturing, particularly in some of the leading sectors mentioned above, offers better earning possibilities to highly-qualified men than most service activities do.

For the countries listed in table V.1, retail trade emerges as the sector with the smallest male-female earnings differentials, and insurance with the largest. The reason for this, as already noted in the 1980 study, is that male salaries have the possibility of rising to a much higher level in large insurance companies than in retail trade businesses where the average size of establishment is relatively small. Women's salaries are also higher in insurance than in retail trade (see figure V.4 illustrating the situation in the Federal Republic of Germany), but they appear to rise at a slower pace than men's salaries. In general, it seems that the pay gap tends to increase where the average salaries of men reach very high levels. This point is also illustrated in table V.5 as regards Sweden, which shows that male earnings are particularly high in the insurance sector. Women's earnings are also relatively

TABLE V.6

**Switzerland: average monthly earnings of full-time non-manual women workers,
as a percentage of those of men, by sector and professional category, 1982**

Sector	Total	Category (1)[a]	Category (2)[b]	Category (3)[c]
Total	67.2	73.2	73.7	74.7
Industry	66.6	72.6	72.6	74.5
Food	59.6	66.0	62.6	75.1
Beverages	67.9	73.4	72.8	..
Tobacco	68.5	..	79.6	..
Textiles	65.7	67.6	69.5	69.3
Clothing and footwear	69.3	69.7	73.2	71.8
Wood and furniture	69.3	75.3	74.3	..
Paper and cardboard	65.7	71.7	71.2	..
Printing and publishing	65.8	74.7	73.5	75.8
Plastics and leather	65.1	70.6	69.6	..
Chemicals	73.3	80.2	79.9	75.8
Non-metal mineral products	70.5	74.8	75.9	..
Metal working and machinery	65.6	..	..	..
Watchmaking	69.3	74.5	72.8	80.3
Other manufacturing	67.0	..	..	..
Electricity, gas, water	67.1	70.2	75.9	..
Construction	65.5	75.5	69.8	..
Services	67.9	73.1	74.5	74.9
Wholesale trade	74.5	78.9	80.5	75.3
Retail trade	63.9	66.3	70.0	73.9
Hotels and restaurants	70.5	80.1	87.6	112.0
Transport and communications	76.7	78.0	81.6	81.9
Banking	78.6	86.4	90.6	72.3
Insurance	73.1	78.5	84.8	78.8
Real estate	75.1	76.4	83.0	..
Counselling services	68.9	74.6	81.4	79.0
Public administration	79.6	93.9	90.0	83.3
Cleaning and sanitary services	58.6	69.7	..	..
Repair services	75.5	75.1	80.7	78.3

Source: Data compiled from *Annuaire Statistique de la Suisse, 1983,* Office Fédéral de Statistique (Berne, 1983).

[a] Qualified, independently-working employees, having completed appropriate studies or training.

[b] Qualified subordinate staff.

[c] Assistant staff.

TABLE V.7

**United States: average annual earnings of full-time female workers,
as a percentage of those of male workers, by industry and professional category, 1981**

Sector	Total	Professional and managerial workers	Clerical and sales workers	Craft workers and operatives
All sectors	59.1	..	..	..
Agriculture, forestry and fishing	61.0	..	..	..
Mining and quarrying	54.4	..	..	..
Manufacturing	56.8	58.9	60.1	57.6
Durable goods	59.9	60.1	63.7	63.4
Non-durable goods	53.7	57.3	55.3	52.4
Construction	64.0	..	56.7	..
Wholesale trade	58.3	58.7	54.6	..
Retail trade	59.7	62.2	56.7	71.7
Transport and communications	68.7	59.3	68.6	78.6
Financial institutions, insurance and real estate	47.8	51.0	45.8	..
Business and repair services	66.4	64.6	60.6	..
Personal services	54.0	66.5	..	57.6
Professional and related services	53.7	57.7	76.5	57.6
Public administration	67.0	67.0	65.5	..

Source: Data compiled from Current Population Reports, *Money Income of Households, Families and Persons in the United States: 1981,* U.S. Department of Commerce, Bureau of the Census (Washington, D.C.).

Figure Ⅴ. 2

Sweden, 1982. Male and female earnings by age in the Trade Sector.

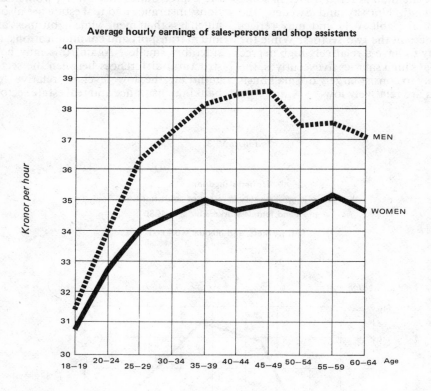

Average hourly earnings of sales-persons and shop assistants

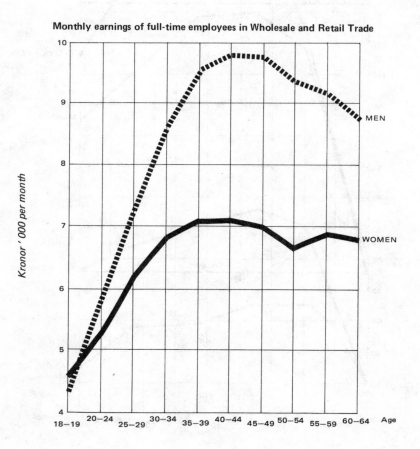

Monthly earnings of full-time employees in Wholesale and Retail Trade

high in this sector but the pay gap remains wider than in banking. In retail trade the gap is relatively narrow, but both male and female salaries are considerably lower than in the insurance sector. Similarly, the earnings gap is generally wider in wholesale than in retail trade. In some countries, such as Finland, Norway and Sweden, the differences are substantial (table V.1) and may reflect basic structural differences in the two sectors. While the wholesale sector is likely to have a relatively high degree of concentration, and pays high salaries to executives, the retail trade sector is likely to consist largely of small businesses where all salaries are relatively low.

As stated in section A.1 above, the smallest male-female pay gap in the United Kingdom is to be found in professional and scientific services while, in insurance, banking and business services, it is surprisingly wide. In the United States (table V.7), women in financial institutions, insurance and real estate are also paid, on average, much less than men, while in business and repair services, and in transport and communications, the pay gap is considerably smaller. Again, this may be explained by the structural differences between the sectors concerned. In addition, the low level of relative female pay in the banking, insurance and real estate sectors may also reflect

Figure V. 3

United Kingdom:
Average gross weekly earnings of adult full-time
male and female workers by age, 1980

(All workers, and manual workers)

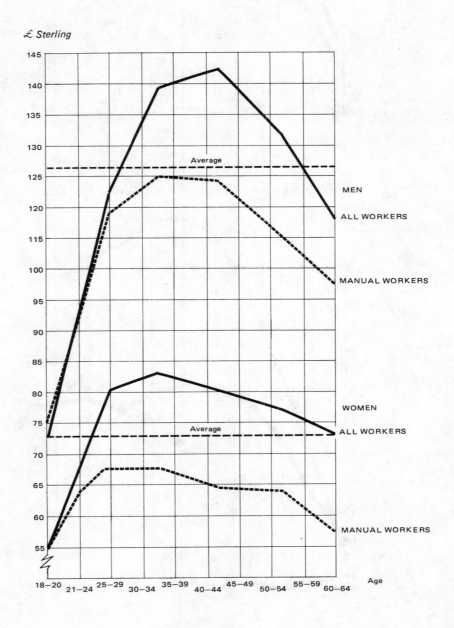

Figure V. 4

Germany, Federal Republic of, 1982.

Average monthly earnings of male and female administrative/clerical (A) and technical (T) workers
in selected sectors.

(DM'000)

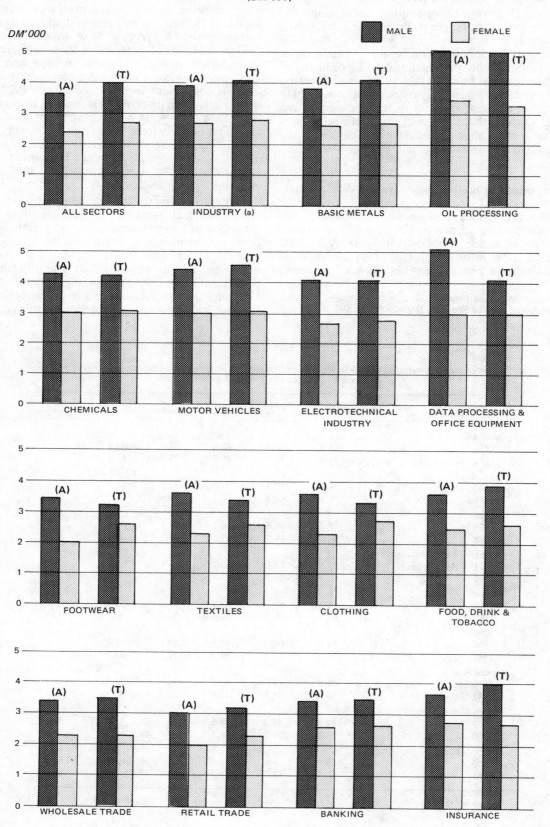

(a) Industry = Mining and quarrying, manufacturing, public utilities and construction.

a certain "overcrowding", i.e. a high supply of female labour, created by the recent increase in female labour-force participation, in sectors offering traditional types of clerical jobs to women which seem more acceptable than, for example, jobs in the transport sector.

Tables V.1–V.7 suggest one other conclusion: the male-female pay gap is generally smallest in public administration. Even in the United Kingdom, where the pay gap in public administration is wider than in other countries, it is smaller than in manufacturing or in any of the service industries shown in table V.1. This is because equal-pay legislation is generally more closely observed in the public than in the private sector. It was observed in a recent OECD study that the size of the public sector was an important explanatory variable associated with the level of relative female earnings in OECD countries.[8]

B. Recent trends in male-female earnings differentials

In recent years, female earnings have improved in relation to male earnings in nearly all the market-economy countries of the region, as shown in tables V.8–V.10. Table V.8 includes information from nine countries on changes in relative female earnings between the early

[8] L. Paukert, "Male and Female Earnings Differentials", *Women and Their Integration in the Economy* (Paris, OECD, 1985).

1970s and years around 1980, covering non-manual workers in manufacturing, in the four service sectors surveyed here and in public administration. Of the 47 country/industry sets of data for the two different years, only two registered a decline in relative female earnings. They declined slightly in the insurance sector between 1974 and 1978 in France; and in banking, insurance and real estate they fell from 51% to 48% between 1970 and 1981 in the United States. In all other cases, there was an improvement in relative female earnings, sometimes of a very pronounced nature. A particularly impressive increase took place in Finland between 1970 and 1981, with relative female earnings increasing in manufacturing from 58% to 76%, in wholesale trade from 57% to 69% and in retail trade from 70% to 87%. Equally impressive was the improvement in Sweden where, over the same period, relative female earnings in manufacturing rose from 59% to 72%, in retail trade from 80% to 92% and in banking from 85% to 93%.

Table V.9 shows the trend in relative hourly earnings of female manual workers in manufacturing. With the exception of Luxembourg, in the 15 countries for which data are available, relative female hourly pay rose between 1975 and 1982. Admittedly, the absolute improvement was only slight in a number of countries (Belgium, Denmark, France, the Federal Republic of Germany and Switzerland), but it was fairly substantial in Ireland, Italy, Norway and Sweden. In most countries the

TABLE V.8

Average monthly earnings of full-time, non-manual women workers, as a percentage of those of men, in selected ECE countries, around 1970 and 1980

Country and year	Manufac-turing	Wholesale trade	Retail trade	Banking	Insurance	Public administration
Denmark						
1974	63.9	71.2	72.6	70.0	63.1	..
1983	71.4	74.4	75.5	76.4	68.1	..
Finland						
1970	58.3	57.3	70.0	75.7	58.0	72.0
1981	76.1	69.4	87.3	78.6	68.5	74.0[a]
France						
1974	58.0	66.6	66.1	71.8	67.6	..
1978	61.7	69.7	67.5	74.5	66.1	83.9
Germany, Federal Republic of						
1971	63.5	67.0	60.1	71.6	73.9	..
1982	66.7	68.3	65.9	77.4	76.8	..
Norway						
1970	55.1	61.3	69.9	71.8	59.1	75.5
1982	65.3	70.5	80.6	77.7	65.5	82.9
Sweden						
1970	58.6	60.9	80.3	84.6	82.4	..
1981	72.1	72.3	92.2	92.5	86.1	88.3
Switzerland						
1970	61.8	71.6	63.4	71.7	70.4	..
1982	66.6	74.5	63.9	78.6	73.1	79.6
United Kingdom [b]						
1971	44.3	44.2	47.1	46.0		56.7
1980	53.2	54.1	56.1	49.9		60.9
United States [c]						
1970	59.4	51.0	52.5	50.5		64.8
1981	60.1	58.3	59.7	47.8		67.0

Sources: As for table V.1.

[a] 1980.

[b] Weekly earnings.

[c] Annual earnings, all workers (manual and non-manual).

TABLE V.9

Average hourly earnings of manual women workers in the manufacturing industry, as a percentage of those of men, in selected countries, 1975–1982

Country	1975	1978	1980	1982	Notes
Belgium............	71.1	71.1	70.2	72.6	October
Denmark..........	84.3	86.1	86.1	85.1	October
Finland	72.6	74.8	75.4	77.2	Industry, mining, quarrying, electricity
France............	76.4	76.6	77.0	77.7	October
Germany, Federal Republic of......	72.5	72.9	73.1	73.2	October
Greece............	69.9	68.8	67.4	73.9	1977: 4th quarter
Ireland	60.9	63.8	68.7	68.5	Adults. September
Italy..............	79.2	85.2	84.6	86.7	October (1978 = April)
Luxembourg.......	60.9	60.4	61.1	60.3	October
Netherlands	73.2	75.2	75.4	75.2	October
Norway...........	78.0	80.2	81.9	83.2	Adults. Including value of payments in kind
Portugal	..	..	72.0	72.8	
Sweden	85.2	88.7	89.9	90.3	Adults. 2nd quarter. Including holidays, sick-leave and the value of payments in kind
Switzerland........	66.0	66.1	66.4	67.0	Adults. October including family allowances
United Kingdom ...	66.9	69.7	69.1	68.8	October

Sources: EUROSTAT, *Wages and Incomes,* Statistical Bulletin, various issues; EUROSTAT, *Hourly earnings – Hours of work, 1 – 1983* (Brussels); and ILO, *Yearbook of Labour Statistics, 1983* (Geneva, 1984).

TABLE V.10

Growth indices of male and female manual and non-manual workers' earnings in manufacturing, in selected market economy countries, 1975–1982

Country	Period covered	Hourly earnings of manual workers			Monthly earnings of non-manual workers		
		M	F	M/F (percentage)	M	F	M/F (percentage)
Belgium	Oct. 1975–Apr. 1982	172.6	173.5	0.5	167.6	170.8	1.9
Denmark	Oct. 1975–Apr. 1982	187.9	189.7	1.0	..	..	
Finland[a]	Average 1975–1982	206.5	219.6	6.3	179.1[b]	197.0[b]	10.0[b]
France	Oct. 1975–Apr. 1982	239.4	245.5	2.5	208.7	220.7	5.7
Germany, Federal Republic of	Oct. 1975–Apr. 1982	148.1	148.6	0.3	152.2	153.2	0.7
Greece	Oct. 1975–Apr. 1982	444.3	465.7	4.8	..	..	..
Ireland	Sept. 1975–March 1982	257.0	288.5	12.3	..	..	..
Italy	Oct. 1975–Apr. 1982	332.0	361.3	8.8	295.5	327.3	10.8[c]
Luxembourg	Oct. 1975–Apr. 1982	166.2	162.1	−2.5	169.8	179.2	5.5
Netherlands..............	Oct. 1975–Apr. 1982	152.3	156.4	2.7	156.0	164.1	5.2
Norway	Average 1975–1982	190.3	202.9	6.6	164.1[c]	187.8[c]	14.4[c]
Sweden	2nd quarter 1975– 2nd quarter 1982	187.5	198.8	6.0	168.7	182.5	8.2
Switzerland	Average 1975–1982	137.6	139.8	1.6	..	..	..
United Kingdom	Oct. 1975–Apr. 1982	222.2	229.3	3.2	231.5	243.0	5.0
United States[d]	1975–1981	158.7	171.9	8.3	158.6	163.7	3.2

Sources: EUROSTAT, *Hourly earnings – Hours of work,* IV–1982, 1–1983 (Brussels); ILO, *Yearbook of Labour Statistics,* 1983 (Geneva); and national statistics as for table V.l.

[a] Includes mining, quarrying and electricity

[b] 1975–1981, office staff in industrial establishments.

[c] 1975–1981.

[d] Annual earnings of all annual full-time, blue-collar and white-collar workers.

progress was steady from 1975 up to 1982 but, in some countries, relative female earnings were affected by the recession and declined in 1980 or 1982.[9] The rising trend of relative female earnings in manufacturing is also illustrated in table V.10, which shows the increases in male and female earnings between 1975 and 1982, and their ratios separately for manual workers (hourly earnings)

[9] For an analysis of the effects of the recession on relative female pay, see L. Paukert, *op. cit.*

and for non-manual workers (monthly earnings) in 15 countries of the region. In the case of manual workers, female earnings increased more rapidly than male earnings by as much as 20% in Ireland and 24% in the United States. In several other countries this differential increase exceeded 10%. Only in the Federal Republic of Germany did the earnings of male and female manual workers increase at the same pace while, in Luxembourg, male earnings rose more rapidly than female earnings. The growth of relative earnings of women non-manual workers in manufacturing was generally even more rapid and occurred in all countries for which data are available. The ratio between the increase of female and male earnings reached 23% in Finland, 37% in Norway and 20% in Sweden. In all countries, with the exception of the United States, the ratio was higher in the case of non-manual workers in manufacturing than in the case of manual workers.

The reasons for the gradual narrowing of the male-female earnings gap have been manifold: institutional, economic, social and political. Most countries have pursued equal-pay policies of some kind, particularly since the early 1970s. Important changes in social attitudes have been brought about by various actions destined to exercise political and social pressure at different levels, and to increase public awareness of the women workers' situation. Moreover, marked changes in the labour force structure have occurred. Women's labour-force participation increased, especially in the middle age groups, which has had the effect of lengthening women's working careers. At the same time, the recession changed the pattern of demand for labour. These factors did not all operate in the same direction, or have the same intensity. The recession, for example, mostly worked against the growth of relative female earnings. An attempt is made below to clarify the respective roles of these factors in changing the earnings gap, by considering the major factors affecting the differences in male and female earnings.

C. Male and female earnings differentials and hours worked

Generally speaking, women work shorter hours than men. On a full-time basis, they work fewer hours per week, as illustrated in the example of European Community countries in table V.11. Moreover, many women work part-time. In 1981, part-time female workers represented over 15% of total employed women in 12 out 16 ECE countries; and in 15 of those countries, between 63% and 94% of part-time workers were women.[10]

---

[10] OECD, *Employment Outlook* (Paris, September 1983); OECD, *Labour Force Statistics, 1970-1981*; and (for Poland) *Rocznik Statystyczny* (1983), p. 57.

However, in this chapter all data on non-hourly earnings refer only to full-time workers. The impact of part-time work on total women's earned income is not analysed here, owing to the lack of statistics thereon in most countries of the region.

As shown in table V.11, the shorter working hours of women working full-time affect women's earnings proportionately more than would be expected on the basis of the difference of hours worked. One reason for this is that the extra hours worked by men are frequently paid at higher rates, e.g. overtime rates. In the United Kingdom, overtime payments and various bonuses, shift premiums, etc., accounted for 26% of male manual workers' average weekly earnings in 1980, and for only 10% of average weekly earnings of female manual workers.[11] Also, non-manual workers' premiums are higher for men than for women, although their impact on average male and female earnings differentials seems to be somewhat smaller. In other countries, the importance of overtime tends to be less than in the United Kingdom, but the general pattern is basically similar: overtime payments (and shift premiums) go mainly to men, and contribute to the widening of the male-female earnings gap on a weekly or monthly basis. An examination of the first two columns in table V.4 shows that, in the Federal Republic of Germany in 1982, the male-female earnings gap was invariably larger on a weekly than on an hourly basis. Evidence from other countries confirms this finding.[12] Table V.11 also shows that, between 1975 and 1981, the differences in weekly hours of men and women working full-time diminished in most countries. Exceptions were the Federal Republic of Germany, where the difference slightly increased, and Italy, where it remained unchanged. The reduction of working hours – due largely to the recession – affected men more than women, and its effect was to contribute to the reduction of the male-female earnings gap.

On an hourly basis, part-time women workers tend to earn less than women working full-time, mainly because of the lower average occupational grading of part-time jobs. However, the pay difference between part-time and

---

[11] United Kingdom Department of Employment, *New Earnings Survey 1980* (London, Her Majesty's Stationery Office, 1981).

[12] See EUROSTAT, *Hourly Earnings – Hours of Work* (Brussels, 1977).

TABLE V.11

Average number of hours worked per week by full-time and part-time men and women workers, in European Community countries, 1975 and 1981

Country	1975 Full-time		1975 Part-time		1981 Full-time		1981 Part-time	
	M	F	M	F	M	F	M	F
Belgium	44.1	41.8	19.2	20.5	38.9	37.2	17.2	18.9
Denmark	44.0	39.6	16.6	21.3	39.9	37.7	16.0	22.2
France	45.5	41.8	24.0	20.7	42.2	39.8	24.4	19.9
Germany, Federal Republic of	43.9	42.4	23.1	22.0	41.9	40.0	21.1	21.3
Greece	..	..	..	..	42.4	39.6	22.0	20.5
Italy	42.8	39.4	28.5	26.4	40.4	37.0	28.2	23.8
Netherlands	42.9	37.1	21.4	18.4	40.6	39.2	27.7	18.9
United Kingdom	44.8	39.5	19.5	19.5	39.5	35.4	15.6	16.8

Sources: EUROSTAT, *Labour Force Sample Survey, 1973–1975–1977* (Brussels, 1980); and *Labour Force Sample Survey, 1981* (Brussels, 1983).

Note: Data refer to all persons with an occupation during the reference week.

full-time women workers is smaller than that of part-time and full-time male workers. This may be illustrated by the following example of Canada in 1981:

Average hourly earnings in full-time and part-time jobs in Canada, 1981[13]

	Men		Women		Women/Men	
			Full-time	Part-time	Full-time	Part-time
	Full-time	Part-time	(Canadian dollars)		(Percentage)	
Total..........	9.39	7.24	7.27	6.66	77.4	92.0
Full year.......	9.93	8.05	7.66	6.95	77.9	86.3
Part year	8.10	6.31	6.31	6.22	77.9	98.6

The situation tends to vary, both between countries and between sectors. The 1974 EUROSTAT survey on earnings in distribution, banking and insurance [14] showed that, in retail trade for example, part-time women workers earned more in most countries than men who worked part-time. In banking, the former also earned more than the latter in Denmark and the Federal Republic of Germany, while the opposite applied in France and the United Kingdom. It should be noted, however, that most part-time women workers are engaged in highly segregated jobs, entirely different from those performed by part-time men workers. Thus, unless allowance is made for the different occupational distribution, it is difficult to draw conclusions from these data.[15]

D. Worker characteristics and the male-female earnings gap

1. THE EFFECT OF AGE ON MALE-FEMALE PAY DIFFERENTIALS

Female workers tend to be more concentrated than men in the younger age groups, where pay is generally lower. For example, in the European market-economy countries taken as a whole, more than 20% of working women but only approximately 15% of working men were under 25 years of age in 1980. In North America in the same year, about one-third of the women, but only one-quarter of the men in the work force were under 25. A much larger share of the male than of the female work force is to be found in the older age groups, where pay is generally higher. Female earnings reach their maximum level mostly between the ages of 30 and 39. The effect of this on average earnings differentials between men and women is not clear. On the one hand, female participation often tends to decline during this age period, as women often leave the labour force either permanently or temporarily. On the other hand, low-earning women tend to leave the labour force more readily than those with better earning possibilities. Finally, it should be noted that, in the middle age groups, many women work part-time while raising a family, which involves an obvious loss of earnings not reflected in the statistics on full-time women workers used in this chapter.

The effect on women's earnings of the concentration of the female work force in the "wrong" age groups can be assessed when the total weighted average of relative female pay is compared with the unweighted average of the male to female pay ratios in individual age groups (table V.12). This method was used in the 1980 study. It was found that, for individual age groups, the male-female pay gap was smaller than the total weighted average. The unweighted average earnings gap for the various age groups was invariably smaller than for the total weighted average. The differences between the weighted and unweighted averages can be considered as a measure of the impact of age distribution on total relative female earnings. As already observed in the 1980 study, the differences vary between countries. For example, in the United States, the effect of age distribution is small whereas, in Norway, it is quite significant (table V.12). In the few countries for which time comparisons can be made (France, Norway, Sweden, the United Kingdom and the United States), it appears that the differences between the weighted average and the unweighted average of individual age groups has declined in recent years. This reflects: (i) changes in the age pattern of female labour force participation; (ii) changes in age patterns of earnings; and (iii) changes in wage differentials brought about by equal-pay policies or by stricter enforcement of equal-pay legislation.

The "unfavourable" age composition of the female labour force is only one aspect of the effect of age on male-female earnings differentials. The pay gap increases significantly with age. This happens up to the age of about 50, when average male earnings start to decline, generally at a more rapid rate than female earnings. The age patterns of earnings are illustrated in figures V.2 and V.3 in respect of Sweden and the United Kingdom. Both graphs show, in particular, the rapid increase of male earnings up to the age of about 35, especially in the case of non-manual workers. This is an important feature to note because, at that age, many married women, their children having reached school age, try to re-enter the labour market or switch back to working full-time. By the age of 35, however, most male careers have already been basically "made", as the graphs suggest. This seems to be one of the most important handicaps for women workers, which is of course reflected in the average level of earnings. At the age when most women become free to concentrate on a career, the majority of good jobs, or the paths leading to them, are already occupied. Figures V.2 and V.3 also show that women, particularly manual workers, seem to reach a certain pay ceiling at a relatively early age in their working life and that this ceiling continues practically until their retirement. It should be noted, however, that the curve, indicating the ceiling, obviously reflects an average trend influenced by earnings both of women with uninterrupted careers and of those with one or several work interruptions. The extent to which women's average earnings would rise more after the age of 40, for example, if they were not lowered by the earnings of labour-force re-entrants, cannot be determined because of the lack of more detailed statistical information.

2. EARNINGS AND LENGTH OF SERVICE

Work experience and length of service are clearly associated with age, and the distribution of the female work force by length of service is likely to play against women because of the age factor alone. Women also tend to have a faster job turnover than men. This means that they are less able to establish enough seniority to qualify

[13] Statistics Canada, "Part-time work in Canada", *Survey of 1981 Work History,* Report of the Commission of Inquiry into Part-time Work, Labour Canada (Ottawa, 1983).

[14] EUROSTAT, *Inquiry into the Structure of Earnings in Distribution, Banking and Insurance* (Brussels, 1974).

[15] L. Paukert, *op. cit.*

TABLE V.12

**Women's average earnings as a percentage of those of men,
by age group, in selected countries, various years**

Age groups	Canada [a] 1979	France [b] 1975	Norway [c] 1982	Sweden [d] 1982	United Kingdom [e] 1980	United States [f] 1981
All age groups (weighted average)	63.3	68.4	67.8	72.7	64.6	59.0
16–17	} 83.7	119.6	..	..	93.0	..
18–19		94.6	99.7	99.5	79.1	} 78.8
20–24	75.4	84.4	86.9	89.3	75.0	
25–29	} 66.9	78.7	81.6	85.8	72.8	73.7
30–34		} 69.9	74.9	81.2	} 65.9	66.3
35–39	} 59.6		} 69.4	76.2		57.1
40–44		} 65.0		73.5	} 62.4	53.0
45–49	} 60.2		66.9	72.6		52.7
50–54		} 63.0		72.5	} 64.9	52.6
55–59	} 65.1		68.9	72.6		51.2
60–64		59.4	72.1	75.2	67.9	57.1
65 +	..	53.6	..	..	..	55.8
Unweighted average	68.5	76.5	77.6	79.8	72.6	59.8

Sources: As for table V.1; also F. Bourit, P. Hernu, M. Perrot, "Les salaires en 1981", *Economie et Statistique*, No. 141 (Paris, February 1982).

[a] Annual average earnings of full-time workers; youngest age group refers to 19 and under.

[b] Net yearly earnings of full-time workers and employees in the private and semi-public sector. Age groups are: under 18; 18–20; 21–25; 26–30; 31–40; 41–50; 51–60; 61–65; 65 +.

[c] Average monthly full-time earnings in establishments affiliated to the Norwegian Employers' Confederation (mostly manufacturing); the last age group refers to 60–66 years of age.

[d] Monthly earnings of full-time employees in industry (ISIC 2 + 3).

[e] Average gross weekly earnings of all adult full-time workers. First age group: under 18; second age group: 18–20.

[f] Average earnings of annual full-time workers; first age group: 18–24.

for promotion, which further accentuates their disadvantage. It is true that job changes are also made because of possible higher earnings elsewhere but many women, particularly the less qualified, tend to change jobs frequently for reasons other than better earning prospects.

Table V.13 provides information on the distribution of the male and female work force, by length of service, in France and the United States. It illustrates the shift of women workers towards the shorter-tenure groups, particularly evident in the case of non-manual workers in France. The available data indicate that length of tenure, contrary to age, tends to close the male-female earnings gap, other things being equal, in most countries and in most sectors. Data on relative female earnings by length of service in the European Community countries in 1974 are shown in table V.14. The information presented shows that it is clearly in women's interests to keep their jobs for a greater number of years. In certain countries, such as Luxembourg and the Netherlands, the propensity of the earnings gap to diminish with the length of tenure appears particularly high. The question arises, however, on the extent to which the narrowing of the gap results from a "weighting" effect, i.e. from the likelihood that better-

qualified women stay on in the same firm trying to make a career while those who are less qualified tend to change jobs more frequently.

Table V.15 shows that, in the United Kingdom for all ages taken together, length of service does not change the earnings gap in any significant way. This may be because the returns for younger age groups are likely to be affected by the length of time spent on education. For example, having spent three years in a job by the age of 18 implies having left school at 15 with a low qualification level. Since men with little education are able to obtain higher pay increases than women with little education (see below), the pay gap is widened after a few years. This appears as one of the reasons, although there are likely to be others, why relative female pay in younger age groups seems to diminish with length of tenure in the United Kingdom. However, after the age of 25, when the length of education factor has been mostly eliminated, length of tenure is very clearly an advantage for women. In general, the proportion of women with adequate education and training, able and willing to keep the same job for a longer period of time, is still relatively low. A large proportion of the female work force consists of young or

TABLE V.13

France and the United States: percentage distribution of the male and female work force by length of service, actually working around 1980

Activity and length of service (years)	Manual workers		Non-manual workers	
	Males	Females	Males	Females
FRANCE, 1978/79				
Manufacturing				
Less than 2	15.3	18.4	9.3	15.3
2–4	18.8	23.4	12.4	18.5
5–9	29.3	33.2	22.6	28.5
10–19	22.9	18.8	29.2	24.6
20 and more ...	13.5	6.1	26.2	12.8
Unspecified	0.2	0.1	0.3	0.3
TOTAL	100.0	100.0	100.0	100.0

	Manual workers, males	Non-manual workers, females
UNITED STATES, 1981		
All wage and salary workers		
Less than 1	13.2	17.9
1–1.9	7.8	10.6
2–2.9	8.0	9.9
3–3.9	6.1	7.0
4–4.9	8.5	7.5
5–9.9	20.4	20.5
10–24.9	26.7	22.0
25 and more ...	9.3	4.6
TOTAL	100.0	100.0

Sources: EUROSTAT, *Structure of Earnings 1978/79,* Principal Results, Vol. 2: France (Brussels, 1983) and N. F. Rytina, "Tenure as a factor of the male-female earnings gap", *Monthly Labor Review* (Washington, D.C., April 1982).

middle-aged women re-entering the labour market with low or inadequate levels of education and training which acts both as a cause and as a consequence of their rapid job turnover. This group suffers from a weak labour-market position and contributes considerably to the lowering of average female earnings.

3. EARNINGS AND EDUCATION

Education appears to be a paramount factor for women's careers. However, because a large proportion of women are not given a real opportunity to develop a career, the average effect of the educational level on female earnings is much lower than would be expected on *a priori* grounds. While high educational levels usually confer a greater relative advantage to women than to men, in comparison with women or men with only compulsory education, the average male-female pay differential is little affected by the rise in educational achievement.

The educational factor, however, influences the male-female earnings gap differently from the other "human capital" factors surveyed above. For example, women workers are not concentrated in low educational categories in the way that they are in low job-tenure categories. Available data indicate that female labour-force participation tends to rise sharply with the level of education while, in the lowest educational categories, it generally tends to remain weak. [16] As a result, at the lower

or intermediate level of education, the female work force can be expected to compare relatively favourably with that of the male work force. In the United States, for example, 18% of male workers have only an elementary education or did not complete high-school education, while only 13% of female workers are in the same situation.

In every educational category, women's average earnings are considerably lower than men's. It follows that, in order to receive the same amount of pay as a man, a woman must reach a much higher educational level. Table V.16 shows *inter alia* that, in Canada, female university graduates earn 33% less on average than male university graduates and in fact they earn only slightly more than a male high-school "drop-out". In the United States, a female college graduate earns little more than a man with an 8-year elementary education, and a woman with a higher academic degree earns, on the average, about as much as a man with a high-school certificate. Data available for Sweden, shown in table V.17, throw an interesting light on a particular aspect of this problem. The data show that, among non-manual employees in Swedish industry, the vast majority of women with a secondary education either went through a general high school or completed a two-year school of commerce. These two educational categories correspond to the two lowest pay levels. Similarly, among university graduates, few women studied technology, science or business administration, which offer the best earning prospects. It therefore seems that, in the field of education, the "unfavourable distribution" effect concerns more the type of curriculum than the length or level of studies. However, even in the case of truly comparable curricula and degrees, women's return on education is generally lower than that of men. [17] This was also found to be the case in the 1980 study.

E. Job characteristics and the male-female earnings gap

The distribution of the female work force by type of establishment, job and job position tends to widen the male-female earnings gap considerably.

1. THE SIZE OF ESTABLISHMENT

As noted above, women tend to be over-represented in small enterprises, where average pay is generally lower than in larger ones. The extent to which this is a matter of larger firms having more employees with high salaries, or small establishments generally paying less for comparable jobs, is not clear. The European Community 1972 Survey of Industry gave some attention to this issue and found a general tendency for small firms to pay lower wages. [18] Recent data available from Sweden corroborate this finding (table V.18), at least as far as the trade sector is concerned. They confirm the tendency for more women than men to work in small establishments and for the earnings of both sexes to increase with the size of establishment. As far as the earnings gap is concerned, there does not seem to be any clear trend. In establishments employing 500 or more people, however, the male-female pay gap is less than 1%. Yet, as most women are to be

[16] L. Paukert, *The Employment and Unemployment of Women in OECD Countries* (Paris, OECD, 1984), table XIII.

[17] D.J. Treiman and H.I. Hartmann, *op. cit.*

[18] EUROSTAT, *The Structure of Earnings in Industry, 1972* (Brussels, 1975).

TABLE V.14

Earnings in wholesale and retail distribution, banking and insurance; corrected gross monthly average pay of full-time female workers in relation to that of male workers (male pay = 100), by branch of activity and length of service, in European Community countries, 1974

Branch of activity and length of service (years)	Belgium	Denmark	France	Germany, Federal Republic of	Ireland	Italy	Luxembourg	Netherlands	United Kingdom
Wholesale distribution..	65.0	71.2	66.6	69.8	56.4	79.0	58.7	61.1	52.3
Less than 2	66.6	77.0	71.9	70.9	58.9	79.8	61.7	65.7	58.4
2–4	66.8	72.2	69.2	69.3	61.0	81.2	62.1	64.0	58.0
5–9	64.9	74.2	67.4	72.3	62.7	82.1	63.6	70.5	51.8
10–19	68.6	72.0	67.8	75.6	60.7	84.8	70.5	76.3	50.2
20 and more	77.7	72.1	66.1	83.7	66.7	88.3	81.3	82.5	51.0
Unweighted average..	68.9	73.5	68.5	74.4	62.0	83.2	67.8	71.8	53.9
Retail distribution	71.1	72.6	66.1	66.4	58.5	85.8	56.3	61.2	55.2
Less than 2	63.7	79.7	73.0	67.1	67.1	89.2	60.3	66.6	61.1
2–4	68.8	76.9	67.5	64.5	62.9	88.6	56.4	63.9	60.3
5–9	72.2	71.4	64.4	66.5	62.4	84.5	53.3	70.3	55.5
10–19	75.2	68.4	63.9	70.0	60.1	87.0	58.8	72.6	50.6
20 and more	80.9	80.1	64.0	77.1	67.9	96.2	66.4	77.1	58.5
Unweighted average..	72.2	75.3	66.6	69.0	64.1	89.1	59.0	70.1	57.2
Credit Institutions	71.2	70.0	71.8	70.9	61.7	79.5	62.4	56.6	53.8
Less than 2	80.0	70.2	79.7	71.9	72.1	94.2	68.8	65.7	61.6
2–4	81.2	83.0	80.5	76.0	76.1	91.8	70.4	65.3	60.3
5–9	79.1	85.6	76.4	80.5	79.1	87.7	69.6	65.6	69.4
10–19	77.3	82.4	71.5	77.3	86.5	84.9	72.8	73.9	71.7
20 and more	74.4	76.0	63.4	74.4	77.3	75.6	86.4	74.3	57.8
Unweighted average..	78.4	79.4	74.3	76.0	78.2	86.8	73.6	69.0	64.2
Insurance..............	68.4	63.1	67.6	71.7	58.9	71.1	54.4	60.4	50.1
Less than 2	77.7	72.9	81.2	74.1	78.3	69.9	62.6	69.5	59.9
2–4	77.2	73.6	74.6	74.9	73.0	76.9	54.2	67.3	56.4
5–9	75.5	71.1	69.1	75.4	65.5	71.9	59.5	74.0	56.4
10–19	73.0	61.9	65.1	76.3	69.7	72.0	66.8	73.0	57.3
20 and more	78.0	68.6	67.4	76.1	60.9	71.0		78.6	51.3
Unweighted average..	76.3	69.6	71.5	75.4	69.5	72.3	60.8	72.5	56.3

Source: EUROSTAT, *Economic and Social Position of Women in the Community* (Brussels, 1981), table 76.

found in small establishments paying low wages to both men and women, the overall earnings differential (based on the weighted averages) is much larger. In fact, it exceeds the differential observed in any of the individual size groups, with only one exception (the 100-199 size group).

Several factors can explain women workers' predominance in small establishments. One is women's lower mobility and their greater propensity to accept the job nearest to their home (or to their children's school), even if the pay is lower than in larger firms located further away. Because of their family responsibilities and the

TABLE V.15

United Kingdom: women's average gross weekly earnings by age group and length of service, as a percentage of those of men, 1979

(All full-time workers)

Age group	Length of service[a]					
	Less than 1 year	1 or 2 years	3 or 4 years	5–9 years	10 years and more	Total
Under 18.........	94.2	87.5	–	–	–	90.8
18–20.............	80.9	81.1	74.8	–	–	78.7
21–24.............	75.0	72.7	73.6	69.2	–	72.4
25–29.............	68.9	69.5	74.4	72.4	68.1	71.0
30–39.............	60.2	60.8	63.2	66.7	69.3	63.8
40–49.............	60.7	60.9	61.3	63.4	63.9	61.3
50–59.............	63.7	64.9	65.1	67.6	63.4	63.5
60–64.............	–	–	62.8	71.5	66.7	66.4
65 and over........	..	..	..	..	..	65.1
All ages	65.7	65.0	66.1	66.8	65.0	63.3

Source: Data compiled from *New Earnings Survey,* United Kingdom Department of Employment (London, Her Majesty's Stationery Office, 1979).

[a] Number of years with the same company or organization.

TABLE V.16

**Canada and United States: annual full-time earnings of male and female workers,
by level of education, around 1980**

Level of education	Men	Women	Female earnings as percentage of male earnings
CANADA, 1979	*Canadian dollars*		
All levels..........................	18 537	11 743	63.3
0–8 years	15 704	8 904	56.7
Some high school	17 214	10 797	62.7
Some post-secondary	19 016	11 851	62.3
Post-secondary certificate or diploma	19 602	12 943	66.0
University degree	26 533	17 842	67.2
UNITED STATES, 1981	*US dollars*		
All levels..........................	22 220	13 117	59.0
Elementary			
Less than 8 years...................	13 561	8 133	60.0
8 years	15 800	9 841	62.3
High school			
1–3 years	16 705	9 690	58.0
4 years	19 545	12 023	61.5
College			
1–3 years	22 166	13 765	62.1
4 years	27 737	15 844	57.1
5 years or more	33 913	20 066	59.2

Sources: Same as table V.1.

TABLE V.17

**Sweden: monthly earnings of non-manual employees in industry, by sex, level of education
and female share of employment in each category, 1982**

	Earnings			
Level of education	Males (kronor)	Females (kronor)	Female earnings as percentage of male earnings	Share of women in employment (percentage)
Average........................,...........	9 501	6 905	72.7	16.0
Secondary education				
Technical high school	10 451	7 968	76.2	2.1
Technical institute	10 333	8 641	83.6	1.0
Continuation school, technical branch .	8 492	7 098	83.6	2.6
Two-year school of commerce	9 390	6 603	70.3	52.3
Three-year high school of commerce ...	9 811	7 176	73.1	45.7
General high school	9 108	6 742	74.0	38.5
Post-secondary education				
Institute of technology	12 494	9 328	74.7	3.8
Science faculty.....................	12 272	9 672	78.8	15.8
Business administration, economics	12 619	9 310	73.8	9.4
Law, social sciences	11 782	9 219	78.2	12.4
Higher course in economics...........	11 259	7 645	67.9	21.3
Other university education............	12 211	9 222	75.5	36.9

Source: Data compiled from Statistics Sweden, *Löner, 1982* (Stockholm, 1983).

double burden of work which they mostly bear, time spent on travelling or commuting represents a greater inconvenience to them than to men. The second reason is linked to the first one: it is easier to combine work and family responsibilities when there is a certain flexibility, perhaps on an informal basis, concerning working hours and work schedules. Such arrangements may be easier to make in small firms than in large ones where personnel management is likely to be more rigid and bureaucratic. Recent research has identified other job characteristics which reduce female wages, thereby demonstrably widening the general male-female earnings gap. Among

them, the findings with respect to the effect of the sex of the supervisor should be mentioned. It has been shown that, *ceteris paribus,* a worker earns more when the immediate supervisor is a man. This is consistent with the hypothesis that the presence of a man in a post confers higher status on an otherwise comparable job. It has also been established that control over money in a job increases men's and women's earnings, but that the rewards are higher for men than for women. [19]

[19] M.A. Ferber and J.L. Spaeth, *op. cit.*

TABLE V.18

**Sweden: average hourly earnings of male and female salespersons and shop assistants,
by size of establishment, 1982**

Number of employees	Males		Females		Female earnings as percentage of male earnings
	Percentage distribution	Hourly earnings (kronor)	Percentage distribution	Hourly earnings (kronor)	
All employees	100.0	36.53	100.0	34.77	95.2
1–4	16.8	34.56	30.0	33.24	96.2
5–9	15.7	35.66	15.7	34.67	97.2
10–19	19.0	36.48	16.5	34.82	95.4
20–49	12.7	36.96	11.4	35.36	95.7
50–99	11.4	37.18	11.6	35.83	96.4
100–199	13.5	38.05	8.8	36.14	95.0
200–499	6.4	38.70	2.6	37.20	96.1
500+	4.5	38.95	3.4	38.65	99.2
Unweighted average....	..	..	..	..	96.4

Sources: As for table V.1.

2. OCCUPATIONAL SEGREGATION

The most evident and widely accepted reason for the low average pay of women compared to that of men is the difference in occupational composition. The preceding chapter discusses the two types of occupational segregation which are usually distinguished: "vertical occupational segregation" and "horizontal occupational segregation" (see Chapter IV, section E). Vertical occupational segregation refers to the fact that few women are to be found in high-status jobs. Management and executive grades account for a much smaller part of the female work force than of the male work force, while the majority of women are in low-status, low-pay occupations. This point can be illustrated, for example, by the case of France in 1978. Table V.19 highlights the concentration of women in low-grade jobs in four service sectors, showing the differences in the weighted and unweighted averages of women's relative pay to which this concentration leads. In each of the occupational status groups listed in the table, the difference between the pay of men and women tends to be smaller than for the total. It is considerably smaller in cases such as those of professional staff in wholesale trade and of employees at middle and lower levels in banking and insurance, where the pay gap is generally less than 10%. For the weighted total, however, the pay gap in the four sectors listed varies between roughly one quarter and one third.

Another illustration of vertical occupational segregation and its impact on earnings is provided in figure V.5, based on data for the United States in 1981. In the chart, the height of each bar corresponds to the year-round full-time level of earnings of men or women in the relevant occupational category. The width of each bar corresponds to the percentage share of each occupational category in total male or female employment. The figure clearly reveals the predominance in total female employment of the lowest-paid manual and non-manual categories, particularly of personal service and clerical workers. As far as female professional and technical workers are concerned, over 50% are nurses and teachers (elementary and secondary), who earn a fraction of the professional income of scientists, engineers, computer specialists, physicians, etc. When the differences between the weighted and unweighted averages of female relative

pay in distribution, banking and insurance in France in 1978 are compared with those for an earlier year (1974), it appears that the differentials have diminished in all four sectors surveyed. As shown in table V.20, total relative female earnings (weighted average) increased more (or decreased less) in all four sectors than the unweighted averages of the six occupational status categories. This would appear to indicate that the occupational distribution of the female work force tended to improve. However, as the unweighted averages of relative female earnings also increased (or diminished more than the weighted averages), there were evidently other factors (effects of equal-opportunity legislation, other distributional factors, labour-market factors, etc.).

Table V.21 provides additional information on the effect of vertical occupational segregation on total relative female earnings for non-manual workers in industry, in five countries of the region. The impact of the unfavourable distribution of the female labour force by occupational status appears greater in France, the Federal Republic of Germany and Sweden than in Switzerland or the United States. In Sweden and Switzerland, somewhat surprisingly, the difference between the weighted and unweighted averages, referred to in table V.21, increased slightly in comparison with 1976/77. At the same time, in both countries, the unweighted average increased more than the weighted average (table V.22). This suggests that other factors (legislative, economic, etc.) caused relative female pay to rise, while occupational distribution may have acted in the opposite direction. With regard to pay differentials in different skill categories of manual workers, the difference between weighted and unweighted averages is generally smaller than in the case of non-manual workers classified by professional grades. This is mainly because the range of occupational pay levels is wider for non-manual workers.[20] The limited evidence currently available indicates that changes in skill distribution were not among the factors of the increased relative pay of women manual workers.

"Horizontal occupational segregation", another important factor in the earnings gap, refers to the fact that more women than men are concentrated in different

---

[20] C. Saunders and D. Marsden, *Pay Inequalities in the European Community* (Butterworth, London, 1981).

TABLE V.19

France: percentage distribution of male and female non-manual workers by occupational status, and male-female earnings differentials, in distribution, banking and insurance, 1978–1979

(Full-time workers)

Occupational status	Wholesale trade			Retail trade			Banking			Insurance		
	Male	Female	Female earnings as percentage of male earnings	Male	Female	Female earnings as percentage of male earnings	Male	Female	Female earnings as percentage of male earnings	Male	Female	Female earnings as percentage of male earnings
Total	100.0	100.0	69.8	100.0	100.0	67.6	100.0	100.0	74.0	100.0	100.0	66.3
Higher management	4.9	0.8	69.8	4.4	0.7	79.6	5.1	0.3	78.3	2.6	0.1	71.3
Executives	12.7	3.9	82.4	9.8	3.1	80.2	17.6	3.8	89.0	19.0	3.1	76.0
Professional staff	12.3	5.8	91.8	12.6	5.1	87.1	34.0	33.4	89.0	25.0	12.4	85.2
Highly skilled employees	17.2	19.7	85.1	20.1	17.7	77.9	16.6	21.6	93.1	9.4	34.5	92.0
Skilled employees	35.5	42.8	86.4	33.1	44.6	79.4	18.8	31.9	95.8	23.7	37.2	88.0
Other employees	19.4	27.0	87.7	20.1	28.9	86.6	7.9	9.1	95.1	10.3	12.6	95.8
Unweighted average	..	..	83.9	..	..	81.8	..	..	90.1	..	..	84.7
Difference of averages	..	..	14.1	..	..	14.2	..	..	16.1	..	..	18.4

Source: EUROSTAT, Structure of Earnings, 1978/79, Principal Results, Vol. 1: France (Brussels, 1983).

types of occupational activities. Few countries provide information on male and female earnings according to a detailed occupational classification. In those that publish such data (including the United Kingdom and the United States), it appears that the pay gap within individual occupations is usually quite small. In fact, the narrower the definition of occupation, the smaller the pay gap.[21] This

[21] N.F. Rytina, "Earnings of men and women: a look at specific occupations", *Monthly Labor Review* (US Department of Labor, Washington, D.C., April 1982).

could be expected for statistical reasons but, in addition, the narrower the occupation, the more likely it is to be either "male" or "female", i.e. the more it is likely to be segregated by sex. Research in the United States has established that there is a positive correlation between the share of women in different occupations and relative female pay levels. In occupations where women predominate, the earnings gap is usually smaller than in occupations which are mixed or where men predominate. Whatever the precise difference between male and female earnings in women-dominated occupations, total average

Figure V. 5

United States, 1981.

Male and female year-round full-time earnings by occupation
and by weight of each occupation in total male and female employment.

(Dollars and percentages)

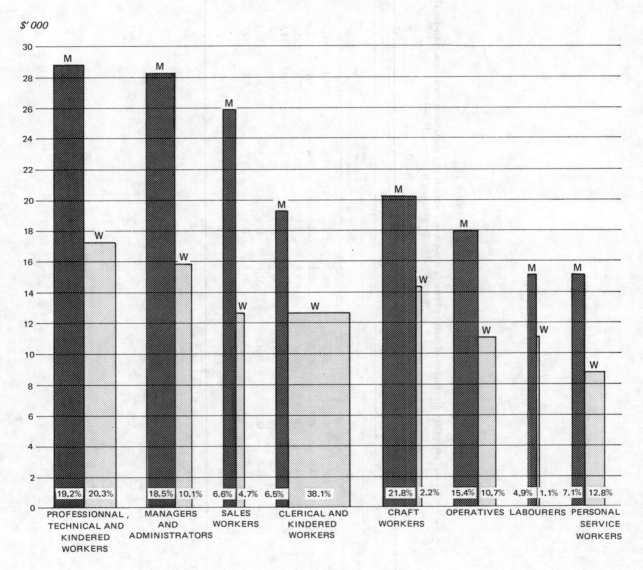

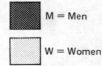

M = Men

W = Women

TABLE V.20

France: relative female earnings in four service sectors, weighted and unweighted averages of six occupational-status categories,[a] 1974 and 1978

Sectors	1974	1978	1978/1974
Wholesale trade			
Weighted average	66.6	69.8	104.8
Unweighted average	85.3	83.9	98.4
Difference.................	18.7	14.1	..
Retail trade			
Weighted average	66.1	67.6	102.3
Unweighted average	81.3	81.8	100.6
Difference.................	15.2	14.2	..
Banking			
Weighted average	71.8	74.0	103.1
Unweighted average	89.8	90.1	100.3
Difference.................	18.0	16.1	..
Insurance			
Weighted average	67.6	66.3	98.1
Unweighted average	90.9	84.7	93.2
Difference.................	23.3	18.4	..

Sources: EUROSTAT, *Structure of Earnings 1978/79,* Principal Results, Vol. I: France (Brussels, 1983); and EUROSTAT, *Structure of Earnings in Distribution, Banking and Insurance, 1974* (Brussels).

[a] As listed in table V.19.

earnings for both men and women in these occupations tend to be low compared to occupations dominated by men.[22]

F. Male-female pay differentials and the labour market

Important as the "compositional" aspects of the male-female earnings differentials may be, they only partly explain women's pay disadvantage. It has often been found that women tend to be assigned to lower-level jobs within each qualification category. Research in the United States and elsewhere has shown that, at any level of human capital, women are concentrated in lower-level occupations and at lower ranks within a given occupation. The proportion of the difference in male and female earnings due to human capital or "compositional" variables has been assessed differently by various authors.[23] It has been found that only about 20% of the difference in male and female earnings could be ascribed to human

[22] N.F. Rytina, "Occupational segregation and earnings differences by sex", *Monthly Labor Review* (January 1981).

[23] See N. Agarwal, "Male-female pay inequality and public policy in Canada and the U.S.", *Relations Industrielles* (Université Laval No. 4, 1982).

TABLE V.21

Earnings of non-manual female workers in industry as a percentage of those of men, in five ECE countries, 1978–1982

France, 1978 (monthly earnings in manufacturing)

Total (weighted average)	61.0
Higher management	70.8
Executives..........................	77.1
Assistants	88.0
Clerical staff	82.3
Supervisors.........................	74.3
Foremen	78.2
Unweighted average	78.5
Difference of averages	17.5

Germany, Federal Republic of, 1982 (monthly earnings in industry)[a]

	Admin. and clerical	Technical
Total (weighted average).....................	68.1	68.1
Executives, staff with responsibility	81.5	86.9
Independently working staff...................	85.5	82.0
Qualified middle-rank staff	85.8	79.4
Other staff................................	82.9	75.8
Unweighted average........................	83.9	81.0
Difference of averages	15.8	12.9

Sweden, 1982 (monthly earnings in industry (ISIC 2 + 3))

Total (weighted average)	72.7
Higher management	83.3
Executives, independently working staff ...	88.5
Qualified staff	91.0
Routine work staff	91.0
Unweighted average	88.5
Difference of averages	15.8

Switzerland, 1982 (monthly earnings in industry and crafts)

	Total		
Total (weighted average).............	66.6	68.1	72.3
Independently working staff	72.6	71.7	83.3
Qualified middle-rank staff	72.6	75.9	75.9
Assistant staff......................	74.4	..	..
Unweighted average.................	73.2	..	..
Difference of averages..............	6.6	..	..

United States, 1980 (annual full-time earnings in manufacturing)

Total (weighted average)	57.1
Professional and managerial workers......	59.2
Clerical and sales workers	61.4
Craft workers and operatives	57.3
Other workers	72.2
Unweighted average	62.5
Difference of averages	5.4

Sources: EUROSTAT, *Structure of Earnings 1978/79,* Vol. 2: France (Brussels, 1983); data compiled from Statistisches Bundesamt, *Statistisches Jahrbuch der BRD, 1983* (Wiesbaden 1983); and from Statistics Sweden, *Löner 1982* (Stockholm, 1983); *La Vie économique,* 8e fascicule, Département fédéral de l'économie publique (Berne, August 1983); and U.S. Bureau of the Census, *Money Income of Households, Families and Persons in the United States* (Washington, D.C., 1980).

[a] Including mining and construction.

TABLE V.22

Switzerland and Sweden: relative earnings of non-manual female workers in industry, by occupational status, 1976/77–1982

Occupational status	1976	1977	1982	1982/1976
Sweden				
Total (weighted average)	71.9	..	72.7	101.1
Higher management	72.5	..	83.3	114.9
Executives, independently working staff	88.5	..	88.5	100.0
Qualified staff	88.9	..	91.0	102.4
Routine work staff	90.5	..	91.0	100.6
Unweighted average	85.1	..	88.5	104.0
Difference of averages	13.2	..	15.8	..
Switzerland				
Total (weighted average)	..	64.1	66.6	103.9
Independently working staff .	..	71.3	72.6	101.8
Qualified middle-rank staff ..	..	69.1	72.6	105.1
Assistant staff	..	69.5	74.4	107.1
Unweighted average	..	70.0	73.2	104.6
Difference of averages	..	5.9	6.6	..

Sources: Data compiled from Statistics Sweden, *Löner 1982* (Stockholm, 1983); and from *La Vie économique,* 8e fascicule, Département fédéral de l'économie publique (Berne, August 1983); also *The Economic Role of Women in the ECE Region* (United Nations publication, Sales No. E.80.II.E.6), chapter IV, table IV.13.

capital variables, most of the difference being due to the fact that women received a lower return on these factors and were given lower-level positions when human capital was held constant.[24] The 1980 study, on the other hand, ascribed a much smaller weight to the non-compositional factors, considering them as a residual which could be taken to measure discrimination.

In recent years, attention has been paid to the discrimination issue by both sociologists and economists.[25] In particular, considerable research has been undertaken recently on the subject of job segregation. The findings suggest *inter alia* that, when followed down to the establishment level, job segregation is much more rigid than the global national data indicate. In fact, it was found that, in smaller firms, very few jobs are performed by both men and women. A research study team recently established that "custom and practice played a major role in explaining any existing division of labour and structure of pay and employment. Most managers did not consciously consider different options for organizing the production process ... until forced to do so by a change in the product market, or by a decision to introduce a new technique ... Thus, women are allocated to particular jobs and excluded from others primarily because this has always been the case, as far as the current management could remember".[26]

In addition, "women's jobs" tend to get "women's wages" (i.e. low rates), particularly in small firms using informal payment systems. Even in larger firms with a formalized payment system, where more attention is paid to job content and skill, women's jobs are generally not carefully assessed and graded according to skill, but pay is determined more or less automatically at "women's rates". A major reason for this seems to be the continued availability of women for employment at low pay, due to women's lower mobility, greater time pressure, etc. Thus, the low status of female jobs is linked *inter alia* to differences in male and female labour supply and to the intra-family division of labour, these factors being further reinforced by women's lack of opportunities in the labour market.[27]

These and other factors contribute to the creation of a sex pattern of earnings which then becomes customary. As women are aware of their limitations, they lower their expectations and tend to accept low pay. They also accept jobs without promotion possibilities, and hesitate to ask for promotion, even when objectively justified. This helps to explain the ceiling of women's average pay illustrated in figures V.2 and V.3. Once it becomes an established custom that women's earnings rarely reflect their real skills and productive contribution, it follows that women will not achieve significant advancement through long service.

Another important factor in respect of male-female earnings differentials is linked to the existence of internal labour markets, which operate particularly in larger establishments. In this system, job openings are usually filled from within the company. In such cases, the length of service acts in women's disfavour, as it tends to be shorter for women than for men. Even a long duration of service does not automatically benefit women, since many other elements are taken into consideration, some of which may be just as, or even more important. The existence of internal labour markets is linked to employers' attempts to minimize turnover and create work incentives by setting up well-defined promotion ladders and prospects, while at the same time reducing training costs. Internal competitions may be determined by many elements, of which a great number may be linked to personal or pre-conceived considerations, such as the assumed possibility to work longer hours, or expected willingness to travel, which often tend to give an advantage to men.

According to some of the models of the dual labour market,[28] employers tend to divide jobs into two categories, primary and secondary. Primary jobs are associated with stability, long or costly training and a quality of performance having a direct influence on the financial results of the enterprise. Employers are inclined to give these jobs to those they consider to be the most productive, promising candidates, ranking them in function of their operational requirements. It has been argued that this type of procedure results in a persistently lower ranking of women, and that this lower ranking is an important factor in explaining women's lower return on human capital. The "queuing principle" in the allocation of jobs is important in explaining women's weaker labour-market position and lower relative earnings.[29]

Moreover, while the primary job holders, relatively few of whom are women, can negotiate for good salaries,

[24] C.N. Halaby, "Sex inequality in the workplace: an employer-specific analysis of pay differences", *Social Science Research* (March 1979) quoted in D.J. Treiman and H.I. Hartmann, *op. cit.*

[25] See for example D.J. Treiman and H.I. Hartmann, *op. cit.,* Bibliography; and M.E. Gold, *A Dialogue on Comparable Worth* (ILR Press, Cornell University, Ithaca, New York, 1983).

[26] C. Craig, E. Garnsey and J. Rubery, "Women's pay in informal payment systems", *Employment Gazette,* United Kingdom Department of Employment (London, April 1983).

[27] *Ibid.*

[28] See for example P.B. Doeringer and M.J. Piore, *Internal Labour Markets and Manpower Analysis* (D.C. Heath, Lexington, Mass. 1971).

[29] See L.C. Thurow, *Generating Inequality* (New York, Basic Books 1975); see also D.J. Treiman and H.I. Hartmann, *op. cit.*; and M.A. Ferber and J.L. Spaeth, *op. cit.*

companies try to compress the wages of the secondary job holders, in order to limit their wage bills. The secondary jobs (cleaning, catering, etc.) require fewer skills, and less or no training. They are largely open to competition and to market pressures, and usually have a high labour turnover. The secondary jobs can be offered to the lowest bidder, since quality of performance is usually less important than cost. The lowest bidders are generally women

and a sufficient supply of women willing to accept employment on these terms is a condition for the continuation of this pattern.[30] The lowest-bidder factor is obviously linked to women's family role and to the fact that relatively few women are the main breadwinners.

---

[30] L. Paukert, *Male and Female Earnings Differentials ...*

CHAPTER VI

MAIN FINDINGS AND CONCLUSIONS

The relative deterioration in economic conditions over the past ten years or so has had a significant impact on the economic role of women in the ECE region. Prior to the economic slow-down, the general economic conditions for the advancement of women were comparatively favourable. Rapid growth and sustained structural change, dynamic labour markets and rapidly expanding social provisions and services created a climate favourable to general progress and the reduction of inequalities, including those affecting women. The deceleration of the pace of economic development and the indications of rather modest prospects for the future imply that the momentum of improvements in the economic situation of women, and men, generated by development will be much weaker in the years to come than in the past. This reduced momentum emanating from general developments signifies that the advancement of women will depend, to an increasing degree, on efforts and policies aimed specifically at improving their economic situation and integration into development. However, slow economic growth also limits the resources available for such programmes, as has already been the case in a number of countries, where policies and measures to control the growth of public or state expenditures have been adopted. The reduction in services and support which might result from such policies would also affect the economic conditions of women not in the labour force, many of whom belong to the lower socio-economic groups.

Another major feature of economic development during the Decade, with significant implications for women's integration in the labour market, was the substantial shift in the sectoral distribution of the economy. Since the early or mid-1970s, many countries experienced a stagnation, or even a contraction, of employment in industry, with the service or tertiary sectors accounting for most new jobs. A large part of the growth in service employment was concentrated in the public sector. The rapid expansion of this sector, which accounts for a considerable and increasing share of women's employment, thus acted as a stimulus for women's integration into the labour market. More recently, however, the expansion of this sector has slowed down as a result of government policies designed to curtail increases in public spending, and public-sector employment can be expected to increase much more slowly than in the past.

The evolution of the economic role of women is also taking place in a different demographic setting, characterized by long-term declining population growth and a continuing aging process. The economic and social pressures created by an aging population may especially affect women, who comprise the major share of the older population, and the poorer groups amongst the aged.

Low fertility and the shortening of the childbearing period will further reinforce the productive potential of the female population. On the other hand, fertility no longer constitutes as much of an obstacle to the integration of women in the economy as it did in the past. Recent experience shows that the presence of young children has become much less of a barrier to female labour force participation.

Other important consequences for the economic role of women may result from the changes in the family which began to emerge in the 1960s and 1970s and which have subsequently become more widespread. The new patterns of nuptiality, divorce, cohabitation and female-headed single-parent families reflect considerable shifts in the social situation of women in society, with potentially important implications for their economic role and independence.

As the United Nations Decade for Women draws to a close, more than 200 million women participate in the labour force of countries in the ECE region. While women's participation in the labour force has been increasing, that of men has declined. As a result, the share of women in the labour force has been growing, sometimes very rapidly in most countries of the region. For the region as a whole, women presently account for close to 44% of the total work force. In a number of countries, women currently outnumber prime-age males among demographic groups in the work force.

Recent developments have highlighted new patterns of women's participation in the labour force, indicating changes which challenge the traditional views of women's economic activity. The evolution in age patterns of female labour force participation which, in an increasing number of countries, is becoming similar to that of men, suggests a more permanent attachment of women to the labour force. The new patterns of female participation in the labour force are also reflected in many countries by the substantial increases in the economic activity of women in their main childbearing years and of mothers of young children. This suggests that the younger generation of women may well follow quite a different lifetime work pattern from that which was typical for their mothers. Also, contrary to expectations based on past experience, in general women did not withdraw from the labour force during the recent recessions. In addition, the rising unemployment rates of women suggest a more permanent attachment to the labour force than has been evident in the past.

Societal expectations play a role in influencing women's participation in the labour force, although economic conditions may be of paramount importance. In many countries, women's paid employment is essential to the financial support of their families, especially in the early years of family formation. In addition, the increasing incidence of female-headed single-parent families means that more and more women have no choice but to engage in paid employment. At the same time, there is concern that high unemployment and slow economic growth may in some countries lead to pressures on women to return to their traditional roles as full-time housewives.

The general economic climate makes it difficult to predict with any certainty future trends in women's labour-force participation. Technological change and declining employment opportunities may increase female and male activity in the so-called "grey" economy, and such activity is not recorded in official statistics.

However, it seems that changing trends in the participation of women in the labour force are now firmly established and unlikely to be reversed. If governments are to develop strategies with respect to women's labour-force participation, their policies will have to be based on the recognition of this new economic role of women. The analysis suggests some key considerations in this regard:

(*a*) Since women currently constitute a significant proportion of the labour force in most countries of the region, labour-market policies explicitly or implicitly focused on male workers ignore a sizeable part of the work force. In particular, policy analysis and development traditionally focused on the "prime-age male" worker should be reconsidered, since these workers are no longer the major demographic group in the labour force of many countries;

(*b*) It is no longer accurate to look upon women as having a tenuous attachment to the labour force, entering, leaving and re-entering several times in their lifetime. There is growing evidence that a new pattern applies to younger age cohorts of women born in the 1950s and 1960s. The apparently weakened connection between fertility and participation in the labour force also implies that even an increase in fertility rates, whether achieved voluntarily or as a result of pro-natalist government policies, may have little impact on the economic activity of women;

(*c*) Policy-makers' conceptions that most employed women work part-time do not hold true for the majority of countries in the region, in many of which between two thirds and three quarters of all employed women have full-time jobs. In some countries, young age cohorts, in their prime childbearing years, have the lowest percentage of part-time work of women in the work force. Moreover, there are indications that part-time employment is increasingly involuntary; economic conditions, rather than family responsibilities, may account for part of the increase in the percentage of part-time employment;

(*d*) The increased labour-force participation of women during their childbearing years, and of women with young children, demonstrates the need for adequate and accessible facilities in this regard, including day care.

Since the beginning of the Women's Decade, the growing employment opportunities for women did not keep pace with the increase in the female labour force, and female unemployment rates therefore rose. In many countries, women's share in unemployment is greater than their share in the labour force as a whole, and their unemployment rates are, in most cases, considerably higher than those of men. Also, most female unemployment is, in many countries, concentrated among younger women and in some of the west European countries, the unemployment rates of young women are significantly higher than those of young men.

As regards policy implications, the following factors merit consideration:

(*a*) Strategies to deal with slower employment growth resulting from the recession and the application of new technology must take into account the growing role of women in the labour market;

(*b*) Specific responses to unemployment should consider the differential impact of such policies on women workers. In some countries, special employment projects and training programmes are focused on specific industries or occupations where male employment predominates, failing to take account of the needs of unemployed women;

(*c*) The increasing prevalence of part-time work makes it even more important to ensure equal treatment for part-time workers, the vast majority of whom are women. Access to benefits, such as pensions and unemployment insurance, are among the measures which should be implemented in this regard.

Since the completion of the 1980 study, there have been several important developments in the sectoral distribution of the labour force and the share of women employed in different sectors. Most notable has been the further increase in the concentration of women in the service sector. Both the percentage of women employed in services and the share of women in service occupations have increased in the large majority of countries in the region. The share of women working in the industrial sector has also increased in most countries, despite the fact that the percentage of women employed in industry tended to decrease. In agriculture, the percentage of women has, for the most part, decreased.

The differentiation between men and women in service-sector employment has also increased further. Between 1970 and 1980, the already high share of women in education, health, community and other social services continued to rise in most countries. Even if the short-term effects of these changes resulted in increased segregation by sex in the labour market, it must not be forgotten that the changes also contributed to a stronger integration of women in the labour market, a strengthening of their economic role and, in that sense, a step forward in the development process.

In general, the evidence from studies does not change the picture of relatively high stability in the structure and overall level of occupational differentiation by sex throughout the 1970s. In this respect, the rather pessimistic conclusions of the 1980 study remain valid, although there are also structural developments which point against overly negative conclusions. A review of aggregate trends shows that the labour market, in most countries of the region, tended towards increased employment in occupations which have traditionally been dominated by women. However, studies also indicate some increase in the female share of male-dominated occupations, although the increases were relatively small and their aggregate effects were negligible compared to the inflow of women in the traditionally female occupations. Whereas such small changes do not affect the polarization by sex of the employment structure, they may be important insofar as they represent an opening up of employment possibilities for women in male-dominated occupations.

Available evidence points to part-time employment as being a contributing factor towards increased occupational segregation. Most part-time work is in the service sector, where there is an over-representation of women, and the shares of women in part-time employment have been increasing in most countries. High degrees of occupational differentiation have been found in the majority of countries where part-time work accounts for a large proportion of women's employment.

Recent data indicate that educational qualifications also continue to have a significant effect on occupational segregation by sex. Although inter-country variations certainly exist, there are large sex differentials with respect to educational qualifications, in terms of both the level of educational attainment and the field of specialization. In particular, at each level, women tend to be concentrated in a narrower range of subjects than men.

The results of the analysis reveal a number of implications for further strategies aimed at reducing occupational segregation:

(a) Several findings suggest the importance of the "role-model" aspect of occupational segregation and point strongly in the direction of active labour-market policies to recruit women into male-dominated occupations. It is assumed that this will have a "snowball" effect and cause more young women to choose these occupations. In terms of the importance of role models, even a relatively small increase of women in male-dominated occupations is a positive development;

(b) The effect of positive action programmes and the active recruitment of women into traditionally male-dominated positions and occupations will be to open up employment possibilities for women. However, the impact of such policies will also depend on the extent to which occupational choice reflects more deeply-rooted differences in occupational orientation and preferences between women and men.

(c) The foregoing suggests that movement towards a large reduction in occupational segregation must have a long-term as well as a short-term perspective. Gender differences in observed occupational preferences which are caused by differences in socialization can hardly be eliminated in the short term. However, the long-term character of this task need not conflict with a short-term policy of reducing occupational segregation through appropriate policies;

(d) Some findings suggest that occupational segregation by sex may be a means of replacing other forms of sex differentiation in the labour market. One indication of such an effect is that countries characterized by small wage differentials between men and women display a greater degree of occupational segregation than countries with larger wage differentials.

Two main conclusions emerge with respect to pay differentials. In the first place, in a number of countries for which information is available, there has been progress during the last decade in closing the male-female earnings gap which, generally speaking, has been reduced from one third to about one quarter. By contrast, in others there has been little progress on an economy-wide level and, in some sectors (such as finance, insurance and real estate), relative female earnings have even tended to decline.

The relatively positive results thus far achieved in many countries of the region have been partly due to a gradual improvement in the characteristics of female workers, such as average age, length of work experience and tenure, and education. Labour-market factors have also played a role. However, the improvement of relative female pay is mostly attributable to the various equal-pay policies adopted in many countries.

The second major finding, although necessarily based on somewhat limited information, is that the improvement of relative female earnings does not seem to have been linked to a reduction in occupational differentiation. Occupational segregation and low pay in "female jobs" continues to be a vital feature of the general male-female earnings gap. The problem of remuneration in predominantly-female occupations appears to be one of the major obstacles to equal treatment.

Some other conclusions and implications can be derived from the analysis:

(a) Further measures should be undertaken to improve the female worker characteristics which have been found to positively influence women's relative earnings. These include, for example, education and training oriented more specifically towards labour-market requirements, effective career guidance, the dissemination of information on women's career possibilities, and other appropriate action designed to increase women's career consciousness and opportunities;

(b) In view of their potentially important impact, the policies formulated and implemented on a national and regional level during the last decade should be studied carefully, their positive and negative features assessed, and their applicability for future action evaluated. Studies prepared at the national level can considerably facilitate such a programme;

(c) Measures aimed at improving female earnings should be accompanied by the regular monitoring of the legal, economic and social aspects of equal access to jobs by men and women. The experience of various countries regarding developments of this nature should be compared and evaluated.